# DIARY OF A SUB-DIVISIONAL POLICE OFFICER

KULDIP SHARMA

Chennai • Bangalore

CLEVER FOX PUBLISHING
Chennai, India

Published by CLEVER FOX PUBLISHING 2024
Copyright © Kuldip Sharma 2024

All Rights Reserved.
ISBN: 978-93-56486-39-3

This book has been published with all reasonable efforts taken to make the material error-free after the consent of the author. No part of this book shall be used, reproduced in any manner whatsoever without written permission from the author, except in the case of brief quotations embodied in critical articles and reviews.

The Author of this book is solely responsible and liable for its content including but not limited to the views, representations, descriptions, statements, information, opinions and references ["Content"]. The Content of this book shall not constitute or be construed or deemed to reflect the opinion or expression of the Publisher or Editor. The views and opinions expressed in this book are the author's own and the facts are as reported by him, and the publishers are not in any way liable for the same and do not make any representations or warranties of any kind, express or implied, including but not limited to the implied warranties of merchantability, fitness for a particular purpose. The Publisher and Editor shall not be liable whatsoever for any errors, omissions, whether such errors or omissions result from negligence, accident, or any other cause or claims for loss or damages of any kind, including without limitation, indirect or consequential loss or damage arising out of use, inability to use, or about the reliability, accuracy or sufficiency of the information contained in this book.

To my father, Nirankarnath Ramlal Sharma, who served as a Sub-Divisional Police Officer at Tharad in North Gujarat, at Morbi in Saurashtra, at Bhuj in Kachchh and Rajpipla in South Gujarat

# PREFACE

Mahatma Gandhi's life and teachings attracted many admirers. He believed that in an independent India, democracy should be practiced from the grassroots. Gram panchayats were his dream. Men and women who represented the voters, he believed, should be leaders of immaculate character and should serve the people with devotion and selflessness. Although the Mahatma did not take part in the debates of the constituent assembly, his vision found its reflection in the constitution, particularly in the directive principles of state policy. It postulates that the state shall promote a social order in which justice shall inform all the institutions of national life and secure the operation of a legal system that promotes it.

The police force is a vital organ of the government that ensures stability in society and creates a level playing field for all individuals through the proper enforcement of laws. It is true that the system of district administration that India adopted after independence was largely a continuation of what existed during the British days. While earlier the aim was propagating a colonial rule, now it was promoting a welfare state. Given the preamble and the fundamental duties chapter of the constitution of India, it is of primary importance to sensitize the police force in all the

States of India to these constitutional values and fundamental duties of the citizens. This can be done by informing the police of what is expected of them and the citizens about what they should expect.

Registration and investigation of crime is the primary duty of the police and the raison d'être of their existence. While the supervisory hierarchy consists of several ranks, perhaps the most important and yet least acknowledged is the role played by a sub-divisional police officer. The supervisory functions entrusted to this rank are such that if discharged properly, it would bring about a quantum jump in the quality of service rendered by the police. The description of the three duties, from amongst various others, expected of this rank should suffice to show their critical role in the control of crime.

The order placing a convict under surveillance and for opening a history sheet is issued by the sub-divisional police officer of the subdivision in which the criminal is living at the time of his conviction, and an entry is at the same time made in the Surveillance Register. The power to remove the name from the said register or continue is also vested with that officer. Similarly, in order to ensure that surveillance is exercised over persons, the knowledge of whose movements will assist in the prevention and detection of crime, the sub-divisional officer is expected to, when he inspects a police station, verify the entries in the register, and remove therefrom after consultation with the officer-in-charge of the police station, the police patel or the officer-in-charge of the Out-Post, the name of any person whose conduct, he considers safely admits of it.

A Known Criminals Register, which is a classified register of criminals known to be active or likely to revert to crime but of whom all are not sufficiently important to find a place in the Surveillance Register, is maintained at all police stations. The entries pertain to house-breakers, thieves, robbers, and dacoits. All persons having one conviction for house-breaking, robbery or dacoity, receiving stolen property, coining and note-counterfeiting or persons bound over under section 110 of the Criminal Procedure Code, persons who have been registered as habitual offenders under section 3 of the Bombay Habitual Offender's Act, 1959 and persons having three convictions for theft will come automatically on this register. In addition to this, it is open to the sub-divisional officer to add to this register the names of persons known to have committed these or other offences, whether they have been convicted or not.

To establish an efficient system of patrol, it is essential in the first place that clear standing orders are issued by the sub-divisional officer laying down the manner in which patrolling is to be done in villages as well as in towns and the nature of the information to be collected and entered in their patrol books or note-books by the patrolling officers. But no system, however good and complete it may be, is ever likely to bear good results unless the work done by the men is constantly and systematically watched and checked by the circle police inspector and the sub-inspector, and the books and men thoroughly examined by sub-divisional officers when on their tour of inspection and at other times as often as possible.

Although the above-mentioned powers are vested in the Superintendent of Police of the district as well, the seminal role of the Sub-Divisional Police Officer is obvious. He is expected to pay particular attention to tracing the whereabouts of the bad characters of his subdivision and impress on all officers in-charge of police stations that enquiry regarding every bad character who has passed out of sight is not to be relaxed until it is conclusively ascertained as to what has become of the individual. Any dereliction on their part, he reminds his subordinates, will render them liable to serious consequences.

Two ranks in the police force, namely, the Superintendent of Police of the district and the Station House Officer, garner the attention of both the public and the media. Movies made by the film industry and fiction in the vernacular languages are mainly about them. The situation is not helped by the fact that even the Government, as also the head of the police force of any state, also focus their directives and orders on these two ranks. This book is to recognize the critical and substantive role played by the Sub-Divisional Police Officer in the maintenance of law and order, and to pay tribute to scores of such officers who work systematically and tirelessly in upholding the highest traditions of methodical policing.

# ACKNOWLEDGEMENT

On completion of basic training at the Sardar Vallabhbhai Patel National Police Academy Hyderabad, I reported, in December 1977, along with my four batchmates, for three months of further training at the Police Training College at Junagadh, Gujarat. While there, we received orders from the Government allotting districts where we would be undergoing practical training. I was assigned to Rajkot City. The Superintendent of Police who was to supervise my induction into the practical aspects of policing for the next ten months was an outstanding officer of the 1963 batch of the Indian Police Service, **Prabhat Kumar Dutta**. Energetic, a man of unimpeachable integrity, he was a true leader of men whose grasp and understanding of public order was extraordinary. I was fortunate to become his understudy during those formative years.

For grasping the method and nuances of the functions of a Sub-Divisional Police Officer, I was attached to **Dilavarsinh Sajjansinh Jadeja,** the then incumbent of the only subdivision of the city-district. He had joined the police force as a directly recruited sub-inspector over two and a half decades ago, and now, in the rank of deputy superintendent of police, he brought to bear incisive knowledge of police functioning at the grassroots level. A simple man with a pleasing disposition, I acknowledge gratefully all that he taught me during my supernumerary days.

On completion of my field training in January 1979, I was posted to Palitana sub-division. This is where I met **Chittranjan Vasantrai Vaishnav**, who functioned as one of the junior clerks in the office of the sub-divisional police officer. A simple, dignified man the likes of whom you do not meet any more, he diligently typed out the crime memos which I wrote in my handwriting describing in detail my visitations of serious crimes for dispatch to superior officers. The contents of this book are based on hundreds of typed pages which I, by some fortuitous circumstance, came to preserve all these years.

A Sub-Divisional Police Officer has a hectic touring schedule visiting serious crime. In those days, subdivisions were quite large in area, and the nature of work required frequent night halts in the vicinity of the scene of crime. There was a practice, not followed by all, to carry a "kitchen-box" containing ingredients like rice, lentils, flour, sugar, tea leaves and other sundry items so as not to depend on local hospitality. Vegetables and milk were purchased fresh at the location where one was camping. During these tours, I was accompanied by **Bachumiya Subalmiya**, one of the two armed police constables allotted to function as orderlies. In his late forties, he was a quiet man who ensured that I was supplied two meals a day which he prepared at every place of camp in makeshift arrangements. Meals were simple and Bachumiya ensured I did not go hungry.

**Preeti, Aarti, Pranay**—wife, daughter and son who constantly goaded me, in that order of persistence, to write again. My

*Acknowledgement*

first book was published in 2006, and although along the way, I drafted manuals for various police organisations where I was posted, I never got down to writing another book. It is their insistence that has made this book possible.

# FOREWORD

Sub-Divisional Police Officer (SDPO) is a crucial link in the chain of cutting-edge level police hierarchy. The official has one of the most important roles to play in ensuring efficient police functioning, but his contribution is rarely acknowledged, while the posts of District Superintendent of Police (SP) and Station House Officer (SHO) garner all limelight. SDPOs are the prime crime officers of the district. They not only personally supervise the investigation of all the serious crimes*, but are also the ones who carry out detailed inspection of every police station under their charge once every year, with an eye on how diligently and sincerely crime work and other policing tasks have been performed by the police station. They are generally the principal aides of the Superintendents of Police in ensuring the efficient discharge of all policing functions in the district.

The posts of SDPOs are manned by newly-inducted officers of either the Indian Police Service (IPS) or the State Police Service (SPS), or by officers promoted from the rank of Inspector of Police. The young recruits of IPS or SPS have no previous experience of police work. The training at the police academies equips them with ample theoretical and conceptual inputs, but not enough empirical guidance. There is also acute dearth of published literature on related issues. I recall my own painful quest for some relevant reading material before joining as a SDPO, when I could find nothing beyond the State Police Manual or some departmental orders. I was, thus, left with no option but to fall back only upon on-the-job learning experience or informal counsel of my own subordinates.

This book, authored by Kuldip Sharma, a seasoned police professional, endowed with exceptionally rich experience of policing at the ground level as well as in conceptual and policy realms, eminently fills the vacuum.

The book empirically describes the various functions of the SDPO, especially the important tasks like grave crime investigation, supervision over other crime work, inspection of police stations. The various chapters of the book cover some important 'visitable' cases investigated or supervised by the author. Each of the cases of 'visitable crime' personally investigated or directly supervised by him, discussed in the book, provides good learning experience to the reader on how to investigate criminal cases of different genres, particularly highlighting the need for and importance of attention to detail.

The book, in chapter after chapter, is also replete with the evidence of wide erudition of the author. The chapter: "The Vice of Gambling", for instance, describes the views on gambling reflected in the verses of Rig Veda, comments of Manu and Kautilya, as well as the opinions of ancient Jewish authorities, Muslim jurists and catholic churches. It also gives a brief account of gambling and its regulation in the United Kingdom, besides the gambling-related enactments in India, starting with the Public

Gambling Act of 1867. It goes on to describe different variants of 'Matka' gambling prevalent from time to time. While narrating the sequence of investigation work in different cases, it also, side by side, gives a brief account of the history of different aspects and components of police work as well as the tools of policing. For instance, the chapter: "An Undetected Robbery" traces the history of use of dogs by the police in various countries of Europe and in the USA, as also its introduction in Gujarat.

The chapter: "Of Criminal Tribes, Police Patels and Wagharies" traces the background of enactment of the Criminal Tribes Act of 1871 and its repeal after Independence, besides describing in some detail the modus operandi of certain criminal tribes. The chapter also explains the duties and functions of Police Patels. The chapter: "Fatal Motor Accident", besides recounting the case of the specific accident and its investigation, expatiates on the legal provisions relating to road accidents in the IPC as also the relevant instructions in the Police Manual and other orders, including, notably the directions to police officers concerning their behaviour in dealing with those cases.

The chapter: "Mistake of Caste – A Tragedy" is utilized to explain the legal aspects of dying declaration. Similarly, the chapter: "The Scourge of Caste" discusses sociological aspects of caste, besides explaining the impact of caste dynamics on crime. This chapter also expatiates on the security provision of Section 107 Cr PC, including what all the police should do while initiating proceedings under this section. Chapter 15: "Correction, Instruction, Stimulation" is devoted to inspection of police stations by the SDPO. The chapter dwells on all the elements of inspection – not just the police station records, but including the inspection of parade, turnout of personnel, squad drill, kit inspection, orderly room etc. – duly explaining the rationale of each such element.

Overall, the book – indeed a magnum opus – is highly educative and instructive and needs to be prescribed as mandatory reading material for not just fresh recruits of the IPS and the State Police Services, but also the officers freshly promoted from the rank of Inspector. The National Police Academy would perhaps do well to include it in the curriculum of the second phase of IPS probationers' initial training. The book, with plenty of real-life crime stories and details of the investigation processes, of course, would be of great interest to general readers as well.

**Kamal Kumar**
*Former Director, SVP National Police Academy, Hyderabad &*
*Ex-Vice Chairman, UN Commission on Crime Prevention &*
*Criminal Justice*

# CONTENTS

*Preface* ............................................................................. *iv*
*Acknowledgement* ........................................................... *viii*
*Foreword* .......................................................................... *xi*
*Acronyms* ...................................................................... *xvii*

**1.** Sub-Divisional Police Officer ............................................. 1
**2.** Accidental Death or Suicide? ........................................... 10
**3.** Of Anonymous Information ............................................ 20
**4.** A Village Bully ................................................................. 33
**5.** An Undetected Robbery .................................................. 43
**6.** Of Criminal Tribes, Police Patels and Wagharies ............. 55
**7.** An Unnatural Death: Too Young to Die ......................... 73
**8.** Fatal Motor Accident ...................................................... 84
**9.** Late Registration of a Crime ......................................... 102
**10.** The Vice of Gambling .................................................. 112
**11.** Prime Crime Officer .................................................... 125
**12.** In a Fit of Anger .......................................................... 139
**13.** The Weekly Diary ........................................................ 153
**14.** Mistake of Caste- A Tragedy ....................................... 165
**15.** Correction, Instruction, Stimulation .......................... 176

| | | |
|---|---|---|
| **16.** | The Scourge of Caste | 190 |
| **17.** | The Offence of Rape | 204 |
| **18.** | Prohibition in the Bi-Lingual Bombay State | 221 |
| **19.** | An Eleven-Year-Old Enmity | 234 |
| **20.** | Temple Theft | 255 |
| **21.** | Infidelity | 274 |
| **22.** | The Offence of House-Breaking | 289 |
| **23.** | Musings | 305 |

*Notes............................................................................324*

# ACRONYMS

AD- Accidental Death

ASP- Assistant Superintendent of Police

CID- Criminal Investigation Department

CrPC- Criminal Procedure Code

CPI- Circle Police Inspector

DD- Dying Declaration

DIG- Deputy Inspector-General

DMOB- District Modus Operandi Bureau

DySP- Deputy Superintendent of Police

FIR- First Information Report

HC- Head Constable

IGP- Inspector General of Police

IPC- Indian Penal Code

IPS- Indian Police Service

*Acronyms*

JMFC- Judicial Magistrate First Class

LCB- Local Crime Branch

MO- Medical Officer

MVA- Motor Vehicle Act

MVI- Motor Vehicle Inspector

OP- Out-Post

PC- Police Constable

PSI- Police Sub-Inspector

PM- Post Mortem

RTO- Regional Transport Officer

SDPO- Sub-Divisional Police Officer

SHO- Station House Officer

SP- Superintendent of Police

UPC- Unarmed Police Constable

# SUB-DIVISIONAL POLICE OFFICER

On the 1st of February 1979 at 11:30 AM, I took over as Sub-Divisional Police Officer, Palitana Sub-Division. Early that morning, I arrived from Rajkot, where I had undergone one year of practical training which is mandatory before one is assigned to an independent charge. Head Constable Bharatsinh had come to receive me at the station, where I had arrived on a Gujarat State Road Transport Corporation bus. Bharatsinh, I remember, was in uniform, tall with an impressive moustache.

Palitana is a town in Bhavnagar district, Gujarat. It is located 56 km southwest of Bhavnagar city and is a major pilgrimage center for Jains. Adinatha, the first of the Jain Tirthankaras, is said to have meditated on the Shatrunjaya hill, where the Palitana temples were later constructed in and after the 11th century CE. It is one of the most sacred sites of Svetambara tradition within Jainism. The dense collection of over eight hundred small shrines and large temples here has led many to call Palitana a 'city of temples.' Before independence, it was a princely state founded in

1194. It was one of the major states in Saurashtra, covering an area of 777 square kilometers. It was the subdivisional headquarters and, therefore the headquarters of the Sub-Divisional Magistrate and the Sub-Divisional Police Officer (SDPO).

Since the inception of the Police Act 1861, the direction and regulation of the police throughout the district is vested in the Superintendent of Police (SP). He has full control over the internal administration of the force under him, including arms, drill, exercise, prosecution, discipline and prevention and investigation of crime. It is in the last-mentioned category, that of controlling crime, that the SDPO plays a vital role. However, the post did not exist in the earlier years of the formation of the police, as we now know. Then, each district was headed by a European officer, designated as Superintendent of Police, who supervised the police stations directly. In the last quarter of the 19$^{th}$ century, police stations were few and had huge territories to cover. Conventionally, crime was also low, and one often found one police station having jurisdiction over a territorial area of what would now make up a full-fledged district.

A deliberate policy had been pursued by the British from the very beginning of the reorganization of the police in 1861 not to develop a superior police service consisting of a body of well-educated and professionally competent officers as a part of the overall scheme of preserving the supremacy of the civil service and the office of the district magistrate for imperial purposes. Direct recruitment was started through a competitive examination in England in 1893, only when it was realized that the existing system did not supply the kind of officers required. Satyendranath Tagore was the first Indian to be appointed to the Indian Civil Service

(ICS) in 1864 and was allotted to Bombay, but the higher ranks of the police were filled entirely by Europeans drawn largely from the commissioned ranks of the native Indian army. Subsequently, some officers were appointed by a system of personal selection from among unemployed European residents in India when it was found that military officers were no longer willing to come, the reason for their unwillingness being the subordination of the superintendent of police to the district magistrate, which the army officers found unacceptable and galling.

Indeed, the Indianization of the police did not happen till 1908 when, as a result of the recommendation of the Police Commission of 1902, direct-entry Deputy Superintendents of Police were appointed by the provincial governments. So far, as the Imperial Police was concerned, it did not have any statutory status like the ICS. It was common to refer to the Europeans recruited to the service in London as members of the Imperial Police. The term 'Indian Police Service' was for the first time formally used in 1912 when a Royal Commission under the chairmanship of Lord Islington was appointed to report on the organization of the Civil Services, with special reference to the employment of Indians in these services. A.K. Sinha, former Inspector General of Police, Bihar, was amongst the first batch of Deputy Superintendents of Police to join in Bihar.

A police station is headed by the Station House Officer (SHO) who in the mofussil is of the rank of a Police Sub-Inspector (PSI) or, in the cities and the towns, a Police Inspector. Due to certain historical reasons, amongst the people they are known to be callous, exploitative, and ruthless. What is less known is that many of those who join as police sub-inspectors are well-educated, come from good families and, are as sensitive and sympathetic to public demands as Indian Police Service (IPS) officers. This is the forefront of police functioning, and these officers command anything from fifty to two hundred men and women, not to speak of being responsible for the safety and security of hundreds and thousands of people in their area. This rank, the SHO, is supervised by the Sub-Divisional Police Officer or the SDPO, as he is popularly referred to.

Each district consists of two or more sub-divisions, and an officer of the rank of Deputy Superintendent of Police (DySP) is appointed as the SDPO. This individual is a police officer who has been through the ranks, having served as SHO and as Circle Police Inspector (CPI), and has a remarkable grip over the subject matter of his jurisdiction. He has a thorough knowledge of the investigation process, sections of law applicable and the manner in which a criminal investigation should proceed, leading to either the submission of a charge-sheet or a final report. He is expected to visit the scene of every serious crime reported in his jurisdiction and is responsible for the efficiency and discipline of the officers and men in his subdivision. He is expected to know the details of every undetected case during the discussions he has with superior officers and during the periodic crime conferences that are held. A competent SDPO is expected to have a general picture of the previous ten years of crime recorded in his subdivision, with precise details of the last three years.

Members of the IPS, designated as Assistant Superintendent of Police (ASP), on completion of institutional and field training, are also posted as SDPO, which, in fact, is the first independent assignment after joining the service. It is in this posting that he or she gets a real grounding of crime work and a taste of the arduous nature of police supervisory duties. Since they are direct recruits who lack the experience of a DySP, it is imperative that they address their duties diligently and take it more as a learning exercise. In any event, an ASP or a DySP in charge of a sub-division handles all crime work in his charge and will visit all the scenes of serious offences as laid down in standing orders. Under the general orders of the SP, he also becomes the first supervisory rank in the police force to inspect a police station at regular intervals and certainly at least once a year. In fact, the inspection lasts for over four days, requiring the SDPO to camp there during the duration and familiarize themselves thoroughly with all the records generated at the station during the year. He also visits all the Out-Posts (OP) of that police station and ascertains for himself, by scrutiny of the Occurrence Book maintained at the OP, that no crime has gone unrecorded. The object of inspection is not merely criticism or correction of faults. It is taken by the SDPO as an opportunity to find what is wrong and give instructions as to the better methods based on the substantial experience that he has. As the SDPO traverses his subdivision camping at various police stations as per a predetermined itinerary—correction, instruction, and stimulation is the essence of this exercise.

One of the positive outcomes of the British administration in India has been the institutionalization of the concept of inspection. No officer can administer his charge properly unless he knows his man and the conditions under which they live and work. Inspection work is required to be taken up early in the year so that it is completed by the time the rainy season sets in. Although the SP also inspects the police station, it is for the

SDPO to inspect in detail each police station and out-post in his charge, recognizing that the maintenance of law and order and the prevention and detection of crimes depends largely on the efficiency of the rank and file of the police station. He will check the First Information Report (FIR), the Cognizable Crime Register, Non-Cognizable Crime Register, Case Diaries, Station (General) Diary, Village Crime Record, and other confidential documents. If, based on the scrutiny of these records, he discovers that a crime has been 'burked,' a term used to describe non-registration of a crime by the police, he will get the same registered and, at the same time, call for an explanation of the SHO for this dereliction of duty. In fact, the Non-Cognizable Crime Register and the Station (General) Diary are ideal places for thorough scrutiny by supervisory officers, for it is here that crime that has not been registered can be discerned. There is another critical record known as *Janva Jog*, meaning worth knowing, register in Gujarat where information received from a member of the public, which neither reveals the commission of a cognizable nor of a non-cognizable crime, is recorded. A diligent SDPO would go through every page of this register to ensure that a crime has not been minimized by the SHO by merely recording the information received from a member of the public in this document and taking no further action.

One of the most important duties that an SDPO performs is that of visiting serious crime. The nomenclature 'Visitable Crime' denotes a category of offences on with special attention is paid by supervisory ranks. Every state police force has provided in the manual meant for police functioning what constitutes a serious crime that requires the visit and thorough supervision by the SDPO. Generally, all cases of murder, culpable homicide, dacoity, robbery, house-breaking with theft involving property of a certain value and serious riots are the focus of visitation by the subdivisional officer. Similarly, any case in which a police officer is accused of an offence, provided a complaint has been registered, is required to be visited. During such visitation, the SDPOs are expected to closely identify themselves with the police enquiry, in the pursuit of truth. Though not as a rule, utilizing the salutary provisions of section 36 of the Criminal Procedure Code (CrPC), they could assume the position of the investigating officers whenever the situation so warranted. Their presence during an investigation must be brought out in the papers of the case either by signing the *panchnamas* or by recording statements of witnesses. Such an action would form a guarantee of the regularity with which such period of investigation came under their personal inspection and control.

Thus, the object of a visitation by the SDPO to the scene of an offence is to personally ascertain the facts of the case from the complainant, witnesses and other sources of information; to ascertain what investigation the police on the spot have made; to assist and generally to direct the investigation and to see that it is being correctly and vigorously prosecuted by suitable officers and to prevent irregularities on the part of the subordinate police and to encourage and guide them in their enquiries.

In addition to the above, sub-divisional officers are responsible for the inspection of public conveyances plying for hire in their charges, inspection of explosives, arms, and ammunition shops, and taking musketry practice.

Some provinces had specific requirements to deal with a problem typical of that area. In the State of Gujarat during the decades of the 60s, 70s and 80s, serious motor accidents where fatalities had occurred, were made a visitable crime. This was because after separation from the bilingual Bombay State, Gujarat was developing at a fast pace with excellent national and state highways laid out. As a result, there was a sudden spurt of fatal motor accidents as many motorists and truck drivers coming from other provinces drove at break-neck speed, resulting in serious accidents. The state had outlawed consumption of alcoholic drinks and it became imperative to take steps to reduce accidents caused by inebriated drivers. Incidentally, fatal motor accidents ceased to be a visitable crime towards the end of 1979.

Similarly, all suicide cases by a married woman below the age of 30 years were also made visitable by the SDPO if the woman in question was residing with her in-laws when the unnatural death occurred. In those times, there were many cases where young married woman ended their lives, either because of the unbearable torture by the in-laws or because they found themselves trapped in a marriage, living far away from their parental homes and the future to them appeared to be bleak. But sometimes, it was not unknown for either the husband or the in-laws to put them to death.

The SDPO, thus, is the *prime crime officer* of the district. If there is any officer in the police who supervises crime recorded and investigated in his jurisdiction in detail, then it is the subdivisional officer. There are explicit instructions in vogue that require him to associate himself more closely with the subordinate police officers in the enquiries, and by throwing himself into the realm of really and personally investigating and supervising serious cases, an SDPO can do much to improve the tone, moral and efficiency of the force. In fact, there is no better way of getting comprehensive knowledge of his men and his area other than the method described.

Palitana sub-division consisted of eleven police stations, the furthest from the headquarters being Paliyad, which is at a distance of 110 km. What follows is the narration of my visits to the scenes of serious crime during the eighteen months that I was posted there.

# ACCIDENTAL DEATH OR SUICIDE?

*T*wo days after taking over as SDPO Palitana, I received a special report. 'Special Report' is a name given to a document that is generated by the concerned police station when any crime or incident that must be visited by an SDPO is registered. It sets in motion the activities of the supervisory officer and lends urgency to the matter at hand. There are instructions given in the police manual and reiterated by the standing orders of the Inspector General of Police that the visiting officer should leave for the scene of the crime within two hours of receiving the special report. I received the said report at 2:45 PM, and by 3:20 PM, I was on my way to the scene of the incident, which was 22 km away.

It was about the death of a married woman aged about 25 years who was living with her husband and in-laws. As I was leaving, my Reader PSI, Mansinh Dabhi, came across to meet me. To assist the sub-divisional police officer in studying and monitoring the crime position of his charge, there is in his office a police sub-inspector who is styled as the "Reader". Dabhi said that this was my first visitation after taking over charge, and it augured well that it was a case of an unnatural death. Apparently, there was a belief prevailing in those parts that if the first case that a police officer handles is the death of another human being, it was considered an auspicious beginning!

I was excited for a less altruistic reason. After completing my probationary period, having taken over my first independent charge, this was the first case that I was about to supervise and get actively involved. I was naturally eager to get started. The incident had occurred in a village called Samadhiala, which was within the limits of Palitana Rural police station and was part of Noghanvadar out-post. On arriving at the village, I was met by Head Constable Mahadev Ganpat, who was the investigating officer and Head Constable Bhikubha, who was in-charge of the out-post. Both briefed me about the incident. A Head Constable (HC) investigates a visitable case only if the SHO, for official and cogent reasons, is not available.

Vijuben, the deceased, was married for the last five years to one Naran Gala. She herself belonged to the village, Noghanvadar, which was not far from Samadhiala. The couple had two children, a girl aged a little more than three years and a boy about one-year-old. They lived in a house located on the outskirts of the village and although there was a courtyard, the premises consisted of one room only. The father-in-law and the mother-in-law of the deceased also lived in the same house. As was the normal practice, Vijuben would rise early in the morning at 5 AM to cook food for her husband, who would leave for work at 6:30 AM. Naran Gala was working as a diamond polisher in Gariyadhar town. On the day of the incident, as Vijuben was cooking, the nozzle of the stove came apart, and her silk saree caught fire. The husband, who was sleeping in the same room along with two children, on hearing the commotion, tried to save her but such was the intensity of the flame that he too got burnt. The father-in-law and the mother-in-law were sleeping on the verandah outside the room. Naran had a brother living nearby, and he proceeded to Noghanvadar to get a vehicle. Vijuben was taken to Bhavnagar, the district headquarters, and admitted in a hospital. On the way, her mother boarded the same vehicle. Unfortunately, Vijuben passed away at 9:30 PM the same day.

The unnatural deaths of women are often the subject of speculation by the public and, at times, condemned by society due to the gender role they play. Mothers, wives, daughters, and sisters – they play a crucial and indispensable role in society. In Saurashtra, there were several cases reported of married women dying due to unnatural causes. When the unnatural death involves a female, it shatters the lives of the survivors or the family. According to the laid down procedure in India, such deaths must be reported to the police station, and it is the duty of the police to conclude whether the cause of demise was natural or unnatural. In the latter case, police are mandated to investigate so as to rule out either homicide or abetment to suicide, both being penal offences. If the unnatural death is that of a married woman below the age of 30 years, staying in the same house as her in-laws in Gujarat, it was mandatory for senior officers such as the SDPO to visit and closely associate themselves with the investigation. This was to rule out any foul play on the part of the family and misdemeanour by way of collusion, on the part of the subordinate police officers.

I began by carefully examining the scene of the incident about which a *panchnama* had already been drawn. Prepared in the presence of two independent witnesses, the only occasion on which a document which is popularly styled as a *panchanama* is required by law to be drawn up is when some articles are seized during the search of a place or an investigation into the cause of death is made as in this case. The holding of *panchnamas* on other occasions is not a duty imposed by law, though in practice a police officer resorts to it as a mode of obtaining independent evidence to corroborate the results of his own inquiry and observation. In such cases, a *panchnama* by itself has no evidentiary value. It is merely a memorandum of what has been observed by the *panch* witness and the investigating officer, who are apt to forget many of the details observed by them in the interval between the events themselves and the day on which they are called on to testify to them in Court. In view of this legal position, the *panch* witnesses to be selected should be of mature age, intelligent, literate as far as possible, respectable, impartial, free from objectionable antecedents, not likely to be influenced by pecuniary or other considerations and should be selected by the police officer and not by the complainant or any other interested person. When the subject matter of the investigation is a woman, preferably a female *panch* should be called in.

The *panchnama* drawn up by HC Ganpat seemed to be in order, and I met the *panch* witnesses to confirm that they had examined the scene of the incident and only after that they signed the document.

I then proceeded to examine the witnesses. The father-in-law of Vijuben was 70 years old and confirmed that he was sleeping on the verandah with his wife when the incident took place. He heard shouts from the room, and along with his wife, when he entered, he found his son, Naran, putting out the flames which had engulfed their daughter-in-law. He further mentioned that his other son, Savji, who stays nearby, went to Noghanvadar to procure a Tempo Traveler for carrying his daughter-in-law to the hospital. Since the latter expired the same day, he, along with all members of his family, had gone to Noghanvadar the following day to attend the funeral of his daughter-in-law. His wife, the mother-in-law of the deceased, corroborated the statement of her husband.

The next witness I examined was the eldest brother-in-law of the deceased. During interrogation, he revealed that his youngest brother, Naran, had come in the morning at about 6 AM and informed him that Vijuben, his wife, had sustained severe burns and was lying in the house, requiring immediate medical attention. He further said that there was another brother named Savji who had already gone to Noghanvadar to get hold of a vehicle. This witness confirmed that he accompanied Vijuben when she was taken to the hospital and that the mother of the latter had also come along. Savji was the next witness to be examined, who confirmed fetching the Tempo Traveler for conveying Vijuben to the hospital at Bhavnagar. In this fashion, close relatives of the deceased were examined, and they corroborated the story so far.

In an enquiry of this kind, it is especially important to question the neighbours and other villagers and ascertain whether the deceased was ever known to complain about maltreatment by the in-laws, including her husband. I, therefore, made enquiries from several people in the village, including the police patel. None of them reported any discord within the family. Since the examination of the parents of the married woman is a vital part of the investigation, I proceeded to village Noghanvadar to meet with them.

Enquiries with the father of the deceased revealed that they had five daughters, of which two were married. Vijuben was the second daughter who was married to Naran Gala of Samdhiayala village. On the day of the incident, he was at the village Jodhavadar attending a marriage when he was informed that his daughter had suffered burn injuries and had been taken to Bhavnagar for medical treatment. He had at once departed to be with his daughter, and on arriving at the hospital, he found her lying in a burnt condition. His daughter informed him that she had sustained these burns while cooking food in the morning. He further reported that his daughter passed away in the same evening at 9:30 PM and that the body was brought back to Noghanvadar for cremation.

The mother of the deceased was also questioned. She disclosed that she learned about the incident early in the morning and confirmed that she travelled in the vehicle that carried her daughter to the hospital and Bhavnagar. Her daughter was burnt all over, and on reaching the hospital, she noticed that her son-in-law, Naran Gala, had also suffered burns. This witness also confirmed her daughter informing her that she was burnt while cooking food.

The cause of the accident was the nozzle of the primus stove that had come apart. Since, in those days, forensic support to the police was not easily available, except for serious cases of homicide, arson or major accidents involving the loss of many lives, police in rural areas depended on the local expertise if one was available. Ibrahim Shah of Noghanvadar village was in the business of repairing stoves widely used in villages for cooking food. This was a time when even the electricity had not reached rural India, and the use of gas cylinders in the kitchen was confined to urban areas. The primus stove that caused the death of Vijuben was shown to Ibrahim, who opined that if the nozzle is not closed properly after the kerosene has been poured into the container, it can come out in the manner that happened in this case.

By the time the above work was completed, and witnesses examined, it had become dark. My subdivisional headquarters, as noted above, was only 22 km away, and since I had a police jeep at my disposal, I could easily return to Palitana. Nevertheless, being mindful of the police manual requirements, in the interest of meticulous investigation, to camp near the scene of the incident, I spent the night at village Noghanvadar in a makeshift facility.

The following day, the remaining important witness, namely the driver of the Tempo Traveler, was examined. He confirmed that on the morning of the incident, his Tempo was requisitioned to carry the deceased to the hospital. He also confirmed that the husband of the deceased, the brother-in-law and her mother had travelled along. This witness further confirmed that the husband had sustained burn injuries on his hands and legs.

In this manner, during my first visitation as an SDPO, it was concluded that the woman in question had died because of accidental burning and that there was no harassment or ill-treatment meted out to her by her in-laws or husband. After initialing the case diaries and the remaining papers of investigation, I departed for Palitana.

Seven years later, in 1986, the Indian Penal Code was amended, and section 304B was inserted to provide for dowry deaths. Where the death of a woman is caused by any burns or bodily injury or occurs otherwise than under normal circumstances within seven years of her marriage, and it is shown that soon before her death, she was subjected to cruelty or harassment by her husband or any relative of her husband for, or in connection with, any demand for dowry, such death was called "dowry death," and such husband or relative are deemed to have caused her death.

That same year, the Indian parliament inserted section 498-A in the Indian Penal Code, which penalizes cruelty by a husband or his relative on a woman for any unlawful demand for any property or valuable security or is on account of failure by her or any person related to her to meet such demand, which forces her to commit suicide or cause grave injury or danger to her life.

Five months later, I had the occasion to visit another case of accidental death which occurred at village Morba within the limits of Gariyadhar police station. According to the information received, Kanchanben Damjibhai, a 22-year-old married woman who was at the house of her in-laws, died due to burns received as her clothes had caught fire while cooking. She had been married for four years and used to live in Surat with her husband Damji, who was employed as an artisan in the diamond industry. On the day of the incident, the latter left the village to proceed towards Gariyadhar en route to Surat. The deceased was to stay behind. He had barely reached there when he learnt that his wife had suffered burn injuries while cooking food and had returned to the village post-haste only to discover that she had passed away.

In this case, too, all the witnesses supported the version that it was a death due to accidental burning while cooking. The father-in-law, mother-in-law, sister-in-law, brother-in-law, the village Sarpanch (headman), and the village chowkidar would corroborate the version. The neighbours, eight in all, and the relatives of the deceased staying nearby would say that they had never heard the deceased complain of any ill-treatment by her in-laws. When I proceeded to Botad, a taluka[1] headquarters town located 80 km away, to examine the parents of Kanchanben, they would confirm that their daughter had no complaints against the in-laws, even though the last rites of the deceased were performed in the absence of the parents. No foul play was suspected, and the case was classified as accidental death.

Forty-four years later, as I write this and recall details of my first investigation in a supervisory capacity, a doubt has entered my mind. Was it really a case of accidental death by burning, or was it a case of suicide? If it was the former, then why was the body of Vijuben cremated at the village of her parents and not at Samdhiayala, where she lived with her husband and children? As far as Kanchanben's death was concerned, it can be safely surmised that she would have been upset at being compelled to stay back and live with her in-laws. Undoubtedly, the quality of life in the village would not be the same as living with her husband in Surat City, and she must have resented the drudgery of a rural existence. My examination of her parents had revealed that she found the mother-in-law irritating. In hindsight, it can be surmised that perhaps this may have been a case of suicide and not of accidental death.

I was just 26 years old at that time, unmarried, beginning a career in the police and not fully familiar with either the intricacies of marital life or the mores of societal pressures on married women living in conservative surroundings.

# OF ANONYMOUS INFORMATION

*E*arly in my career, I became aware of the importance and the relevance of information received from anonymous sources. Ordinarily instructions in vogue were that anonymous applications are to be filed away without taking any action thereon except when specific instances capable of verification are mentioned and are of sufficient public importance to be investigated. When a signed application is proved to be pseudonymous, it is to be treated in the same manner as an anonymous application.

In the first week of March 1979, Z S Saiyed the Superintendent of Police, Bhavnagar had received an anonymous application conveying that a married woman had been done to death in village Kanad falling under the jurisdiction of Sihor police station. The SP on perusal of the unsigned and undated letter concluded that it required to be inquired into, and entrusted CPI Palitana with that task. The incumbent G S Ahuja, an energetic and a sincere police officer, proceeded to the village and within the course of a day, he was able to conclude that there was substance in the allegations made. A woman had indeed been done to death and the fact concealed not only by the members of the family but by the neighbours as well. Nobody had come forward to file a complaint. Section 154 CrPC, which pertains to the registration of FIR contemplates that the person giving first information should be personally present before the officer-in-charge of the police station. Where, therefore, information is sent to the police station by a letter, or through a verbal message by a servant, or by telegraph or telephone, it is for the Police Station Officer to judge, on the facts or each individual case, whether the information is genuine and to treat it accordingly. If he thinks that the information so received is dependable, he need not refuse to act upon it, but may, for the purpose of fulfilling the requirements of the law, record the information as given either by himself or by any of his subordinates. Similarly, information received through anonymous or pseudonymous communications or from rumours or from the personal knowledge of the Police Station Officer or any other policeman may in appropriate cases, be treated as first information and acted upon after recording it in the same manner. In this case, Ahuja had personally verified allegations and therefore became a complainant himself, filing the same on behalf of the state.

Before embarking on narrating the details of this case it is necessary to clarify the nomenclature commonly used amongst the *darbar* community to avoid any confusion. Traditionally, *ba*, which in the Gujarati language stands for mother is suffixed to the names of females out of a sense of respect and regard. Similarly, *bha* is often suffixed to the names of the males instead of *sinh*, meaning lion, to display deference and status as a respected or an elderly person. Thus, in the same family *sinh* could be suffixed to the name of one male member, usually the son and *bha* suffixed to the name of another, in all probability the father.

The special report which would manifest into a visitation by me was received on a Sunday just two weeks after the receipt of the application by the SP. This would show how promptly and efficiently the system worked in those days. I was already busy supervising a murder case registered with Palitana Town police station. Since that was a detected case and all the important witnesses had been examined, I decided to conclude that visitation and proceed to village Kanad. This turned out to be a medium-sized village of about 243 families located 9 km north of the police station, most of whose vocation was agriculture. The prominent residents were Rajputs, locally known as *darbar*. On arrival I was met by the CPI who apprised me of the facts.

Sarojba (name changed) was only fifteen years old when she was married to Bharatsinh Bhikhubha who resided in the village with his brothers and parents. She belonged to Jamnagar district, and this was a case of an arranged marriage. Neither the bride nor the bridegroom had seen each other before the wedding. That apart, amongst the *darbar* community to which they belonged, the marriage ceremony is consummated in the absence of the bride who is later taken to the bridegroom's house in a formal ceremony. The bride was good-looking, well-built, vivacious, and tall. On the other hand, Bharatsinh possessed a puny physique; he was shorter in height and weighed much less than his wife. They had been married for five years and over a period Sarojba became disgruntled and irritable. It was suggested that because of physical disparity, the marriage had not been consummated.

The family found the new daughter-in-law to be dominating and demanding. The latter came from a comparatively well-off family and did not find either the social standing or the financial position of the family into which she had been wedded inspiring. Her marital home consisted of, in addition to her husband, the mother-in-law, two brothers-in-law and a widowed sister-in-law. Customarily and traditionally, for reasons which in today's time are difficult to understand, the bulk of the household chores had to be done by Sarojba. While initially she fell in line and met the requirements of the family, over a period she began to assert her individuality. It was reported that she developed illicit relations with a certain individual, and this was objected to by the elder brother of her husband. About a year ago, the objecting sibling had been done to death allegedly by her paramour, Ramsingh, who was undergoing a life term for the said murder. Normally this should have been ground enough for Sarojba and Bharatsinh's marriage to end. However, in a conservative environment which existed in those days in rural India, and particularly amongst the rajputs, such a move for such a reason would have brought calumny to the reputation of the family.

Sarojba, at least at home, did not change her attitude and there were instances when she would react violently with members of the family, especially with her husband. The latter, already suffering from an inferiority complex because of his physical attributes, did not make an issue out of such instances, fearing gossip in the village and so appearing to be pathetic in the pitying eyes of the villagers. However, one day, about a month before the crime came to be reported, when Bharatsinh came home in the evening just as it was getting dark, he found his wife standing outside the house with a stick in her hand and banging the door, shouting upon her mother-in-law to open it up. Her widowed sister-in-law was also inside and apparently there had been a disagreement amongst them. Saroj was threatening to thrash them and was shouting abuses. On seeing this, something snapped in the husband. From a diminutive and a mild person, he transformed into an aggressive and violent one. He approached his wife to beat her up with a *lathi* that he was carrying, but instead got knocked off to the ground by a blow that she delivered to him with the stick that she was holding. Standing in the proximity was Chandubha, the younger brother of the husband, a lad of hardly fourteen years age and one Fatehsinh Amarsinh, a first cousin. Since all were tired of the licentious and shrewish behaviour of this daughter-in-law of the family, they decided to finish her off that day.

Sarojba must have sensed this and ran to take shelter in the house of a neighbour, Jasuba Ranubha. She bolted the door from inside, despite the objections taken by the latter, who, sensing something untoward was about to happen, began shouting and crying. By now another cousin of the husband, namely Nanbha Amarsinh, had also arrived. Around that time, one Dilubha Dilawarsinh, a well-regarded villager, who was passing by intervened and asked the husband Bharatsinh and others to exercise restraint. He, in fact, rebuked them for such behaviour and told Saroj to come out of the house and resolve the issue. It seems that the latter had not sensed or had underestimated the collective fury of the family. Assured by the presence of an elderly villager like Dilubha, she stepped out. The moment she did so, all four, that is Bharatsinh, Chandubha, Fatehsinh and Nanbha, set upon her and continued beating her with their *lathis* till she became lifeless. Thereafter the husband along with his two cousins went to the Sarpanch, the village headman, and conveyed that he had killed his wife. This village official, whose duty was to ensure that the crime is reported to the police, instead told them to do as they deemed fit.

This was a case where a serious crime such as a murder, committed in the presence of so many witnesses, had remained unreported till the receipt of the anonymous application and subsequent enquiry by the CPI. The latter accompanied me to the scene of offence which was inside a large courtyard with stone-studded flooring in which the house of the deceased, accused Bharatsinh and Chandubha was located. Opposite of this was the house of witness Jasuba Ranubha. In fact, the distance between the deceased's marital home and that of the first cousins of her husband, Fatehsinh and Nanbha, was barely thirty feet. A fourth house located at some distance to the south-east was that of Jesubha Mulubha. I verified the *panchnama* of the scene of offence for its accuracy and comprehensibility.

The body of the deceased had been disposed of in what can be described in a summary manner. While all the four accused led by the husband were discussing the next step forward, a distant relative Ratansinh Jamsinh, who also lived in the vicinity, arrived. After confabulations, shortly after 9 PM, they simply picked up the body, proceeded to the designated spot outside the village where cremation was usually done and consigned the mortal remains of Sarojba to the flames without even bothering to change her clothes or follow any ritual connected with the last rites according to the Hindu religion. It must be understood that these villages were without any electricity and after nightfall within homes, the source of illumination was kerosene-based lanterns and candles. It was therefore not difficult to go about this business without either being seen by anybody or being accosted. I decided to visit the cremation ground and confirm for myself of such a possibility. Before my arrival, the investigating officer had succeeded in collecting bones from the pyre for medical and forensic examination. This had been possible although almost a month had passed by since the deceased was cremated because of two reasons. Firstly, no other cremation has taken place in the intervening period. And secondly, because the family had not bothered, for obvious reasons, to collect the bones which in the normal course is done for a subsequent ceremony of immersing them in a river.

Ratansinh Jamsinh was not party to the murder but was certainly an abettor for an offence defined in section 201 IPC. This section relates to causing the disappearance of any evidence of the commission of an offence and includes the giving of false information with the intention of screening an offender. On questioning, he admitted his culpability saying that he had known the family for generations and was part of the ceremony five years ago when Sarojba and Bharatsinh were married. He explained that when he arrived, in the courtyard he found the dead body of the deceased on the floor while her husband and others were discussing in an agitated manner what was to be done next. He said that Sarojba was not a woman of good character and was a nagging and a disobedient wife. When he learnt that she had been killed a little while ago, he cooperated with his distant relatives to quietly cremate her. The next day they spread the word that the deceased had died because of serious gastric problems.

Gulabsinh Jorsinh was the village headman, the *Sarpanch*. He was examined in some detail because as an elected functuionary employed in connection with the affairs of the village, there were certain legal obligations for him to discharge. He said that on the day of the incident around 8:30 PM the husband of the deceased accompanied by Fatehsinh and Nanbha came to him and revealed that they had killed Sarojba. According to this witness, he asked them to report this to Sihor police station and abused them for such a heinous act. He further testified that he was aware of the general bad reputation of the deceased and the fact that she was not in the control of her husband. Gulabsinh, however, could give no explanation as to why he did not report the crime to the police station, despite the lapse of more than three weeks before eventually the police swung into action after being alerted by an anonymous application. There exists a salutary provision in section 40 of the CrPC which casts a certain duty on village officers and persons living in the village to immediately give information about certain offences and about certain state of things to the nearest magistrate or police officer. The duty cast by law is absolute and immediate. However, the provisions of this section are not intended to be punitive; they are intended to facilitate the receiving of information about offences and consequent taking of steps either for prevention of the same or apprehension of the offender. The *Sarpanch* was clearly at fault.

Interestingly, the barber of the village, Arjun Sukha was present at the residence of the *Sarpanch* when the three accused came to speak with him. He reported that at that time he was serving meal to the latter and had heard them convey to Gulabsinh about the killing of the deceased. According to this witness, the

Sarpanch asked them why they did so, to which the husband Bharatsinh responded that in a fit of anger they just did it. The witness further stated that at this point of time he went home to have his dinner, and when he came back, the *Sarpanch* informed him that the accused had indeed killed Sarojba.

In those days, every village had a watchman, locally called chowkidar. The incumbent in village Kanad then was Pathubha Aderaj. He was summoned for examination. He reported that the day after the murder, he had heard people talking in the village that somebody had died. He thereupon contacted Gulabsinh, his boss, and asked him about it. The latter told him that Sarojba had died due to "gas" trouble. Nevertheless, by evening he had heard that she had been killed by her husband and other family members, and hurriedly cremated without informing the police. This witness, also being a village official, was duty-bound to convey the information to the police station but had failed to do so.

In the FIR recorded at the police station on the complaint filed by Inspector Ahuja, one Manubha Daulatsinh was cited as the fourth accused. During detailed questioning it had been possible for me to figure out that Bharatsinh, the husband, had given the name of this person only to shield his adolescent younger brother Chandubha. Manubha in fact turned out to be a valuable witness. It happened that around the time when the crime was being committed towards the evening, he was returning with his cattle and was passing nearby when one of his cattle strayed towards the residence of Ranubha Kadabha, the husband of Jasuba. He heard a woman shouting for help. When he got there, he found the Sarojba lying on the ground and all the four accused beating her up mercilessly. This witness claimed that since he could not stomach the sight, he made a hasty retreat and went home.

Although by now it was late in the night, I could not have completed the first day of business without questioning the "good samaritan," Dilubha Dilawarsinh, on whose assurance the deceased walked out of the neighbour's house where she had taken shelter. He reported that he was passing by the courtyard when he heard Jasuba Ranubha shouting for help. He had gone there and found that Sarojba had locked herself in while all the four accused were outside carrying *lathis*. He testified that he tried to pacify the husband and his family members and assured Sarojba that no harm would come to her if she now came out and tried to resolve the issue with them. She expressed apprehension that they would kill her but finally agreed to do so after she sensed that Bharatsinh and others had retreated. The witness said that Saroj came out and was walking away when suddenly her husband and the other accused returned and started hitting her with their *lathis*. Realizing that there was nothing much that he could do, this witness simply walked away.

Bharatsinh, Chandubha, Fatehsinh and Nanbha were taken into custody, and I left with them for Sihor, along with Ahuja and the investigating officer, to put them in the lock-up and camp for the night.

Next day I returned to the village along with the accused to recover the weapons used for committing the crime, in this case, the *lathis*. This was done under a *discovery panchnama*, the legal relevance of which has been described in some detail in the following chapter. There were two important witnesses who had to be examined and their statements recorded. The first was Jasuba Ranubha in whose house the deceased had taken shelter. She said that her husband Ranubha being away, she was cooking food for the family when suddenly the deceased came running, entered another room in the house and locked it from inside. Her small children were also inside there, and she had seen all the four accused armed with lathis chasing the deceased. She somehow sensed that they were going to kill Saroj. She feared for the safety of the children and started shouting. The husband of the deceased had approached her and told her to let them in or else she too would be assaulted. After the intervention of Dilubha, the deceased opened the door, whereupon she collected her children and hastily left for the house of her sister living in the same village. This witness said that as she was exiting, she could hear blows being rained on the deceased. She did not return home that night.

The other important witnesses who had to be questioned was another neighbour living near the scene of offence, Vajuba, wife of Jesubha Mulubha. She, however, claimed that though she heard shouts and screams as well as the sound of beating, she did not venture out of her house out of fear. I was struck by the realisation of one common feature emanating out of the testimony of this witness and that of Jasuba recorded earlier, as also the hearsay evidence of what the deceased said to Dilubha before she was done to death- that there was an abject fear of what the men folk could do, including causing grievous injuries or death. This was a manifestation of community norms that privilege or ascribe higher status to men and lower status to women, and a preconceived notion about how a woman should conduct herself especially in conservative and traditional societies.

It was therefore not surprising, that when I questioned Jikuba, the mother-in-law of the deceased, there was no remorse about the death of a member of the family, only a reiteration of the deceased's shrewish and bad character. Since this witness was the cause of the events that led to the murder, it was important to examine her to establish the motive.

As a visiting supervisory officer, I had completed all that was expected of me. All the accused had been arrested, important evidence taken on record, and weapons used for the commission of a crime recovered. They would be charged with the offence of murder and for destroying evidence by cremating the body. Before leaving, I directed the investigating officer to prosecute under section 201 IPC, Ratansinh Jamsinh as well, for the role he played in quietly cremating the body and thereby destroying the evidence. I also directed that action be taken under section 176 IPC against the Sarpanch and the Chowkidar of the village for not reporting the crime to the police station. This provision of law applies to all persons upon whom an obligation is imposed by law to give certain information to public servants, and the penalty which the law provides is intended to apply to parties who commit an intentional breach of such obligation. Section 40 CrPC provides that every officer employed in connection with the affairs of a village, and every person residing in a village shall forthwith communicate to the nearest magistrate or to the officer-in-charge of the nearest police station, any information which he may possess respecting the commission of, in or near such village, of any non-bailable offence or the occurrence of any death under suspicious circumstances. Both these village officials were duty-bound to inform the police.

I did not understand then and perhaps do not understand even now why section 176 IPC is preferred over section 202 IPC. The latter is a similar provision which makes it an offence if a person legally bound to give information about the commission of a crime omits to do so. Back then, as a young officer, I presumed it had to do with the chapters of the Indian Penal Code wherein these provisions are included. Section 176 IPC is part of chapter X which deals with contempt of lawful authority of public servants whereas section 202 IPC is contained in the next chapter dealing with false evidence and offences against public justice.

Technically almost the entire village could also be prosecuted similarly. Within twenty-four hours everybody knew that Sarojba had been done to death. And yet such are the traditions, perhaps emanating out of fear of antagonizing a prominent community like the *darbars*, and amongst them the fear of calumny, and the desire to retain the male hegemony, that total silence prevailed throughout the village. *Omertà* may have been an Italian code of honour for a conduct that places importance on silence in the face of questioning by authorities or outsiders, especially during criminal investigations; what happened at Kanad village was evidence enough that it existed in India as well.

# A VILLAGE BULLY

*M*urder is a crime that generated considerable interest in those days. Although the killing of another human being catches eyeballs even today, earlier, it was not so ordinary and was not treated in such a mundane manner as it is done now.

It may be of interest to know that the Indian Penal Code describes two kinds of homicide. Lawful homicide is committed where death is caused by accident or misfortune and without any criminal intention or knowledge that the perpetrator is doing an unlawful act. This covers cases where a person in good faith believes that he is doing a lawful act. Unlawful homicide, on the other hand, is resorting to an intentional act which either results in death or causes such body injuries as to cause death.

Although I was posted as SDPO Palitana sub-division, it sometimes happened that I was deputed to supervise a visitable offence in another subdivision of the district. This was the case when the SDPO of that subdivision was either busy supervising another serious crime or happened to be on leave at the relevant time. In this case, it turned out that the incumbent SDPO was required to ensure that no untoward incident happened at an ongoing Swaminarayan festival. On a particularly warm day in May 1979, I received directions from the office of the Superintendent of Police to proceed immediately to Talaja police station of Mahuva sub-division as a murder had been reported, and the accused were not known. So it was that I found myself in the village of Borla where the crime had occurred. It was at 8 PM in the night when I reached the scene of crime.

I was met by PSI Parmar, who was the SHO of Talaja police station and the investigating officer. After the perusal of the FIR, I questioned Parmar about the incident. It transpired that the body of one Koli Chithar Dama was recovered on the morning of the previous day from the bushes beside the road connecting village Trapaj and village Kathava, the village to which the deceased belonged. Apparently, the deceased was returning in a bullock cart after meeting his sister, who lived in village Babariyat. The cart belonged to one Mangalsinh of village Trapaj, and on the day of the incident, the bullock cart returned to Trapaj empty and without the deceased. The owner discovered bloodstains on the cart, and he at once informed the local police. Inquiries further revealed that Chithar Dama did not enjoy a good reputation in that area and was despised and feared by many. Very often, he had beaten up the villagers and even compelled married women to enter into illicit relations with him. The husbands could not say anything to him because they were mortally afraid.

Before we continue with the narrative, it is important to mention here that Bhavnagar district is a part of a region called Saurashtra. This is a peninsular region of Gujarat located on the Arabian Sea coast. It covers about a third of Gujarat state, notably 11 districts.

It was formerly a State of the Union of India before it merged with the erstwhile Bombay state. In 1960, it separated from Bombay and became part of Gujarat. The peninsula is sometimes referred to as Kathiawar after the kathi darbar, a caste that once dominated the region. However, Saurashtra is not entirely synonymous with Kathiawar since a small portion of the historical Saurashtra region extends beyond the Kathiawar peninsula. Before independence, this region consisted mainly of princely states, 217 in all, and therefore, there were several instances of the upper-class rajputs and the kathi darbars displaying belligerent behaviour towards the common man and exploiting their relative inferior status. This situation continued for a couple of decades, even after independence.

The *koli's*, on the other hand, belong to the 'other backward classes' category. Sources from the medieval period suggest that the term *koli* was applied generically to lawless people, whilst British colonial studies considered it to be a vague collective noun for varied communities whose sole common feature was that they were inferior to the *kunbis*[1]. At some stage, *koli* became accepted as a caste and thus superior to the tribal *bhils*[2]. Although not rajputs, they claimed the status of the higher-ranked rajput community, adopting their customs and intermixing with less significant rajput families through the practice of hypergamous marriage, which was commonly used to enhance or secure social status. The *kolis* now constitute over 22 per cent of Gujarat's population. They are evenly spread across all regions of the state. Socially, they are divided into several sub-sections like chumadia koli, tadapada koli, patanvadia koli, baria koli, thakor koli and koli patel. Occupationally, there are two sections: sea-based *kolis,* those settled in the long coastal belt and engaged in fishing activities, and land-based *kolis,* small, marginal farmers and landless labourers. The deceased belonged to this community.

Since it was already dark, the examination of the scene of crime was postponed to the following morning. This revealed that the road connecting Borla village, and the highway ran along a canal emanating from Shetrunji Dam. Near the village, the road goes into a steep decline and then rises again to come on level ground. It is in this depression, which cannot be seen by anybody standing on level ground that the crime was committed. Bloodstains were still visible on the road as also evidence that the body had been dragged into the bushes. I examined the *panchnama* of the scene of crime and noted that blood caked in mud had been seized for forensic examination. I also went through the inquest report and other papers connected with the case. The deceased had been delivered a blow on the base of his skull with a sharp-edged weapon, and both his legs had been nearly severed.

There were no houses near the place where the murder had been committed, nor were there any eyewitnesses. Accompanied by the investigating officer, I visited all the wadis nearby, which are cultivated agricultural land, hoping to find some witnesses. Unfortunately, this did not result in anything worthwhile. Inquiries were also made in the village of Borla. The nature of the murder made it clear that it was a case of personal enmity, and often, questioning the close relatives of the deceased leads to detection of the crime. Since the deceased belonged to village Kathava, further inquiries there was the next best option.

Kadviben Dama was a widow and mother of the deceased. Distress was writ large on her face as we approached her. It happened that she lived in that house along with the deceased son and another younger son, Mohan. She revealed that Chithar Dama was employed by one Mangalsinh of Trapaj and that on the day before the crime, he was to go to visit his sister, who was married and lived in another village nearby. She claimed that while she had no personal knowledge about why her son was killed, she did suspect one Hamji Sursinh of the same village.

Next to be questioned was Mohan Dama, the brother of the deceased. He corroborated the statement of his mother and indicated that Hamji could be the murderer since there was enmity between him and his brother. It was learnt that about a year ago, the deceased had attacked Hamji with a *dhariya*, a sharp-edged, sickle-shaped weapon. In the resultant police complaint, the deceased Chithar Dama was arrested and spent some time in judicial custody.

The brother-in-law of the deceased, who lived in the village of Babariyat, was examined, and he confirmed that on the day prior to the murder, the deceased had come to visit him. He had come on a bullock cart and was carrying two maunds of *bajra* (millet) for them. The wife of this witness was the sister of the deceased, who said that her brother stayed overnight and left the following morning at about 8:30 AM. Both witnesses also stated that the only person who could have a grudge against the deceased was Hamji.

In the meantime, inquiries were made with the ladies of the village who often visited the canal near the scene of crime for washing clothes. It was learnt that one Nanduben Koli had indeed taken a bag of clothes for washing but, on questioning, said that she was there at 7:30 AM in the morning and returned soon after without having seen anything. Another witness, Kantilal Vejnath, was found. He was an employee of the irrigation department and worked as a chowkidar near the canal. He claimed that, on being summoned by his superior officer, he was away from the village and returned only in the evening.

Although there were no eyewitnesses nor was there any circumstantial evidence available, it was decided to interrogate Hamji Sursinh. This was a prolonged exercise as the suspect initially declined any knowledge. But on sustained interrogation, he finally broke down and revealed that a few days after the deceased was released from judicial custody, he met him on the road to the village. At that time, the deceased had taunted him and said that there was nothing the police could do to him, and now that he is out on bail, he proposes to visit the house of the suspect and force himself on his wife. He also threatened that if he found the suspect's wife alone anywhere while farming, he would most certainly dishonour her. The language conveying such intentions had enraged the suspect. Given the notorious reputation of the deceased, Hamji believed that the deceased would do to his wife what he had done to other women in the village. Since he was a rajput, he was not able to tolerate such a threat or even the possibility of dishonour. He therefore decided to kill him.

Hamji revealed that he had seen the deceased travel towards the village of Babariyat and knew that the latter was going to the village of his sister and would certainly return the following day by the same route. The next day, around daybreak, the suspect lay waiting for the deceased, hiding himself behind some bushes beside the road. The deceased was soon sighted returning on a bullock cart, and as soon as he passed by the suspect, the latter came up behind and delivered a powerful blow on the base of his neck with an axe. Before the deceased could react, he delivered two more blows on the body. Chithar Dama fell out of the cart, and the suspect then dragged him behind the bushes and tried to cut off both his legs using the same weapon. He did not wait to see whether the deceased was dead but went ahead immediately to wash the bloodstained axe and clothes in the canal and then fled from the scene of offence.

The statement of the accused was recorded, and he was placed under arrest. There were literally no eyewitnesses, and under the laws applicable in India, confession before the police is not admissible in evidence. It should, however, be noted that a statement that amounts to a dying declaration under section 32 (1) of the Indian Evidence Act, though made to a police officer in the course of an investigation, and a confession relevant under section 27 of the Evidence Act, can be used for evidentiary purposes in the inquiry or trial against the accused. The only way forward would be to recover the weapon used in committing the crime in the presence of two independent witnesses. This is described as the *discovery panchnama* and is admissible in evidence as per section 27 of the Evidence Act. The object of this section is to admit evidence, which is relevant to the matter under the enquiry, namely the guilt of the accused, and not to admit evidence which is not relevant to that matter. Confessional statements made to police officers are admissible in evidence, but only that part of the confession that leads to the discovery of property or other relevant facts is admissible. Information supplied by a person in custody that "I will produce a knife concealed in the roof of my house" does not lead to the discovery of a knife. It leads to the discovery of the fact that a knife is concealed in the house of the informant, and if the knife is proved to have been used in the commission of the offence, the fact discovered is relevant.

So, where a confession in the form of a statement of an accused person is recorded by a police officer to the effect, "I stabbed Pratap with a spear. I hid the spear in a yard in my village. I will show you that place," the first sentence is inadmissible, but the second and the third sentences are admissible under section 27.

Since the strength and credibility of this vital piece of evidence depended on obtaining two impartial and independent witnesses, efforts were made to find the same in the village. The accused then led the police party to the scene of crime where he indicated the spot where the deceased was killed, and the bushes behind which the body was hidden. This was methodically recorded in the *panchnama*. Next, Hamji proceeded to produce the axe used in committing the crime. There were no blood stains on the same, although the clothes that he produced contained signs of washed-away stains. These articles were seized in the presence of the *panch* witnesses.

Since it was almost dark, I proceeded to Trapaj to spend the night at a government guest house. On the following day, being my third on this investigation, we made efforts to ascertain whether the accused had acted on his own or whether somebody assisted him. This was a case where there were no eyewitnesses, nor was circumstantial evidence forthcoming. It was, therefore, decided to search the house of his brothers, three of them, on the possibility that it could lead to something incriminating. However, nothing was found. Not resting with this, several people were questioned. One Ravji Rukhad confirmed that he had a tiff with the deceased eighteen months ago as the latter had cut electric wires on his farm. A police complaint was lodged. The witness, however, could not reveal anything more beyond confirming the nefarious reputation of the deceased. Another person whose daughter was supposed to be involved with the deceased was also questioned. He denied the rumour or any knowledge about the crime. The villagers apparently were not above gossiping!

A statement of Mangalsinh, the owner of the bullock cart, was recorded, who confirmed that the cart had returned without the deceased and contained blood stains, upon which he informed the police. Anuben Hamji, the wife of the accused, was also examined, and she revealed that the accused had left the house on the day of the crime before sunrise on a cycle. She denied any further knowledge about the whole incident, including the motive. She did confirm that her husband was at loggerheads with the deceased. Three witnesses, all rajputs and distant relatives of the accused, living in village Borla, were interrogated to ascertain whether the latter had gone to them after the offence. They denied any such contact with Hamji.

In all twenty-four witnesses belonging to four villages were examined, the weapon used in the crime recovered, and all possible theories tested against ground realities before it was concluded that the crime had been committed by Hamji alone, the primary motive being a sense of self-esteem as a rajput. In the meantime, I had received another special report of a murder committed within the limits of Bagdana police station, also not of my subdivision. After initialing the case papers, case diaries, *panchnama* and instructing the investigating officer to get the confession of the accused recorded before a judicial magistrate, I departed from the scene of the crime.

CHAPTER 5

# AN UNDETECTED ROBBERY

Robbery is a special and aggravated form of either theft or extortion. The chief distinguishing element in robbery is the imminent fear of violence. However, there can be no case of robbery that does not fall within the definition of either theft or extortion, but in practice, it will be perpetually a matter of doubt whether a particular act of robbery was a theft or extortion. The offence carries a punishment of 10 years imprisonment and is a visitable crime by the SDPO.

During the British period, it was legal, under a regulation promulgated in 1827, to levy fines in case of robbery committed within the bounds of a village and collect the same from the villagers. Thus, if a robbery was committed within the boundary of a village, or the perpetrators of a robbery had been satisfactorily traced thereto, and neglect or connivance was proven against the inhabitants with regard to prevention, detection or apprehension, it was competent for the district or sub-divisional magistrate to investigate the matter as a criminal offence, and, if the fact be well substantiated, to exact a fine not exceeding the value of the property lost, the whole or part of which could be awarded in compensation to the owner. Further, if the fine was awarded against the inhabitants at large, it was realised by the Collector in the same manner as revenue demands. Uniquely, similar fines could be levied on members of the police establishment if found negligent in preventing or detecting a robbery.

Independent India, of course, did not have any such provisions. It was, however, a visitable crime and, as per the provisions of the Bombay Police Manual, then applicable to Gujarat, it was mandatory for an SDPO, the officer visiting the serious crime, to associate himself with the investigation for minimum five days in case the same is not detected before that. Thus, it was that when I received a special report about the occurrence of a robbery within the limits of Gadhada police station, I departed within two hours for the scene of crime as prescribed.

Jalalpur was the village where the offence was committed. The complainant in this case was one Laghtabhai Ramjibhai aged 55 years. His house was situated outside the village and was generally isolated from the rest of the houses. His main occupation was buying and selling cattle, which in those days was a profitable business. Therefore, by normal standards, he was well-off and lived in the village with his wife and six children. His fortuitous situation becomes significant when one considers the fact that he belonged to a community called *vedva wagharies*. The latter are categorised as 'Other Backward Classes' within the scheme of reservations in India, and that perhaps explains the isolation of his house from others in the village. From the police point of view, there was a perception that they were given to committing property crimes, although they were never known for widespread depredation.

On a warm night in the summer of 1979, Laghatabhai and his family were sleeping in the house, which consisted of a courtyard and four rooms, which all opened into a verandah. The room on the extreme left was where all the valuables were kept. Around midnight, Laduben, the wife of the complainant, who was sleeping in one of the rooms with her daughter, heard some noise outside. She woke up the latter and told her that there was somebody moving outside the house with a torch light. The daughter, Vasantben, had gotten up to check but had not found anything untoward. She had gone to sleep. Shortly after that, three people had jumped into the courtyard, of which two were armed with sticks and one with an axe. They first approached the bed where the complainant, Laghatabhai, was sleeping and assaulted him. As the remaining members of the family woke and began shouting, the robber with the axe assaulted Laduben with the same. To facilitate escape, one of the culprits unlocked the courtyard door from the inside.

I reached the village at 7:30 PM. and the first thing to do was to remove all superfluous persons and post guards to protect the scene of offence. The investigating officer apprised me of the facts of the case. The room from where valuables were stolen had been thoroughly ransacked. Wheat grains were scattered all over since the culprits had emptied gunny bags in their search for the valuables. Clothes previously contained in a cupboard were thrown all over, and other articles of domestic use were noticed on the floor.

After questioning the complainant, who had survived the assault, it was necessary to speak in detail with his wife, Laduben. She was evidently in a state of shock not only because both she and her husband had suffered physical injuries but also because she had lost valuables and her jewelry. The *panchnama* of the scene of the crime indicated the value of the property stolen as Rs. 22,160. Although this might appear to be a small amount today, in those days, it was a huge amount and especially for the station from where the complainant came, it was a substantive loss.

Since Laduben required some time to recover, her daughter Vasantben, aged 18 years, appeared to be both knowledgeable and alert. Her examination revealed that she had gotten up in the middle of the night at her mother's prompting to check out the noises emanating from outside the house but could detect nothing. She revealed that later, when the culprits entered the house, her mother was almost hysterical with fear and screaming loudly, so one of the culprits hit her with an axe, after which Laduben ran to one of the rooms and locked herself in. The culprits had then threatened her younger brother to give them the key to the locked room containing the valuables. The child, along with his other siblings, were so terrified that they would not speak. The culprits then broke open the window of the room, entered the premises and committed the robbery. On a detailed examination, she revealed that the robbers had covered their faces, but otherwise, they were dressed like normal villagers. In the morning, at daybreak, she went to the house of the Sarpanch, the village headman, and informed about the incident.

In the meantime, the dog squad had arrived from Bhavnagar, the district headquarters. A word about the use of canines in the detection of crime will be useful. Dogs have been used by law enforcement agencies for over one hundred years. The English used bloodhounds while searching for Jack the Ripper in 1888, and during that time, they allowed canines to accompany bobbies, as the English policemen were then called, on patrol. In 1899, in Ghent, Belgium, police started formally training dogs for police work. By 1910, Germany had police dogs in almost all their largest cities. In the United States, however, it was only in the 1970s that the use of dogs in law enforcement took a foothold.

The introduction of canines in Gujarat was due to the initiative of K S Pavri, who was the Inspector General of Police, Gujarat State, from June 1969 to June 1971. He introduced two breeds, German Shepherd, and Labrador. Originating in Germany, the Shepherds are often preferred by law enforcement because of their strength, intelligence, and obedience. Around the world, they are utilised often in the detection of narcotics and explosives. Earlier, they were also used in tracking and apprehension of human suspects. On the other hand, a Labrador is considered even-tempered and well-behaved even around children and the elderly. Their athletic, playful nature makes them one of the most popular breeds. Labradors are often trained for detection work in law enforcement and for tracking suspects.

That night, Dimple, a German Shepherd, was sent to assist with the investigation. She was taken inside the ransacked room and made to smell several articles. During the crime, a shirt pocket of the culprits had been torn off by Ladhuben, which was recovered from the scene of the crime. Also recovered was a bundle of *bidi*, home-made cigarettes, left behind by one of the accused persons. Dimple was made to smell these as well. She led the police party towards the highway, about 2 km from the village, and then stopped near a well. She would not go any further, and it became clear that the culprits must have fled from there in a vehicle.

Nevertheless, on returning to the village, the canine was shown five suspects. However, nothing conclusive came out of this exercise. Since it was quite late, I decided to make a night halt at the village.

The following day, I re-examined the complainant and studied the scene of the crime once again. This was followed by examination of nine witnesses who we thought could help with detecting the crime in some manner. Witness Vashram Duda did confirm that at 1 AM in the morning, he heard people shouting and screaming from the direction of the house of the complainant, but since it was not uncommon for the *wagharies* to fight amongst themselves, he took no notice of the same. It was only the next morning that he learnt about the offence. Two other witnesses, Purshotam Bhima and Manji Hira, when examined by me, said the same thing. They too had heard the screaming and shouting but attributed it to internal issues amongst the *wagharies* and, therefore, took no notice.

The investigating officer was instructed to send an "E" report to the District Modus Operandi Bureau (DMOB). In those days, before the advent of computer-based databases, details mentioning the way an undetected crime had been committed were sent to this bureau located within the office of the superintendent of police. After scanning the records manually for offences having similar modus operandi, the names of suspects available with them were sent. So, it would happen that if there was no other clue or suspect found, the investigating officer spent considerable time locating the suspects mentioned in the list received from the DMOB and questioning them. This, more than anything else, served the purpose of proving to the supervisory officers that a thorough investigation was being done and that a sincere attempt was underway to trace the culprits.

The village headman was the next to be questioned. He confirmed that the daughter of the complainant, Vasantben, had informed him about the occurrence at 6 AM in the morning and along with the village chowkidar, he had visited the house and surveyed the scene of crime. He had found the complainant and his wife injured and bleeding and had arranged to send them to the hospital. Thereafter, he went ahead to notify the police. The village chowkidar, when questioned, corroborated these details.

Information was received that one Bhikha Lala and the complainant's son had a dispute over ₹ 10,000, which the former owed to the complainant. The suspect was interrogated at length and was also exposed to the police dog, Dimple. He confirmed his presence in the village during the night but resolutely denied any knowledge, culpable or otherwise, about the crime.

In the morning, when the complainant was examined again, he had mentioned the name of one Waghari Samta Laghra, a known criminal. It appeared that he had visited the village twice during the previous 10 days. The suspect lived in a place called Lathi in the neighbouring district, and I went there along with the investigating officer. He was found, questioned in detail, and his house searched, but nothing incriminating was noticed. The house of his brother was also searched with the same effect.

My next place of halt was Damnagar police station. There was a considerable population of *wagharies* in the jurisdiction, and therefore collected names of persons who were previously arrested or known to have committed similar offences using identical modus operandi.

It was clear that the investigating officer and his team would not be sufficient, in terms of menpower, to trace the culprits since it was apparent that they had come from some distant place. As SDPO, I supervised the police stations located at Gariadhar, Songadh, Vallabhipur and Sihor. The Station House Officers of these police stations were summoned to report to me at the village the following day. As it was late in the night, I made my second night halt at the scene of the crime.

On the third day, early in the morning, efforts were made to find out where the *bidis* left behind by the culprits at the scene of the offence could have been made. This was not an easy task as these home-made cigarettes are routinely made in many households across Saurashtra. A *bidi* (also spelled beedi) is a thin cigarette or mini cigar filled with tobacco flake and commonly wrapped in a Tendu leaf tied with a string or adhesive at one end. They were invented after Indian tobacco cultivation began in the late 17$^{th}$ century. Tobacco workers were the first to create them by taking leftover tobacco and rolling it in leaves. *Bidi* smoking tends to be associated with a lower social standing, and these tobacco-filled leaves are inexpensive when compared to regular cigarettes.

A police constable was deputed, with a description of the culprits, to check all highway hotels and eateries. In the meantime, a special messenger arrived from the district headquarters carrying names of suspects as deemed by the DMOB, to whom details of the crime were sent the previous day. Since each one of them lived far apart, the list was divided amongst three teams, with me heading one of them. Each of the suspect mentioned in the list received were thoroughly interrogated, and their premises were searched but to no avail. Towards early evening, all the teams collected at a place called Dhasa, which, apart from being a railway junction, was also a police out-post. A review of the work done by other teams was undertaken. During this discussion, it was decided to enlarge the ambit of the investigation and look at "*dafers*" as suspects as well.

Dafers are a semi-nomadic community found in Gujarat, with hunting being their subsidiary occupation. Earlier, they were recognised as one of the ethnic groups which routinely resorted to crime. The dafer claim to have immigrated from Sindh and settled in Saurashtra. The community is sub-divided along religious lines, with there being both Muslim and Hindu dafers. They are settled in the Vanthali and Talala talukas of Junagadh District. The community speak Kutchi, while most also speak Gujarati. They are known for migrating short distances and have encampments at the edges of villages.

Two teams, each headed by a PSI, were dispatched to look for dafers in the vicinity. Several villages located within a radius of 50 km of the scene of crime were visited and searched for any information that could establish the presence of this nomadic community. While this effort did not reveal the presence of dafers in the area, speaking to villagers and perusing the crime reported in neighbouring police stations and district, it became clear that a gang of three persons was certainly operating in that part of

Saurashtra, committing such crimes. The name of the suspect, Koli Mohan, came up, and although he was not a dafer, it soon appeared that he was assisting them in their nefarious activities.

Since it was late in the night, I made a night halt at Dhasa out-post.

Today being the fourth day of my visitation of this crime, the SHO of Songadh police station, who had earlier been included to assist with the investigation, reported back with one Koli Jiva, who confirmed that Koli Mohan was indeed moving with the dafers and now lived in village Muliyapet. Intensive combing of the area was undertaken, although whether the dafers were involved or not was yet in the realm of conjecture. Returning to the scene of the crime and the village of Jalalpur, I once again closely questioned the complainant and members of his family, who by now had recovered considerably from the trauma, in order to glean any information that could give some clue about the identity of the culprits. As often happens in the rural social milieu, doubts about the amount of property stolen were being raised in some quarters, but this in no way could deny the fact that a robbery had been committed with injuries caused to the complainant and his family members. In fact, the medical certificates received after the injured had been examined by the medical officer at the government hospital revealed that a hard and blunt substance had been used on the complainant and his son, and a sharp instrument had caused injury to his wife, Laduben.

After spending the night at Gadhada the following morning, I decided to conclude the visitation as I had to proceed to

Bhavnagar, the district headquarters, to attend a crime conference called by the SP. Before departure, I gave detailed instructions to the investigating officer, guiding him on the further course of action and laying emphasis on the fact that the culprits must be traced and that I shall be regularly checking up on the progress through the case diaries that are received periodically by the office of the SDPO.

The above narration should reveal how sincerely and seriously property crime was dealt with in earlier years. In social terms or as a man of any substance, the victim was of little consequence. What, however, mattered was that a crime had been committed which, according to the norms of those days, was a visitable crime, and no efforts had to be spared to detect it. During that time, I made strenuous efforts to locate the culprits in this case and similar cases throughout my career. I was often reminded of what N Rama Iyer, who belonged to the 1939 batch of the Indian Police, said in one of the crime conference several years before I joined the police. The year was 1964, and during a monthly review, the legendary police officer is reported to have remarked that while ₹ 500/- maybe nothing for the rich but for the poor, it is all that they have. He directed that it is the duty of every investigating officer to pay more attention to the depredations suffered by the poor by way of robbery, theft or house-breaking than to worry about the losses of the rich. Such was the leadership and empathy of those days!

Narayanswami Iyer Ram Iyer was a member of the Indian Police and had earlier, in 1956, served up as Inspector General of Police, Saurashtra. He held a graduate degree in science from Mysuru and was known for his impeccable integrity and professional competence. On the formation of Gujarat State, in May 1960, he became the first Commissioner of Police, Ahmedabad City and later Inspector General of Police, Gujarat State. Many years later, during my visit to Bengaluru in 1994, I went to meet him as he had settled down there after retirement. He received me dressed in a lounge suit. Before I left, he gave me the IP sword, which had become part of his accoutrements after joining the police. That sword is now displayed at the office of the Director General of Police, Gujarat, at Gandhinagar.

# OF CRIMINAL TRIBES, POLICE PATELS AND WAGHARIES

*H*on'ble Mr. T. V. Stephens, the then Member for Law and Order, while introducing the Criminal Tribes Act of 1871 bill, observed, "The special feature of India is the caste system. As it is, traders go by caste: a family of carpenters will be carpenters, a century or five centuries hence, if they last so long. Keeping this in mind the meaning of professional criminal is clear. It means a tribe whose ancestors were criminals from times immemorial, who are themselves destined by the usages of caste to commit crime and whose descendants will be offenders against law, until the whole tribe is exterminated or accounted for in the manner of the Thugs. When a man tells you that he is an offender against law, he has been so from the beginning, and will be so to the end, reform is impossible, for it is his trade, his caste, I may almost say his religion to commit crime."

The Criminal Tribes Act of 1871, expanded in scope through the 1920s, targeted numerous castes in colonial India. The law declared everyone belonging to certain castes to be born with criminal tendencies. The colonial authorities prepared an extensive list of criminal castes living in various parts of India. Those who were members of such tribes were restricted in terms of movement and people they could socialise with. A paper published in 1952 by K M Kapadia on the criminal tribes has given some details of the *modus operandi* adopted by different tribes:

> *The Bhamptas are railway thieves par excellence. The Minas of the Punjab are the most skilful burglars and dacoits known. The Sansis in the Punjab and the U. P. are more prone to dacoity. The Kalian considers robbery a duty and a right sanctioned by descent. The Jadna are swindlers who pretend to turn metals into gold. The Gopalas engage themselves only in cattle-stealing. The Manggarudis are cattle - poisoners and cattle-lifters. The Kolis commonly steal only bullocks and buffaloes: the Manggarudis goats and sheep. The Chhapparbands are known for pilfering and petty larceny, though at times, they take to counterfeiting coins. The Lamanis kidnap women and children. The Baurias engage only in house burglary and cattle-stealing at night. They are experts at wrenching jewellery off the persons of sleeping women. The Oudiahs engage in house-breaking and theft only during the day. The Soonarias are daytime pickpockets and petty thieves. The Sansias often disguise themselves as constables and, in the course of a mock search, rob travellers. The Harnis are adept at masquerading as religious mendicants.*

> *The Kaikadis, who take to robbery and dacoity, disguise themselves as Jungums (Lingayat priests), fortune-tellers, medicine-men, or shepherds to pick up information. A Chandrawedi will often disguise himself as a woman and travel in the third-class women's carriage and carry on his trade.*

For four decades after independence, police academies and training institutions across the country included the subject of criminal tribes as a part of the basic course syllabus. The lectures revealed that the *bhamptas* were not only railway thieves but were also masters of disguises and experts in tricks. Their favourite trick is to kick babies and make them scream, causing the mother to put them on the floor to suckle them to sleep. While there, they use a small, curved knife to slit up the travellers' bags and bundles. They are trained to carry a tiny knife concealed between the gum and the upper lip. The stolen articles are concealed in the expanded orifices of the body. Or, again, when a *bhampta* sees a well-to-do person in the street, he makes a great show of brutally beating a small boy. The boy screams and yells and rushes for protection to the prosperous-looking person. The *bhampta*, in apparent anger, tries to snatch away the boy from his protector as the boy struggles. When the sympathiser lets the child go, he finds, much to his chagrin, that his purse has disappeared.

Similarly, in addition to larceny, the *chhapparband* was known for his sleight of hand as well. He would, for instance, ask a woman to give him a rupee in exchange for a rupee's worth of copper, promising her a commission. The 'holy fakir,' as she takes him to be, looks at the rupee that she hands to him and, with simulated surprise, says that it is not current in his part of the country and expresses his inability to accept it. He takes the copper back, but in lieu of the woman's good rupee, he palms off on her by sleight of hand one of his counterfeits. Likewise, the *baurias* sometimes posed as members of high castes and managed to marry their daughters to well-to-do people whom afterwards they plunder in collusion with them.

A *soonaria,* well-dressed to present an appearance of respectability, accompanied by a couple of boys, enters a fair. The attendants pretend to be strangers to him and follow at a distance. Having selected a stall which, he considers would suit his purpose, the leader enters into a conversation with the owner. One of the boys, having casually strolled up, stands either close in front or by him, the others being some distance off. The merchant produces his goods for inspection. The stranger is difficult to please as he appears to evaluate the articles laid out in front of him. He begins to scratch his hand as if perplexed, this is the sign for the boy to be alert, and by conversation attracts the attention of the merchant. At an opportune moment, he either touches the boy with his elbow or makes a sign with it when the young urchin adroitly purloins unseen by the owner, whatever is nearest, and slips quietly away. He at once passes the stolen article to the other boy or to the man, who runs off in the opposite direction with it. The *soonaria* calmly leaves the stall, expressing his regret that there is nothing in the shop he likes. If, however, the loss is discovered before the former leaves, he condoles with the shopkeeper on his loss, being himself never suspected.

The Government of the day made two assumptions. First, all persons born in a particular group or caste are criminals by birth and second, once a criminal, always a criminal. The law, therefore, provided for registering all the members of the tribe or tribes declared as Criminal Tribes. It further required such registered members to report themselves to the police authority at fixed intervals and to notify their place of residence or any change of residence. Contravention of these provisions could result in imprisonment up to three years or a fine, which could extend to Rs. 500.

Besides the family and the group to which they belong, the society at large also provides a favourable climate for their anti-social activities. The Hindu community, and to a certain extent even the Muslims, regard it highly meritorious to give alms to beggars and to show respect to the *sadhus* (mendicant). It is this conception of charity and the spiritual belief that have encouraged the swelling of the fraternities of the sadhus in India and have facilitated the operation of their anti-social activities under the guise of a mendicant or as a poor beggar. In fact, the Bombay Police Manual directed that whenever a child is reported as missing, enquiries must be continued until the child is found or its disappearance is accounted for and further that in checking gangs of *sadhus, bairagis, iranis* or other tribes known to kidnap children, careful enquiries should be made with a view to ascertaining that the children found with the members of the gang belong to them.

The social system of the Hindus, namely the caste, stresses exclusiveness. The people who belong to the lowest rung of the caste hierarchy have been tolerated as the dregs of society. While, on the one hand, the social system does not allow free social intercourse with them, on the other, they have been kept at a distance out of fear. In the popular mind, murders committed by some of these people and tales of their heinous crimes are fresh and form the basis of contact between them. People's attitude to or sentiment toward these criminal tribes is, therefore, a blend of hostility, contempt, and fear. The reaction is one of shunning and segregating. Consequently, instructions were in place for special surveillance over all wandering communities, such as Baurias, Bhamptas, Berads, Budduks, Rhatores, Lamanis, Wanjaras, Kaikadis, Kunjars, Minas, or Sonnerias. Whenever suspicious persons from such communities are found at or near a village, the police patel was to inform the police station or out-post in the local limits of which his village is situated. It was essential for the police to keep a constant watch at all railway stations, *dharmashalas* and landing places, noting particularly any strange or suspicious persons who may arrive, making every possible enquiry about them.

The most crucial factor that helps to perpetuate the criminal propensity of the members of these groups is the social security provided by their *panchayat*[1] organisation. When a member happens to fall into the hands of the police and is sent to jail, his family is properly looked after during his absence. It is this security that provides against incapacity and destitution and the guarantee of the dues that prompt the members of these tribes to risk their lives in criminal acts and to place their loyalty to the tribe above that of their families. This scheme of social security is made possible by the efficient organisation of the *panchayat*, which many of these tribes have evolved and supported. The *panchayat* keeps a record of the members of the tribe, organises crime, deputes active members on missions to rob, steal or commit dacoity, disposes off the booty and distributes the sale proceeds among the members according to their respective shares.

When any member is arrested for the commission of a crime, the *panchayat* arranges and supports the litigation involved. The organisation is held intact not merely by its strict discipline and punishment of the recalcitrant members, but by individual obligations to contribute to the *panchayat* fund to meet its expenses for litigation when its funds are found to be insufficient. The importance of the *panchayat* as an incentive to crime lies in the fact that it trains men and women in crime and criminality and regulates their criminal activity.[2]

Such provisions as treating a section of our people as criminals only because they were born in that tribe ran contrary to the provisions of the constitution that India had adopted after independence.

Dr. K. N. Katju, then Union Home Minister, once remarked: "It is an insult to God and humanity to treat innocent children of criminal tribes as born criminals."

Pandit Nehru said in 1936: "I am aware of the monstrous provisions of the Criminal Tribes Act which constitute a negation of civil liberty. Wide publicity should be given to its working, and attempt made to have the Act removed from the Statute book. No tribe could be classed as criminal as such, and the whole principle was out of consonance with all civilised principles of criminal justice and treatment of offenders." Later, in January 1947, the Government of Bombay set up a committee, which included B.G. Kher, then Chief Minister, Morarji Desai, and Gulzarilal Nanda, to examine the matter of 'criminal tribes.' This set into motion the final repeal of the Act in August 1949, which resulted in 2,300,000 tribals being decriminalised.

A new law, however, came to be notified. The Habitual Offenders Act, 1952 states that a habitual offender is one who has been a victim of subjective and objective influences, has manifested a set practice in crime and presents a danger to society. Some believe that the massive crime wave after the criminal tribes were de-notified led to a public outcry, resulting in the new enactment.

Despite the de-notification of the criminal tribes, investigative practices in the police department followed the age-old tradition of viewing members of such communities with suspicion. Often, such doubts were not completely misplaced. These aspects I discovered when I was required to supervise a house-breaking that had occurred within the limits of Sihor police station at village Valavad. The complainant, Nandram Vidyaram, was a retired railway employee, and since he was a Brahmin, post-retirement, he had taken up duties of a *pujari* at the village temple. On a scorching summer day, the family had locked up the only room on the temple premises, which was their home and slept outside in the open courtyard.

On arrival at the scene of offence, PSI Suresh Vyas met me. A direct recruit in that cadre, he was energetic and enthusiastic by temperament. After being briefed by him, I proceeded to examine the witnesses whose statements had already been recorded by Vyas. This included the wife and son of Nandram, who, in material terms, corroborated the complaint. They revealed that the complainant rose early at 3 AM in the morning to commence his daily prayers and rituals when he discovered that he could not open the room. This came as a surprise, and on peering through the windows, he found that the door had been bolted from inside, and in the opposite wall, there was a gaping hole.

Nandram thereupon walked behind the house and entered the room through the same hole that the house breakers had made for committing the crime. The premises had been ransacked, and the culprits had decamped with booty worth ₹ 7750. The family was distraught as this amount in those days, given their circumstances, was a substantial loss.

An examination of the surroundings revealed a set of footprints which led to a section in the village called *waghari vaas*, a collection of huts where the *wagharies* lived. Listed in the past as a criminal tribe, they were once guards of the hill forts of the Marathas. With the advent of British rule, modernisation and the changes that began to come about due to modern transport, many tribes lost their traditional means of livelihood. The *wagharies* now lived by stealing. Their women were persistent beggars and cleverly stole ornaments worn by children. The father is more often a drunkard and a prison-bird; the mother is known for her illicit sex relations and, at times, criminal propensity. The parents, therefore, not only failed to provide a sound moral foundation but, on the contrary, stimulated immoral tendencies.

It was, therefore, decided to concentrate on *waghari* settlements in a radius of 50 km from the scene of offence. This was an undetected property crime which would prove tough to solve. In the meantime, the fingerprint operator scanned the scene of crime but could not trace any worthwhile fingerprints. I sent a message to the district headquarters to dispatch the dog squad.

Regular recruits of the IPS, when posted to a subdivision, are expected to personally investigate six cases in a year. Although they are sub-divisional police officers who are expected to supervise, it was necessary for the young direct recruits to grasp the fundamentals of the investigation procedure. This would involve writing the case diaries, recording statements, drawing up a *panchnama*, submitting a charge-sheet if detected, or a final report if the offence could not be traced, and even tendering evidence in the court of law. I decided to take over the investigation from PSI Vyas.

Scrutiny of the inhabitants of the huts revealed that one Waghari Bachu Kana was missing. However, a search of his house revealed nothing incriminating. Interrogation of his mother resulted in no headway, except for learning that the former and his wife had gone out of the village. She claimed she did not know where. In the meantime, one Vala Bhima, who stayed in the neighbourhood, revealed that two days prior to the occurrence of the crime, some strangers had come to visit Waghari Bachu Kana. He was able to surmise from their conversation that they had some connections with Ramdhari village and Gadhada town. He further revealed that during the night of the crime, he had heard dogs barking, indicating that certain people were moving in the vicinity. This bit of information was also confirmed by another witness, Deval Vala, who lived behind the house of Waghari Bachu Kana. She also had heard the dogs barking during the night. The next morning, she learnt that the complainant's house had been burgled.

On the next day, the dog squad arrived. The canine was made to smell certain select portions of the scene of the crime. Interestingly, it led from behind the house of the complainant to the *waghari vaas* and to the house of Waghari Bachu Kana. This naturally supported the belief that this individual could have something to do with the crime.

Several persons belonging to the community were questioned, which revealed the name of one Kalu Shera, a notorious criminal who was wanted by the police in several cases. It was time now to extend the enquiry outside the village. I, therefore, proceeded to Songadh police station, within the limits of which Ramdhari village was located. A thorough search of all the houses of *wagharies* was carried out, but no significant progress was made. On return to Sihor police station, suggestions received from the DMOB were waiting to be scrutinized. The bureau, in those days, would deal with eight types of offences, namely cheating, criminal breach of trust, counterfeiting, dacoity, robbery, house-breaking, receiving or disposing of stolen property and theft. In addition, I directed scrutiny of the police station records of the last ten years to show those who had been arrested for the offence of house-breaking.

Further, a 'Hue and Cry' notice was sent to all the police stations of Palitana sub-division as well as the Lathi and Damnagar police stations of the neighbouring district of Amreli. The purpose of such a notice was to alert other police units about the occurrence of a crime, the intention being that either during their interrogation of criminals arrested for similar crimes or through their network of informants, information could be obtained that could result in detection. It should be noted that this was a time when there was no social media as is available now, and even the newspapers sometimes did not carry the stories of such crimes. The two police stations of Amreli mentioned above were included in this communication since there was a large concentration of *wagharies* in that district.

Along with a suitable police party, I first proceeded to village Gangli to locate and question one Bharwad Popat Karna, who figured as a suggestion received from the DMOB. There, it was discovered that the suspect had not lived in the village for the last fifteen years, having relocated to Surat. Next, I proceeded to the village of Maglana to tackle a suspect by the name of Jesang Bhana. His demeanour and manner of speaking conveyed the impression that he had not been active for a very long time, perhaps for many years. Normally, such persons should not have figured in the list, and this only proved that the records maintained by the office of the SP were not regularly updated.

In the mofussil, often useful information is obtained from influential persons, community leaders and village functionaries. Inquiries had revealed that the police patel of village Navgam had some hold on the *wagharies* of that area. In those times, the police patel was an important functionary in the village. The relevance and importance of this remarkable village institution needs to be narrated.

The Indian police owes its existence to the Police Act of 1861, enacted in the aftermath of the Crown taking over the governance of India from the East India Company, a direct consequence of the uprising of 1857. One of the salutary enactments of the Bombay Presidency was the Bombay Village Police Act of 1867, which laid down a proper procedure for policing rural areas. It should be obvious that given the length, breadth, and size of the country, it was not possible to get information about crime and criminals from far-flung areas, nor was it economical to deploy a policeman in every village or even for a group of villages. This new law allowed for appointments of a police patel, and the powers to do so were conferred on the Sub-Divisional Magistrate. In time, a certain prestige came to be associated with this appointment.

The police patel had a variety of duties. If he heard of the advent of a suspicious stranger in the village, it would be his duty to question the person regarding his antecedents and residence and to send to the police station, with as little delay as possible, all the information obtained by him. He was expected to be in the know of illicit distillation going on in his village, and it was his duty to inform the police of commissions of such offences promptly to enable the latter to take necessary action. Under section 10 of the Bombay Village Police Act, it was the duty of the police patels to preserve all incriminating articles found at the scene of offence till the police reached there and took charge of them. When a person gave any information to a village police patel, the latter was expected to send his report about the information to the police station. In such cases, that report could be treated as first information for the purposes of the law. However, in practice, police patels were instructed to bring the complainants to the police station for proper recording of the FIR.

Whenever any temporary regulations for the prevention of the outbreak or the spread of cholera in any local area were promulgated by the government, it was the duty of all police patels of that area to assist the controlling officer appointed under the regulations in carrying out the provisions of those regulations. As regards calamities such as an earthquake, floods, fires, or frost, the primary responsibility was that of the village *talati* (patwari), a junior revenue officer. However, in villages in which there was no *talati* or if the latter was absent on the date of the occurrence of the calamity, the police patel of the village was required to submit a report in the same way as the former.

The importance of a police patel for law enforcement can be gauged from the fact that the Station House Officer was mandated to supply the former with the names of surveillees residing in the respective villages to enable the Patel to keep a watch on the persons and report their movements. The police are duty-bound in the interest of efficient detection of crime, to keep their eyes on all anti-social elements, and the classification 'surveillee' is only intended to mark out the more active of criminals. The patrol policemen, visiting the village, were required to see that the police patel has with him a copy of the booklet entitled *Instructions for the Guidance of Police Patils*, the FIR book and the Wandering Gang Register, and repeatedly instruct him in the method of writing up of the book and the register with the help of the instructions contained in the booklet. Before leaving a village, it was the duty of the patrol policeman to write up the village Visit Book and his own patrol book, in which he would enter the substance of all information or complaints received and action taken there on, all acts done, and all facts observed in his official capacity. The entries must not be confined to information about cognizable crime but must cover the whole field of work, which the Police officer must address. The signature of the police patel was required to be obtained below the entry. If the Patel was illiterate, a responsible man's signature could be taken on his behalf. The former would be required to read the entry before signing it. If he could not read, the person who signed for him would be required to read out the entry to him.

I have always maintained that the key to the success of the British administration in India was the system of methodical touring by the district officers. It is well-known that as they began enacting laws to govern this country, at the onset of winter, British officers used to leave their headquarters, often along with their families, with enough horses and carriages to inspect their charges. They would set up camp in different villages, settle land revenue claims, arbiter disputes and then move on. It was not unknown for such official tours to last for as long as three months.

A competent system of touring was also developed for the police. All villages within the limits of a police station were divided into three categories:

Class A: (important villages), Class B: (unimportant villages) and Class C: (deserted villages)

All sub-inspectors and inspectors, when they passed through villages, were expected to instruct Patels in their duties and, by enquiries, check whether the patrol policemen's visit to the village was nominal or done with intelligence and thoroughness. Supervisory officers had a role as well. When certain occurrences came to notice in the villages, the SP and the SDPO were expected to make a practice of sending for the patrol books of the head constable or the police constable concerned so that they would see if that officer had been performing his duties satisfactorily or otherwise. Another check was to compare, during inspections, the entries in patrol books with those in the various registers usually kept by police patels, such as the visit book, surveillance register, register of convictions, register of wandering gangs, and register of arrivals and departures. Such a practice would prevent subordinate ranks from making misleading or incorrect entries or work perfunctorily.

Hence, my decision to meet the police patel of the village in Navagam. This meeting turned out to be fruitful as he came up with the name of Waghari Kehu, who would provide information about the whereabouts of Kalu Shera. He accompanied us to the part of the village where the wagharies lived. In the meantime, Kehu had already heard about the arrival of the police party and the ongoing discussions with the police patel. So, when he saw the latter accompanying the police as we approached the part of the village where he lived, he made good his escape, despite a good chase given by couple of police constables. A discussion was held, and it was concluded that Kehu, in all probability, would go to the village Chogath under Umrala police station. Without wasting any further time, I proceeded to that village where there were substantial numbers of *wagharies* residing. By the time we reached there, it was dark. With the limited men at my disposal, we tried to encircle that encampment. It was learned later that Kalu Shera was there but made good his escape under the cover of darkness.

Not having been satisfied, I decided to check the residences in that area in the morning and returned to Sihor for the night. There, I met police constable Arjan Harsur, who reported seeing one Waghari Moti Thula that morning near the state transport depot. He further reported that although he was not sure, a person accompanying the former looked like Kalu Shera. Thula was a resident of Palitana. The constable should have attempted to question the suspects there and then, which he unfortunately did not. There was no option but to dispatch him along with PSI Vyas to locate Thula.

The following morning, at 4.45 am, taking two police vehicles with me, I proceeded to village Chogath in the hope of tracing Kalu Shera. It often happens that a suspect returns home late in the night once the police have departed from his locality the previous day. Earlier, Vyas had returned and reported that he could not locate Waghari Moti Thula at Palitana. This time, we had sufficient manpower and encircled the encampment to prevent any escape. To our surprise, all the huts in the area had been abandoned before the arrival of the police. While this gave an indication that we were on the right track to detect the offence, it was nevertheless disappointing to miss the target so narrowly.

We returned to Sihor. Enquiries about Bachu Waghari revealed that he had not yet returned to the village. Thereupon, before the end of the day, I visited Palitana and the villages of Jivapur, Thorali, Samdhiyala, and Khara Na Jaliya to interrogate more *wagharies* to get a sense of the whereabouts of the suspects. It was in the last-named village that we found Moti Thula. A detailed interrogation followed, but no concrete headway was made in tracing the culprits.

By now, it was the fourth day since I had taken over the investigation of this case. In the following two days, I interrogated history-sheeters of Umrala police station, Sihor police station, and Jesar police station, which is part of the adjoining Mahuva sub-division. En route, I visited the villages of Katrodi and Bhilwada to tackle suspects of past crimes and meet with informants.

The above narration brings out vividly how seriously a crime like house-breaking was taken even if the property stolen was a small amount and even though the complainant was not of such stature that he could have brought to bear any pressure on the police to pursue his complaint. It was done in the normal manner, with every crime, big or small, given priority and attempt at detection pursued vigorously. Before I turned my attention to other important matters, I had made five night-halts in that area and been on the move for six days. During this time, the culprits could not be traced, but it was clear that *vedhva wagharies* were involved. Therefore, instructed the Station House Officer to be on the lookout for Kalu Shera and Bachu Kana and keep me posted on the efforts made in this regard.

As I returned to my headquarters town Palitana, the first shower of the season was received. It was a heavy rainfall which lasted for more than two hours and inundated all the main streets of the town. Arriving at my office, I sent word to the Deputy Engineer of the Public Works Department to meet me at the police lines. Together, both of us inspected each residential quarter of the constabulary to check if there was any leakage and a list was prepared to provide details of the repair work required. I also proceeded to the sub-jail and inspected the guard room to ascertain if that needed any attention. The Deputy Engineer promised to commence repair works wherever required in two days' time.

CHAPTER 7

# AN UNNATURAL DEATH: TOO YOUNG TO DIE

The law identifies two kinds of deaths: natural and unnatural. Regarding the former, there are no issues, but about the latter, often it becomes important to be sure that no crime has been committed that resulted in such an unnatural death. A person can commit suicide or be killed by an animal or by machinery or through an accident. There may be circumstances which raise a reasonable suspicion that some other person is involved. It is the duty of the State to ensure that no foul play has resulted in such an event and that duty has been entrusted to the police. Section 174 CrPC is a salutary provision that empowers the police to conduct an enquiry into accidental or suspicious deaths without registering a FIR, which in the normal course allows the police to start investigation in those cases where it has the power to take cognizance. This section and the provisions of section 175, which allows the police to summon witnesses for such an enquiry, supply a complete and autonomous code.

The law allows the State Government to make suitable rules to facilitate inquiries into such deaths. This has allowed provinces to prescribe procedures depending on the local social conditions and customs. In Gujarat, all cases of deaths that prima facie appear to have been caused by an accident can be enquired into by an HC. In all other cases of unnatural deaths, the investigating officer is bound to delve deep to find out the cause of the demise. An offence of murder is at once registered when there is the slightest suspicion to that effect. All cases of suspicious deaths are, as far as possible, to be personally investigated by the SHO.

The year was 1979, and I had just returned from a short leave home when I received a special report of a double suicide committed by a recently married couple. Kanchanben was twenty years old and had married a young man, Labhshankar, who was two years older than her. The couple lived on the premises of a quarter allotted to Gaurishankar, the father of the husband. This gentleman, a brahmin, worked as a cook at the K J Mehta TB Hospital, located at the village of Amargadh. It was a joint family where both Labhshankar and his elder brother Babulal lived in the same house as their parents, along with their wives. In fact, both the brothers were also employed with the hospital and going by the socio-economic conditions prevalent in Bhavnagar district, this was one happy and satisfied family. Ranjanben, their sister, also lived in the same house.

However, the younger son's marriage to a lively young lady caused some consternation primarily due to the free and open way the couple conducted themselves in public. Obviously, in love, they were found sometimes expressing their feelings for each other within the eyesight of other members of the family. The constraint of space at home did not help matters, and for this reason, the young wife was often rebuked by other members of the family, especially by the mother-in-law. A couple of days before the incident, the sister Ranjanben's marriage was celebrated, and during that time, Kanchan and Labhshankar were found moving around together, which was disapproved, according to the family members, by visiting relatives from the extended family and friends.

May is quite warm in Gujarat, and on one such day, the ladies of the house prepared to attend a ceremony in the village. Lalitaben, the mother-in-law of Kanchan, asked her to come, but the latter declined. It could be surmised that there must have been some clash between the two, which resulted in such a refusal on the part of a young and new entrant to the family. In the social milieu of that area, it is generally not acceptable for a daughter-in-law to decline to participate in ceremonies in such a manner. In the event, the mother-in-law, Lalitaben, accompanied by her elder daughter-in-law, Manjula, departed from the residence. It appears that half an hour later, Gaurishankar, the father-in-law, came home and, after enquiring from Labhshankar where the ladies of the house were, went to sleep. The latter and his wife Kanchan went to sleep in an adjoining quarter that had been temporarily acquired for the purpose of marriage ceremonies. Sometime later, the two ladies who had gone out also returned and went to sleep.

Somewhere around midnight, the sound of vomiting and retching was heard from the quarter occupied by the young couple. Both Gaurishankar and Lalita went over to inquire. They found their son Labhshankar unconscious, while his wife Kanchan was conscious. She conveyed that both had consumed some medicine. At this, the father removed them immediately to the hospital on whose premises, in any case, they were living. After a preliminary examination, Dr. A N Mandke, who was on duty, recommended that they move the patients to a government hospital at Sihor, a town nearby. On arrival there, it was found that Labhshankar had died on the way while Kanchan breathed her last shortly after being admitted.

On reaching the village, I proceeded to the residential area where Class IV employees of the hospital were allotted quarters. In the governing system of India, government employees and civil servants were divided into four categories in those days, ranging from Class I to Class IV, with the senior officers being in the first category. The classification was also essentially salary-based. Gaurishankar, working as a cook, was in the last category of government servants. Right from the days of the British, a happy approach had been to provide residential accommodation to all, even if modest, but especially to Class III and Class IV employees. This allowed such individuals to live a comfortable life despite the low salaries that were the order of the day in those times.

I met the parents (and parents-in-law) of both the deceased. The father, Gaurishankar, could not understand why his younger son committed suicide. The latter earned the highest salary amongst the three male members of the house, and therefore, according to him, there was no question of ill-treatment. Lalita corroborated her husband's statement, claiming that there was no ill-will between any members of the family.

The obvious next to be met with and questioned was Babulal, the elder brother of Labhshankar and his wife, Manjula. Between the two, interrogation of the latter was more relevant, as being the eldest daughter-in-law of the family, she would be privy to instances of real or imagined slights inflicted on the young bride, which is, at times, normal in such households. It transpired that on the night of the incident, after having attended a ceremony in the village with her mother-in-law, Manjula went ahead to be with her husband at the sanatorium where he was on night duty. She spent the night there with him and, only after learning about the incident late in the night, came to the hospital. She could not understand why the young couple had committed suicide, although she confirmed that both were found to be more liberal in their interpersonal behaviour in public and in the house. Her husband, Babulal, corroborated her statement.

Suicide in the family invites stigma and criticism of society. There is, therefore, a normal tendency to pass off suicides as natural deaths if that can be done. None of the surviving family members could explain from where the couple had obtained the poisonous substance, which was apparently used for committing suicide. It is necessary to emphasize how important it is for a police officer to have basic knowledge of the diverse kinds of poisonous substances available. During the initial stages, there is no medical assistance available, and a police officer may have to act without the support of an expert. That apart, in the earlier days, it was troublesome to prove poisoning through chemical analysis or microscopic examination. In such a scenario, evidence of dependable witnesses helps even the expert in making conclusions either way.

I met Dr Mandke to ascertain whether the deceased's statement in any form had been recorded and if they revealed anything that could explain the reason why they took such an extreme step. An order issued by the Home Department in August 1958 directed that the dying declaration of a married woman committing suicide should not be recorded in the presence of her mother-in-law, father-in-law, husband, or any other influential person in the family of the husband. As far as possible, a well-respected non-partisan social worker, if immediately available, should be asked to serve as a *'panch'* when such a dying declaration is recorded. It further mandated that in cases of suicide, police investigation should be more elaborate and conducted in the spirit of discovering the cause of the social evil and should invariably reveal details of family relations, the economic conditions of the family and the physical and mental condition of the victim This was a case of a husband who was twenty-two years old and a wife who was twenty years old, both very fond of each other and in the prime of their life. The doctor revealed that when he examined the young couple, they were barely conscious and were merely nodding their heads when called by their names. Both had symptoms of poisoning, and he did not see any signs of violence on their bodies. He confirmed that he recommended their removal to a regular hospital immediately, as the one they were brought to was meant for treating tuberculosis patients.

K J Mehta T B Hospital Trust today has advanced healthcare facilities with a team of good doctors, including specialists who are equipped to manage complex medical cases. However, in 1979, although it was a well-known center for tuberculosis, the facilities there were basic. It did, however, have a medical store to dispense medicines to the patients, and it is in this store that I discovered that the store also had strychnine powder normally used to kill dogs. The medical superintendent, Dr. Trivedi, claimed that all medicines, including any poisonous substance, were dispensed under the strict supervision of the matron and, therefore, there was no chance of any pilferage.

Examination of witnesses in such cases needs to be done with sensitivity, especially if they are neighbours. Although privy to arguments, quarrels and the tensions that prevail in families living around them, they are often reluctant to speak up as they have lived in the neighbourhood and do not wish to antagonize the community. One such witness was Balabhai, who also worked at the T B Hospital. That night, when he heard the commotion, he went to the home of the deceased and discovered that they seemed to have consumed something poisonous. On detailed questioning, he expressed astonishment as to why such a young couple should have decided to end their lives. In this manner, as many as nine witnesses, including the superior of Labhshankar at the hospital, were examined, but not one person said that they had any clue as to why such a step was taken by the former and his wife.

As explained earlier in this book (Chapter 2), such cases of consuming a poisonous substance and committing suicide would not have warranted the visit of a senior officer, such as the SDPO. The local sub-inspector of police of the concerned police station could have investigated the said incident. However, since one of the deceased was a married woman below the age of thirty years and living with her in-laws, it became imperative to ascertain that there was no foul play in the death of the woman. This was in the context of widespread unnatural deaths and sometimes even murders reported from that segment of society. In such cases, the statement of the parents of the deceased woman is always recorded to give them an opportunity to express their views and doubts, if any, about the death of their daughter. This is normally to be done by the visiting officer, the SDPO. However, in this case, it was clear from all accounts that no foul play could be attributed to any member of the family or to anybody else. I, therefore, decided to conclude the visitation with a direction to the investigating officer to proceed to Kodinar, then in district Amreli, where the parents of Kanchanben resided and record their statements.

In all such cases, post-mortem is always done, and viscera is collected and sent for chemical analysis to decide what substance was consumed by them. The autopsy report would also confirm that there were no other injuries on their bodies, thus laying at rest any speculation in this regard. The investigating officer was therefore instructed to get this done and send a report by way of compliance.

The sub-divisional police officer is one of the busiest touring officers that the system has generated. He is expected to be constantly on the move, as one visitable crime after another comes to be reported. This would be in addition to those visitations where the crime has not so far been detected. In the untimely demise of the young couple, clearly nothing sinister could be discerned. On the other hand, the robbery at the village of Jalalpur (Chapter 5) remained undetected. Efforts were already on, and based on some information received, I departed and visited villages Pipardi, Sarvedi, Sarkadia and the town of Songadh to trace a *waghari* who was strongly suspected of being involved in the robbery. Although no success was achieved in this regard, it was a matter of satisfaction that these efforts resulted in the detection of another robbery in which the victim had sustained grievous injury and had survived. A part of stolen property was also recovered.

Both Labhshankar and Kanchanben were a happily married couple who probably possessed an independent thought process which did not sit well with the conservative societal norms in which they were destined to live. Although not one witness mentioned about any tension in the family or about any ill-treatment being meted out specially to the deceased wife, it would be safe to assume that they came under pressure and stress due to the abuse they suffered for not conforming. In rural settings such a situation can be excruciating. It does not help if the mother-in-law is dominating. This results in controlling and then invading each other's space to lessen the threat they feel from each other. The daughter-in-law is raised in a different environment than the home where the mother-in-law raised her own children. Many times, the presence of another lady married into the family, as in this case Manjula, results in an unfair comparison and criticism.

I moved on to investigating and supervising other cases and probably never checked back to find what was the cause of suicide given in the report submitted by the investigating officer to classify these deaths as suicide. My guess is it would have vaguely referred to domestic issues resulting in mental stress which led them to take this extreme step. In today's times, however, such fatalities would invite a more thorough examination of the mental condition of the deceased couple.

In 1983, section 174 CrPC was amended to provide that where the woman has been married for seven years and the case involves suicide by a woman or relates to the death of a woman in any circumstances raising a reasonable suspicion that some other person has committed an offence in relation to such woman, or any relative of the woman has made a request in this behalf or there is any doubt regarding the cause of death, or the police officer for any other reason considers it expedient so to do, he shall forward the body for a post-mortem. It is significant that what was considered a special report crime or incident in Gujarat State eventually found its way in the statute books. This is without doubt a tribute to the farsighted vision and proper understanding of the societal issues, on the part of the senior officers of the home department and the police force.

Suicide is the act of intentionally causing one's own death. Mental disorders, including depression, bipolar disorder, schizophrenia, personality disorders, anxiety disorders, nihilistic beliefs, physical disorders, such as chronic fatigue syndrome, and substance use disorders are risk factors. Some suicides are impulsive acts due to stress, such as from financial difficulties, relationship problems or harassment and bullying. Those who have previously attempted suicide are at a higher risk for future attempts.

Several questions are raised about the philosophy of suicide, including what constitutes suicide, whether it can be a rational choice, and the moral permissibility of suicide. Arguments as to acceptability in moral or social terms range from the position that the act is inherently immoral and unacceptable under any circumstances, to regarding suicide as a sacrosanct right of anyone who believes they have rationally and conscientiously come to the decision to end their own lives, even if they are young and healthy.

Suicide is considered a cowardly act and strangely its attempt is made an offence in the penal laws of several countries including India. Defined in section 309 of the Indian Penal Code, it is used only if the perpetrator survives the attempt. The punishment can extend up to one year. However, the Mental Healthcare Act, 2017 has decriminalized suicides. Section 115 of the said Act overrides the provision of section 309 of the Indian Penal Code (IPC) and provides that a person committing suicide shall be presumed, unless proved otherwise, to have severe stress and shall not be tried. However, abetment of suicide, dealt in section 306, is seen as a more serious offence. For those who aid a person in taking his or her own life, they can be sentenced to up to ten years in prison.

CHAPTER 8

# FATAL MOTOR ACCIDENT

*H*omicide by negligence has been dealt with by section 304A of the Indian Penal Code. This provision was added in 1870 to deal with those cases where there is no intention to cause death, and no knowledge that the act done in all probability would cause death. For such fatalities, the offender can be sentenced to a maximum of two years in prison. In case of murder, the maximum punishment can be death by hanging while in case of culpable homicide not amounting to murder, and offender can be sentenced to life imprisonment.

Ten days after taking over as SDPO Palitana, in the second week of February 1979, I received a special report about a fatal motor accident. In my tenure of eighteen months in that subdivision, I was to supervise many more. This particular incident was reported at Vallabhipur police station and had occurred on the Ahmedabad-Bhavnagar highway. It transpired that truck bearing number GTS 6031 had been leased by one Jaisukhlal Gandhi. It was loaded with onions at Trapaj, a village in Talaja taluka of Bhavnagar district and located 45 km from the district headquarters. The consignment was to be taken to Surat, and the journey began at 9 PM that night. The driver was Harshvadan Navnitrai, and Bijal Nanji functioned as the cleaner. Jaisukhlal also sat in the cabin of the truck. They reached Vallabhipur shortly after midnight and decided to take a rest.

Unknown to them, the patch of road between Km 145 and 146 on the forward journey was under repair. The work had been assigned to a firm called Mahesh Quarry. During the daytime there would be about thirty labourers working on resurfacing of the road. After sunset, two of them would stay back at the site to look after the equipment and other material while the remaining would go away to return the following morning. There were two heavy pieces of machinery, a thirteen-ton paver and a ten-ton roller. In the evening after work was over, both would be parked, one behind the other, on the left side of the road. The road was freshly paved and was thirty-one feet wide. That night it was the turn of two labourers, Panchu Narshi, aged 19 years and Soma Narsingh, aged 18 years to spend the night at the site. As per the practice in vogue, these two boys spread a mat between the paver and the stationary roller and went off to sleep. Presumably, they could not have conceived of any safer place as they were shielded from the upcoming traffic from Bhavnagar side by the paver and from Ahmedabad side by the roller.

At 5.15 AM the next morning, the truck driven by Harshvadan began its onward journey. They were coming from the Bhavnagar side. The truck was driven at high speed, and in the darkness the driver did not notice the two heavy pieces of machinery parked on the left side of the road. Fifteen minutes later the collision occurred. Such was the impact that the paver machine was flung twenty-one feet away while the other heavy piece of machinery, the roller, was flung thirty-six feet away. Both Panchu and Soma were crushed and suffered grievous injuries but were yet alive. The truck also turned and lay on its right side. All the three occupants crawled out by pushing out the right side of the windscreen. They also saw the two labourers lying injured nearby. Jaisukh made attempts to stop passing vehicles to convey them to the hospital, but nobody stopped. Thereupon both he and the driver left the place, walked some distance towards Vallabhipur, before they got a lift. The driver got off there and went ahead to the police station to inform them about the mishap. Jaisukh went ahead to Bhavnagar to contact Dhirajlal Tamboli, the owner of the truck. In the meantime, at 7.15 AM, the other workers who had retired for the night the previous evening arrived to resume work in another truck. They were naturally distraught on seeing the site of the accident. Both Panchu and Soma had expired from the injuries sustained.

PSI G L Khunti, SHO of Vallabhipur police station at once proceeded to the scene of offence. He became a complainant on behalf of the state and registered an offence under section 279, 304A of the Indian Penal Code and sections 112, 116 of the Motor Vehicle Act (MVA). Section 304A of the IPC is a provision which applies to cases where there is no intention to cause death, and no knowledge that the act done in all probability will cause death, and yet because of the certain actions of the accused person, fatality has occurred. Therefore, when the act is in its nature criminal, the section has no application. In simple terms, this section deals with homicide by negligence. Section 279, on the other hand, is about riding or driving a vehicle on a public way in a rash or negligent manner. Negligence is an omission to do something which a reasonable man, guided by those considerations which ordinarily regulate the conduct of human affairs, would do, or doing something which is imprudent, and a reasonable man would not do. Both these sections of law apply to even horse-drawn carriages or bullock-carts and that is why the provisions of sections 112 and 116 of the MVA are invoked to cover motor transport. The latter section makes it culpable for any person to drive a motor vehicle at a speed or in a manner which is dangerous to the public, having regard to all the circumstances of the case including the nature, condition and use of the place where the vehicle is driven and the amount of traffic which actually is at the time, or which might reasonably be expected to be in the place. In other words, it defines reckless or dangerous driving.

On my arrival at 4.15 PM the same day, I was met by Khunti who apprised me of the accident. The truck was still lying on its right side on the highway, blocking most of the road. All traffic had been redirected towards a temporary diversion prepared alongside. On both sides of the highway were barren fields or cultivated agricultural land. The owner of Mahesh Quarry, Kantibhai Patel, the one who employed both the deceased, was also present. On questioning him, it was learned that both Panchu and Soma belonged to Panchmahal district and had been working for him for the last five months. The bodies of both had been conveyed to the government hospital at Vallabhipur and a preliminary report had been received about the cause of death. Soma had died due to hemorrhage of the head and fracture of the skull, while Panchu due to hemorrhage of the lungs and the head.

Khunti had drawn up the *panchnama* of the scene of offence and I carefully examined it for accuracy which included questioning the *panch* witnesses. In the case of a motor vehicle accident, two legal requirements must be met with. One is about sending intimation to the Regional Transport Officer (RTO) to check whether the vehicle involved in the accident was roadworthy. Therefore, I checked with the investigating officer whether the RTO had been informed. Inspection of the vehicle must mandatorily be done by personnel of that office. Khunti conveyed that a police constable had been dispatched to Bhavnagar for this purpose. In those days there were hardly any telephone connections in the rural areas and the best mode of communication was by sending a special messenger. Thereafter, I proceeded to Vallabhipur where the driver Harshvardhan and the cleaner had been detained at the police station. Jaisukhlal had also returned after his visit to Bhavnagar. All three were questioned in detail and their statements recorded. It was ensured that there was no contradiction to obviate any difficulty in securing a conviction during trial.

The driver was placed under arrest for causing death through his rash act of driving at great speed. The second legal requirement is about issuing a notice under section 131 MVA which provides that no person prosecuted for an offence punishable under section 115 or section 116 shall be convicted unless he was warned at the time the offence was committed that the question of prosecuting him would be taken into consideration. Frankly, bare reading of this section made no sense to me then. During the probationary days as a supernumerary ASP at Rajkot city, I had not come across this provision nor had anybody bothered to explain the same. Such ambivalence was understandable as MVA was not a priority subject for the police as far as training is concerned, the assumption being that many things are to be learnt on the job. I therefore decided to just go along with the flow. That night I camped at Vallabhipur, and the following day once again returned to the scene of offence where the co-workers of the deceased were available. They were questioned and it was heart-rending to note that among them were two brothers of Panchu Narshi, and the mother of Soma Narsingh. Shortly after their statements were recorded, they left for Panchmahal with the dead bodies. There were 275 km away from home, a long-distance in those days.

During the examination of the scene of offence, it was noticed that the management had not made any arrangements for placing a night reflector or a lantern to warn the oncoming traffic of a stationary object on the highway. This was corroborated by the driver, the cleaner and Jaisukhlal as well. Other than documenting this fact in the statement of the witnesses and reflecting the same in the case diary, nothing more was done. I had no clear idea whether Kantibhai, the owner of Mahesh Quarry, could be held accountable or whether there was any civil or criminal liability on his part or on anybody else's. Both Khunti and I were too fresh and too young in the system.

I decided to remove this lacuna in my professional profile. The study that I undertook over the next few weeks revealed some interesting facts.

Locomotive and automobile development have a common time-frame with the former taking precedence for obvious reasons of commerce and industry. Nevertheless, the 19th century saw several attempts to come out with steam-powered vehicles.

Such innovation resulted in fatalities on the road hereinbefore unknown, and regulations to control the same. In the United Kingdom, Locomotive Act (1865) was enacted, which required many self-propelled vehicles on public roads to be preceded by a man on foot waving a red flag and blowing a horn.

During the beginning of the 20th century, cars were imported into India primarily by the British, the royalty and the business tycoons. Later, the number increased especially in the Presidency towns of Bombay, Madras and Calcutta. With the shifting of the capital to Delhi in 1911, there was a quantum jump of vehicular traffic in that region. Gradually, it became obvious that roadside killings due to rash or negligent driving became commonplace. Since the punishment, as discussed above, was maximum two years in prison, if the driver of an automobile killed a person in a road accident, there came a time when many such fatalities were suspected to be homicides. It was in this backdrop that in the Bombay Presidency during the British rule, and later after independence, in the bilingual Bombay State, fatal motor accidents were made visitable by a sub-divisional police officer. This was done to rule out any foul play in such incidents.

The Public Conveyances Act, 1920 dealt with animal-driven transport. In urban and semi-urban areas, a horse-driven cab was the most convenient mode of transport. The SDPO was the licensing authority and I recall fixing a day once a year in each town of Palitana sub-division when all the *tongas* were called in an open ground for inspection. This would include observing each horse-carriage on the move to judge the robustness of the cab and the health of the horse. Offences under this law were cognizable meaning thereby that the police could arrest a defaulter without a warrant. In the rural areas there were bullock-carts, but this was outside the ambit of the 1920 legislation.

In 1939, the British enacted the Indian Motor Vehicles Act to deal with influx of automobiles across the country. This dealt extensively with all aspects touching the licensing, manufacture, possession, and maintenance of motor vehicles and created for the first time a Regional Transport Authority. Certain violations of this law were made cognizable when committed in the presence of a police officer. This included driving dangerously, recklessly or under the influence of alcohol or drugs. The flexibility of this enactment can be adjudged from the fact that the Commissioner of Police, Mumbai, was authorized to withdraw a prosecution under section 113 of the Indian Motor Vehicles which dealt with disobedience of orders, obstruction, and refusal of information.

Although India was a British colony, even in those days there was a genuine concern for the working class. This is borne out from the fact that, through a standing order issued by the then Inspector General of Police, Bombay in May 1936, all Superintendents of Police and the Commissioner of Police, Bombay, were expected to report to the Commissioner of Workmen's Compensation, Bombay, any motor accident occurring in their respective jurisdictions involving death or injury to driver or cleaner of any motor vehicle. To remove any doubts and to facilitate the members of the public, a March 1951 order directed that request made by insurance companies and other private persons for the supply of extracts from police records concerning motor accidents, on payment of prescribed fees, should not be refused. It was conveyed that the term 'police records' was not limited to case or inquiry papers but included all entries in authorized police registers and files.

In 1941, a pamphlet entitled "Instructions for the guidance of Police officers regarding the control of Motor Vehicles Traffic" was supplied to all Police officers. The police manual directed that drivers and conductors of the nationalized transport undertakings could be straightaway prosecuted for offences under the provisions of the Motor Vehicles Act, 1939 except those falling under Chapter VI of the Act, in which case the matter should be referred to Government in the home department directly by the district Superintendent of Police or the Commissioner of Police for sanction to prosecute. This latter category dealt with regulatory provisions such as traffic signs, speed limitations, signals and signaling devices. Any police officer in uniform was empowered to stop any motor vehicle and satisfy himself that the tax due had been paid. All police officers were to report to the SP, the registration numbers of all motor vehicles on which current tax tokens were not displayed, for communication to the RTO concerned. Although this provision came to be extensively abused with the police setting up points on the highway and other roadways to collect illegal money, it illustrates the point how thoroughly the senior leadership was keen to implement a new law governing public transport and private vehicles.

It was not as if no directions were given to the police officers for reasonable behaviour. A police officer was expected to not resort to impounding of driving licences in petty cases. Whenever he did so, he was expected to furnish the driver with an official receipt or temporary authorisation in accordance with motor vehicle rules. Similarly, motorists offending against minor requirements, such as a broken side-mirror or absence of a bulk horn when there is an electric horn were to be ordinarily dealt with by giving them a warning for the first offence and an opportunity to make good the deficiency. The police and especially the traffic police should concentrate their attention more on important cases, such as over-speeding, over-loading, plying without permit or without payment of tax or without insurance. They were encouraged to pay particular attention to motor vehicles with raucous horns and report them to the RTO for action and act against drivers under Rule 149 (2) of the Bombay Motor Vehicles Rules for indiscriminate use of horns.

There was an emphasis on cooperation between the police and the RTO. All police officers were expected to offer full and active co-operation to the Motor Vehicles staff in all ways, as for example, checking fitness certificates of motor vehicles, evasion of tax and breach of conditions of license, and checking and detecting traffic offences. Inspectors of the Motor Vehicles Department, when on tour, could contact the local police officers, for assistance. As early as 1949, for the quick disposal of cases, it was directed that resort should be had to departmental action against the defaulters, as far as possible, rather than to prosecuting them in courts of law, which involved delay and inconvenience to all. Clearly judicial delay was an issue even in those days.

In 1958, the Government of Bombay enacted the Bombay Motor Vehicles Tax Act. Under section 15 of the Act, any police officer, or officer of the Motor Vehicles Department, in uniform, not below such rank as may be prescribed by the State Government in this behalf could enter, at any time between sunrise and sunset, any premises where he had reason to believe that a motor vehicle was kept, or require the driver of any motor vehicle in any public place to stop such vehicle and cause it to remain stationary so long as may reasonably be necessary, for the purpose of satisfying himself that the amount of the tax due in accordance with the provisions of this Act in respect of such vehicle, had been paid.

Such was the importance given to plying of automobiles on Indian roads, and the role expected of the police in enforcement of laws that were more regulatory in nature. It was in this backdrop that when I received a special report of the next fatal motor vehicle accident that occurred on the Bhavnagar-Rajkot highway near village Limda within the limits of Umrala police station, I was better prepared to discharge my supervisory duties. Early that week in June 1979, I commenced inspection of Vallabhipur police station. This involved an elaborate procedure of scrutinizing every single record, accoutrement, and personnel. Necessarily it required at least four night-halts at the location to complete the task effectively. Nevertheless, in the scheme of things, a special report crime took precedence. Thus, within forty-five minutes of being intimated, I departed for the scene of the incident.

On arrival, I was met by the investigating officer who apprised me of the facts. The complaint had been lodged against one Nathubhai Badrubhai, aged 55 years who was the driver of a truck bearing number GTZ 673 and Bhavanbhai Bharvad, aged 25 years who drove a bus bearing number GTX 3061. The truck was not loaded and was coming from Gadhada, a taluka headquarter town within Bhavnagar district whereas the bus carrying a marriage party was returning from Ahmedabad and headed for Dhasa junction, then an important out-post village. It was a bright day and yet shortly after noon, while passing each other from the opposite direction, both the bus and the truck collided. As a result, the truck swerved off the highway and fell in a ditch. Sitting at the back was Maganbhai Govindbhai, who had taken a ride in the truck earlier and was seriously injured. He was removed to the hospital at Bhavnagar where he died. He was only 40 years old.

In most crimes, there are two parties namely the victim or the complainant, and the accused. In motor accident cases such a clear division of roles becomes difficult, as was the case with the incident I was visiting, since both sides must have seen the vehicle approaching from the opposite direction. The police station while registering an offence of rash and negligent driving which resulted in a death, had made the drivers of both vehicles culpable. I noticed that the highway was twenty feet broad and strewn with glass pieces all over. Facing towards Rajkot on the left side, the bus was perched precariously on the edge of the highway. Its glass panes as well as the windscreen were shattered. The right side of the vehicle was crumpled and had caved in. Nevertheless, nobody in the bus was injured, and all the passengers along with the driver had proceeded to their destination Dhasa, taking a lift from other vehicles plying on the road. The truck, on the other hand, was standing in the ditch but devoid of its fender. There were bloodstains seen on the driver's seat.

In establishing who was at fault and the degree to which they were at fault, an examination of the scene of crime becomes critical. During the basic training at the National Police Academy while attending forensic science classes, a trainee is introduced to some rudimentary aspects of examination of the scene of crime. However, it was during my practical training at Rajkot city that

I acquired sufficient knowledge which enabled me to give some meaningful guidance to the investigating officer. This was my third visitation of a scene of a fatal motor accident and being a greenhorn newly appointed officer, I was not only keen to use what I had learnt but also, I suspect, to show off!

In road accidents three aspects are important. First, and not necessarily in that order, is the examination of skid-marks. These marks are due to a thin layer of rubber deposited on the path by the heat of friction between tyre and roadway, when brakes of a moving vehicle are forcefully applied. These lines will give an indication of the point at which the brakes were applied, and they are also indicative of the speed at which the vehicle was travelling. The length of each skid mark should be measured, and the distance recorded. The scene must always be sketched as it throws light on the length of skid-marks and many other vital facts such as the position of the vehicles at the time of collision and their dimensions. Similarly, impressions on mud, dirt, on wet roadway and on the surface of a tarred road on a sweltering day may give valuable information such as the make or brand of the tyre, its condition, the size of the track of the car, the direction of approach or departure of a vehicle from the scene. If the tyre marks show evidence of unusual wear, defects or cuts which correspond with the condition of the traced vehicle, they will contribute useful evidence. Such marks on the roadway must be protected against rain, traffic or pedestrians until casts can be made.

Second is the examination of the glass fragments. Pieces of glass from the damaged head lamp, side mirror, windows, or windscreen are very often detached from the automobile by the force of impact and even in quite minor accidents the glasses of side lamps are smashed. Fragments of glass from the "scene" should be collected and carefully preserved. A note should be made of the exact spot where they are found. This information may suggest the speed and position on the road of a vehicle when the accident occurred. Every piece must be collected to enable an expert to determine the type and make of the glass by piecing together the fragments as in a jig-saw puzzle. In the case of fragments of glass from a head lamp, it may be possible to figure out from this glass, the type of lens and from this fact the year and the type of cars involved in the accident. Fragments of glass found at the scene may have to be compared with glass remaining in the windows, windscreen or lamps of a vehicle suspected of having been involved in the accident. But more often in such cases, it is a matter of deciding by means of physical examination whether the fragments in question could have come from a suspected source.

Finally, paint chips are found in motor car accidents, for example, when the painted metal surface of the automobile comes in contact with either inanimate or animate objects like lamp-posts, other moving or stationary vehicles, animals and human beings. These should be carefully collected to make possible a future microscopic and spectrographic comparison by an expert for colour, sequence of the layers, constituent elements of flakes of paint at the scene with the control samples of the suspected vehicle. The paint flakes found on the road should be preserved since it may be possible later to show that the flakes fit accurately with others still adhering to the vehicle or to the outlines of the area of the bare metal surface. Traces of paint on tools that have been used in forcing open doors, windows or safes may be helpful in connecting the crime with a person in whose possession the tools have been found.

Visitable offences are always investigated by the SHO, who is the officer-in-charge of the concerned police station. In this case the incumbent, having been summoned by the SP, was away at the district headquarters. HC Gadhvi was entrusted with this case. In the scheme of things, fatal motor accidents are not high on police priority primarily because there is absence of criminal intent to commit the crime and is accepted by all and sundry that the unfortunate incident happened because of negligence or rashness on part of the automobile driver. Oftentimes such cases were entrusted to one rank lower. A head constable is an individual who has put in more than twenty years of service and is therefore quite experienced. Conversely, as the source of recruitment for joining the force was as a police constable, most of them had limited formal education. Several aspects of forensic examination appeared completely alien to them and sometimes unnecessary, given the facts and circumstances as was in this case. For Gadhvi, this was a simple case of two vehicles colliding while approaching from opposite directions. Excepting that it was not that straight forward. Not only the deceased Maganbhai but three other people were travelling as passengers in the truck, something which the provisions of the Motor Vehicles Act or the rules made thereunder, did not allow. Although the *panchnama* of the scene of offence had been prepared, I suggested additional evidence be recorded for subsequent forensic examination.

Next, the inquest *panchnama* was perused to get an idea about the kind of injuries suffered by the deceased. The document revealed that the brunt of the impact on the deceased was around the waist and over the eyes. I examined two witnesses who were sitting on the back of the truck along with the deceased. They broadly corroborated the sequence of events as narrated above. The fourth person sitting with them was the son of the truck driver. He, along with another person had helped in shifting the injured persons, the driver, and the deceased to the hospital.

Next destination to visit was the Civil Hospital at Bhavnagar. There, I was able to interrogate one of the accused that is Nathubhai who was the driver of the truck. The cleaner of the truck, Devji Mansingh was also there for some minor injuries, and he too was questioned. Both insisted that their truck was moving at a slow pace and that they had kept on the left side of the road. Such assertions are on expected lines, and I departed from the hospital after informing the medical officer in writing, that the truck driver is required to be taken into custody after he is released from the hospital and therefore, that fact should be communicated to the police well in time. The son of the truck driver resided at Kumbharwada, a locality within the city. He gave a statement that tallied with that of his father.

I returned to the scene of crime and continued to verify the statements of witnesses already recorded by the investigating officer. This included the owner of the bus who had come down from Rajkot, the driver of the bus who was the other accused in the case, and the cleaner of that vehicle. The deposition of the last two was relevant as they had witnessed the unfortunate incident. The bus driver, Bhavan was placed under arrest.

After spending the night at Umrala, the following morning, I proceeded to Dhasa and tried to locate bus passengers who were part of the marriage party. In this connection, I examined the bridegroom Vinodrai Gangadiya who claimed that because of the marriage ceremonies in Ahmedabad and the long journey, he was sleeping and awoke only after the collision. He heard people shouting and women crying. He later helped the ladies exit out of the bus, stopped a State Transport bus which was proceeding towards their destination and put the passengers on the bus. He followed suit too. Three other bus passengers were also located who corroborated what Vinodrai had said.

In motor accident cases, there is a normal practice of informing the Regional Transport Authority about the incident who then dispatches the Motor Vehicle Inspector (MVI). It is the function of this individual to examine the vehicle and conclude whether before the accident, the vehicle was travel-worthy. The MVI in this case inspected both the vehicles and promised to send the report at the earliest. Another official who is required to visit and assist with the investigation is the CPI. This officer is one rank subordinate to the SDPO and supervises four or five police stations which are part of his Circle. He is usually an officer who has risen to the position he holds owing to his ability to deal with crime and criminals. He is employed mainly for crime work and for surveillance over the activities of the bad characters and the gangs. He is present during the investigation of serious crimes, such as murders, dacoities, highway robberies, and crime suspected of being the work of professional criminals. Incidents of motor accidents involving loss of life occurring in rural areas, also require his attention so that he can direct and advise the sub-inspector and his staff. He would thus supply a much-needed check in supervising and co-ordinating crime work of the different police stations in his Circle. Such was the seriousness attached to fatal motor accidents involving loss of life that, in November 1948, in an order issued by the Inspector General of Police, Bombay State, it was directed that in cases of motor accidents involving loss of life occurring in rural areas, intimation should be sent to the CPI at once by telegram and by special report. In the instant case, CPI Botad had been informed but being busy elsewhere, he had not turned up. As this was a case of accident caused due to a rash or a negligent conduct with no criminal intent, it was not thought necessary to insist on that officer's presence.

It was decided to prosecute both the drivers although it is possible that one of them was more negligent and therefore more culpable than the other. It had not been possible to bring out this differentiation within the parameters of the existing law. My role as a supervisory officer had concluded. The above narrative brings out the effort put in for investigation of fatal motor accidents in those days. It might come as a revelation that police stations used to maintain separate maps and graphs in respect of motor accidents. These were also maintained by the office of the superintendent of police for the entire district. Fatal accidents were shown in red, serious accidents in green, and minor accidents in blue.

Just as I was hoping for some respite, I received intimation from the Superintendent of Police, Bhavnagar, to proceed to supervise a murder offence within the limits of Palitana Rural police station.

CHAPTER 9

# LATE REGISTRATION OF A CRIME

*T*here are three supervisory characteristics of a Sub-Divisional Police Officer's functioning. The first is through the medium of visitation, as discussed in the preceding chapters, when he or she proceeds to the scene of crime and examines witnesses when a serious crime is reported. The second is through the medium of inspection of each police station and out-posts under his charge, once every year. We shall discuss this in a subsequent chapter. The third method is by proper scrutiny of papers of investigation received by him, through regularly writing up of crime registers which he is required to maintain in his office and through scrutiny of case diaries which are written by an investigating officer for every cognizable offence.

Palitana sub-division consisted of eleven police stations and with special crime being reported on a regular basis, I was away from headquarters sometimes for two and sometimes for three weeks in a month. Regardless of whether I was able to attend my office or not, letters and other mail that was received in my office would be brought to me at my place of camp by a special messenger, usually a police constable. Reports regarding crime, accidental or unnatural deaths, closure of cases when on completion of the investigation no charge-sheet could be submitted, had to be regularly attended to and a decision taken. The SDPO's office maintained an important document called the crime register, one each for every police station wherein details of cognizable crime recorded by that police station had to be entered. The entries therein were made by the Reader PSI, who assisted the SDPO with the supervision of all the police stations as far as crime work was concerned. In addition, there was the Serious Crime Register where details of all visitable offences were to be personally entered by the incumbent SDPO.

The importance given to prevention and detection of crime in those early days can be gauged from the fact that every sub-inspector and inspector of police in the Greater Bombay was required to maintain a record in a book of all offences personally investigated by him, with their results from time to time. The record was continuous, that is, if he were transferred to some other police station, the officer concerned would continue his record in that police station also in the same book. Police Commissioner's instructions mandated that the book be divided into six parts and consisted of cases under the Indian Penal Code, Prohibition Act, Gambling Act, Local Acts, Preventive action, and miscellaneous cases such as accidental deaths. It is not without reason that once upon a time, Bombay Police had a formidable reputation amongst police forces in the country.

In the mofussil no such instructions were in force and yet there was proper emphasis on effective supervision of crime. Every investigation must be completed without unnecessary delay. Investigating officers are expected to, when applying for extension of time for investigation, show concisely in their application what they have attempted and what they have achieved during the first fourteen days of their investigation, or the extension of previous to the one applied for, as the case may be, and for the same period to quote the diaries in which their movement and the results of their enquiries have been recorded.

I had received closure report of an investigation conducted by PSI Brahmbhatt of Sihor police station about an incident that was of more than a year ago. In this case no offence was registered as the death of Koli Dhirubhai Keshubhai was treated as an accidental death. A perusal of the case papers revealed that the deceased used to work as a cleaner with Virani Transport, Bhavnagar. A cleaner is a person whose responsibility is to keep the vehicle clean and spruced up and assist the driver during their long journeys. On 14 April 1978, the deceased Dhirubhai was asked by the owner of the transport company, Kalubhai Virani to take a message to Nesda, a village located nine kilometres north of the police station and deliver the same to the driver of the truck number GTS 5522. The instructions given to the former was that he should go to the house of an acquaintance Khimabhai Ahir in that village and await there for the driver. Those were the days when there were no cell phones or internet. Pagers, which had made a brief appearance in the 1990s, had not yet been invented. Special messengers back and forth ferried important messages.

Mehboob Hussain, the driver of the truck, reached the village Nesda at about 8.15 PM and on reaching the house of Khimbhai, did not find the deceased there. Shortly after midnight Mehboob departed from the village and as he entered the highway, he saw a dead body lying on the road but did not wait to ascertain who it was. Early next morning a vehicle belonging to the State Traffic Police passed by. PSI V C Gohil who was patrolling the highway reported the occurrence to Sihor police station. Consequently, an accidental death case was registered.

When a person does not die due to natural circumstances, that person is considered victim of unnatural death. This would include accidental death, murders, animal attack, complications of surgery, suicide and many more. Accidental deaths are covered under section 174 CrPC. It provides that when an officer-in-charge of a police station or some other police officer specially empowered by the State Government receives information that a person has committed suicide, or has been killed by another or by an animal or by machinery or by an accident, or has died under circumstances raising a reasonable suspicion that some other person has committed an offence, that officer after giving intimation to the concerned executive magistrate empowered to hold inquests, shall proceed to the place where the body of such deceased person is, and there, in the presence of at least two respectable inhabitants of the neighbourhood, conduct an investigation, and draw up a report of the apparent cause of death, describing such wounds, fractures, bruises, and other marks of injury as may be found on the body, and stating in what manner, or by what weapon or instrument, if any, such marks appear to have been inflicted. This report in popular understanding is called the *Inquest Panchnama*.

The inquest proper is what is done by the executive magistrate which is to determine the cause of unnatural death. The magistrate shall examine the body and upon investigation conclude as to the reason which caused the death of the person. His role is limited in its scope; therefore, it is restricted to ascertaining the circumstances that caused the unnatural death of a person. He is neither required nor has any authority under the law to trace the person who has so caused the death. The latter obligation is that of the police. In the same manner as done by the police officer, the magistrate must conduct the investigation in presence of two or more respectable inhabitants of the neighbourhood. In case when no resident is there on the spot or when no one volunteers to be a witness of the investigation, the inquest report may be prepared without the presence of such citizens. The magistrate need not examine all the witnesses while performing investigation for a cause of unnatural death. In case no foul play is found, the dead body must be handed over to the legal heirs of the deceased. In cases where there is suspicion over the death of the deceased, then the dead body must be sent to the government medical officer for post-mortem.

A post-mortem is necessary when there is doubt as to the cause of death, or in the cases of suicides where there is no direct evidence to show that the death was due to suicide, or if, though there is no such doubt, the police officer thinks it expedient to do so, for instance, in order to procure expert medical evidence as to (a) the period of time that might have elapsed since death; (b) whether the death was homicidal, suicidal or accidental; (c) the identity of the deceased; (d) whether the deceased, in a case of infanticide, was born dead or alive; or (e) whether the death was due to the accident, when a prosecution is intended in a case of a motor accident. No examination was ordinarily necessary in cases of motor car or other accidents, where no prosecution is intended and there is unambiguous evidence of the cause of death. In an order issued by the Inspector General of Police, Bombay State, in March 1954, it was directed that copies of post-mortem notes and medical certificates may be supplied to the relatives of the deceased after the case is classified as an accidental death and a summary is issued in that behalf by the competent magistrate.

In a nutshell, section 174 is limited in scope and lays down the procedure that a police officer must follow on the unnatural death of a person. The section does not lay down the procedure for tracing of the accused. In the SDPO's office, cases enquired into under this provision are entered into the crime register, in a separate portion reserved for this purpose. This portion is further divided into two parts- (a) accidental deaths, and (b) other unnatural deaths. However, in case there is slightest suspicion of foul play, offence should be registered.

In this case post-mortem of the deceased Dhirubhai Keshubhai had been conducted. The investigating officer had forwarded the case papers to my office for endorsing his conclusion that this was a case of accidental death. It was made out that the deceased could have been fatally injured while either trying to climb on or getting down from a running truck which he may have planned to board for his onward journey or in which he may have arrived. I examined the papers carefully. The inquest *panchnama* itself revealed that the deceased had died a violent death. It indicated that the skull was broken and that there was a hole in the head. Since the dead body was found on the highway, it could have been safely concluded that this was a hit-and-run case, and as it had resulted in the death of the victim, an offence punishable under section 304A IPC, should have been registered. The postmortem report listed the cause of death as due to intracranial haemorrhage and fracture of the skull. There were descriptions of other injuries on the body and mutilation of other parts of the victim's anatomy.

There were other circumstantial reasons also for concluding that it was not a case of accidental death. Pratapsingh Prakaramsingh was a driver employed by the same company for which the deceased worked, Virani Transport. On 14 April, the day on which the deceased was to meet Mehboob, he had passed village Nesda, driving his own truck and accompanied by his cleaner. This was about 11 PM in the night and his cleaner told him that he saw the deceased sitting at the bus stand which was adjacent to the highway. The driver decided not to stop the vehicle but head home. The evidence of this witness made two things clear. Firstly, that the deceased had reached Nesda and was alive till late night and secondly, based on the evidence tendered by Mehboob Hussain, the death must have occurred between 11 PM and shortly after midnight, as the latter saw a dead body while departing the village, the identity of which he had not waited to check. The acquaintance Khimabhai on the other hand reported that the deceased never came to his house as he was supposed to. Since Mehboob had departed after midnight, it was not clear and therefore suspicious as to why the deceased did not go to meet the former at the house as prearranged. Further, the deceased was 25 years old, physically fit and his vocation being a cleaner, it was difficult to believe that he could have suffered such serious injuries while attempting to climb up or getting down from a truck as deemed by the investigating officer. By nature of his vocation the former is a sort of an expert as far as boarding or deboarding a goods vehicle is concerned. He cannot in the normal course be expected to suffer fatal injuries of the nature described in the post-mortem note.

This was clearly a case of minimisation of crime, and I therefore directed that an offence be registered under sections 279 (rash driving on a public way) and 304 A (causing death by rash or negligent death) of the Indian Penal Code read with sections 114 and 116 of the Motor Vehicle Act. So, it came to be that more than a year after the dead body of the deceased was found on the highway, the said offence was registered at Sihor police station on 6th June 1979. I had just concluded the inspection parade of Vallabhipur police station, when I received the special report, this time through a telephonic message, of the registration of the said crime. I therefore departed to visit the scene of crime near village Nesda.

Two witnesses who owned a cycle repair shop and a *paan* (betel leaf) shop near the scene of offence were located. Both reported no knowledge of any accident, fatal or otherwise, before they closed for the day. One witness, Arjanbhai Vashrambhai, stated that on the day of the incident, an acquaintance had come to visit him at village Nesda. He had later that night accompanied his guest up to the highway to help him with directions. The witness reported that he saw no dead body lying on the highway and returned home at about 11 PM. Thus, the testimony of this witness corroborated what Pratapbhai, the driver of another truck had stated. Khima Ahir confirmed that Mehboob had come to his house to meet the deceased but had departed after waiting for some time when the latter did not turn up. It was customary during such investigation to speak with the police patel and the Sarpanch (village headman). The latter reported that he was informed about the incident early next morning and on visiting the spot, was unable to identify the victim as he did not belong to the village.

My next port of call was Bhavnagar for the purpose of examining Kalubhai Virani, the owner of the transport company, as also to verify the statement of Pratapbhai. I had by now examined a total of nine witnesses, apart from visiting the scene of crime and verifying the *panchnama*. While it was clear that in all probability a moving vehicle must have hit the deceased, it had not been possible so far to ascertain who was the culprit. The other intriguing part was, why did he not visit the house of Khima Ahir at all, though he had come to village Nesda. Further enquiries revealed that rest of the witnesses who could throw some light thereby leading to the detection of the case, were in Surat and Ahmedabad. This required permission from the SP to travel out of the district. The latter however was of the view that this was an incident which was more than a year old and as there were other pressing engagements which needed my attention, I could conclude the visitation. The investigating officer PSI S V Vyas, the Station House Officer of Sihor police station, was instructed to proceed to the two destinations and make sincere efforts to detect the offence.

This was a case where an offence should have been registered at the relevant time which was more than a year ago. If that had been done, the chances of detection would have increased as it would have been possible to trace transient witnesses passing by that area. Further, with the passage of time, the memory of stationary witnesses also comes into question. The deceased obviously came from a humble background with nobody to pursue his case to seek justice. If any crime is committed, the crime is against the state. If a person dies due to unnatural circumstances, the state is burdened to identify the cause of death and if there lies suspicion as to the cause of death, the state must take appropriate steps to punish the guilty. The only satisfaction I could derive was that a crime had been brought on record and the demise of the unfortunate victim did not pass off as an accidental death. Once a crime is registered, there is always hope that it might be detected sometime in the future.

CHAPTER 10

# THE VICE OF GAMBLING

*F*rom times immemorial gambling has been considered a vice which human beings are expected to avoid. The Mahabharat deprecates gambling by depicting the woeful conditions of the Pandavas who had gambled away their kingdom. In fact, the judiciary also has used the Mahabharat to justify the prohibition of gambling and allied games terming it as *res extra commercium*, outside the fundamental right to free trade and commerce guaranteed by the constitution. However, a deeper examination of the Mahabharat and other ancient religious texts reveals that this statement may not entirely be true. Gambling was neither frowned upon nor considered immoral by ancient Hindu culture. Gurcharan Das through his research on the Mahabharat claims that playing dice was part of the ritual and imperial consecration required of the king in the Vedic *rajasuya* ceremony. Nevertheless, Shakuni uses Yudhisthir's love for gambling and the knowledge that he does not know how to play, as a strategy to get the better of the Pandavas. He advises Duryodhan that it is useless to brood over the good fortune of his cousins. They are invincible in battle;

they are far superior warriors and have made important alliances which give them immense power. One needs clever means, and he suggests a gambling match. Thus, religious texts accept gambling as a social reality and have never entirely prohibited or criminalised it, though many Rig Vedic verses and comments by jurists like Manu and Kautilya dwell upon ill effects of gambling addiction.

Ancient Jewish authorities frowned on gambling, even disqualifying professional gamblers from testifying in court. Although different interpretations of Shari'ah (Islamic Law) exist in the Muslim world, there is a consensus among the 'Ulema', that is scholars of Islam that gambling is *haram*-sinful or forbidden. In assertions made regarding its prohibition, Muslim jurists describe gambling as being both un-Qur'anic, and as being harmful to the Muslim Ummah. The Catholic Church, on the other hand, holds the position that there is no moral impediment to gambling, so long as it is fair, all bettors have a reasonable chance of winning, there is no fraud involved, parties involved do not have actual knowledge of the outcome of the bet, the gambler can afford to lose the bet and stops when the limit is reached, and the motivation is entertainment and not personal gain or for making a living.

The history of gambling in the United Kingdom goes back centuries, as do efforts to deplore it, and regulate it. Gambling was legal under English common law but the government worried that it interfered with military training. The Unlawful Games Act 1541 made virtually all gambling illegal. The Gaming Act 1845 legalized games of skill, made cheating a crime, simplified the regulation of gambling houses, and made gambling contracts legally unenforceable.

Gambling has been defined as something which involves not only chance, but also a hope of gaining something beyond the amount played. Gambling consists of consideration, an element of chance, and a reward. The Supreme Court has held that even though the most important aspect of gambling is chance, it does not mean that it is completely devoid of skill.[1] Hence, there are games which require skill, coupled with chance, up to a certain degree and such games are not illegal. The British enacted the Public Gambling Act, 1867 which incidentally does not expressly refer to "game of chance" or "game of skill".

For the Bombay Presidency, the British enacted the Bombay Prevention of Gambling Act, 1887 to consolidate and amend the law for the prevention of gambling. In the earlier days, a dice or birds or cards were used as instruments of gaming. In 1947, after independence the law was re-enacted. The manner of gambling also progressed with changing times and now included gaming on the market price of cotton, opium or other commodity, the digits of the number used in stating such price, the amount of variation in the market price of any such commodity or even on the digits of the number used in stating the amount of such variation. Extraordinary as it may seem, gaming included within its ambit the occurrence or non-occurrence of rain or other natural event, or the quantity of rainfall or on the digits of the number used in stating such quantity, occurrence, or non-occurrence of any uncertain future event.

One of the most popular forms of gambling was 'worli matka'. It was started in 1961, by a man called Ratan Khatri. Little is known about his origin except that he was born in what is now Pakistan probably in 1933 and started as a small-time operator who rose to become the mastermind behind a vast gambling network. Khatri had taken matka betting to the whole country and had complete control over it. He is famous for his 'matka king' nickname and is credited with transforming this form of gambling. During the decades of the 1980s and 1990s it had reached its peak. The precursor to worli matka was kalyan matka. This was started somewhere around 1950. The people then used to place bets on the opening and closing rate of cotton. The practice made its way to the Bombay Cotton Exchange right from the New York Cotton Exchange, via teleprinters. When the New York Cotton Exchange stopped the practice in 1961, gamblers and punters started using pieces of paper to keep this gambling business alive. In 'satta matka' gambling, numbers from 0-9 are written on pieces of paper. The papers are then placed into a matka (earthen pot). An individual is assigned the task to pick out a piece of paper and read out the winning numbers. The practice evolved over a period. Offline three numbers are drawn from a pack of cards to announce the winner. This form of gambling grew at a huge scale during 1980s and 1990s. Betting volumes touched to Rs 50 crore-range every month during that period. Over the years technology has taken over. Instead of using pieces of paper, winning numbers are randomly generated now.

Back then three numbers that were drawn by Ratan Khatri every morning used to be published in several well-known newspapers across the country under the misleading title *Shubh*

*Rashi* (auspicious zodiac sign). I however do not recall a single instance of a newspaper being prosecuted for aiding and abetting this crime. Such was the craze for matka betting that it became a positive threat to the economy in the sense that it generated a huge amount of black money, part of which was deployed to compromise police officers and politicians. In 1972, section 3A was inserted in the main statute which made printing or publishing, of pictures, digits or figures relating to worli matka, a criminal offence. Special gambling squads were set up in the police forces of metropolitan areas and the mofussil. And yet, mainstream police organisations, such as police inspector and sub-inspector at the police station level, were exhorted through provisions in the police manual to have no doubt that the work of controlling gambling was a part of their duties. They were expected to get the necessary information and help the special staff in that work. Failure to do so would amount to neglect of duty.

In Greater Bombay, Mawali Register maintained at the police station contained the names of persons known or believed or reported to be habitually involved in acts of violence, intimidation, extortion, or other illegal pursuits likely to affect adversely, the peaceful living of law-abiding citizens. Habitual gamblers along with violators of the prohibition law, and prostitution would also come within definition of a mawali. Policemen on duty in a town were expected to move on their beats, keeping their eyes and ears open to what was going on around them. They were directed to keep an eye on brothels, *dharmshalas* and the houses of suspected or known receivers of stolen property, and on thieves, gamblers, and other bad characters, taking note of those who enter such places. Even for the criminal procedure code proceedings under sections 109 and 110, which is a useful means at the disposal of the police for checking and controlling crime, a person who was habitually gambling and depended on this activity as a source of living, was considered a fit person to be proceeded against.

The week ending 7$^{th}$ of July 1979 had been particularly busy one. On Sunday, I had left my head-quarter town at 8 AM in the morning to visit a fatal motor accident which had occurred within the limits of Vallabhipur police station. Same day I also had to proceed to Bhavnagar to conduct the departmental proceedings of Constable Balwantsinh Ladhubha. Although I was able to return to Palitana later that evening, the following day I had to proceed to Jesar police station to supervise the investigation of yet another fatal motor vehicle accident. This was not my jurisdiction. However, the SDPO of the adjoining Mahuva sub-division was on leave. Such was the seriousness attached to the supervision of serious crime, that it had been mandated by a circular issued by the Inspector General of Police, Bombay State that if the incumbent subdivisional officer was not available for any reason, SDPO's of other subdivisions who were at that time not actively involved in supervising or visiting a serious crime, should be sent.

Tuesday was a rather quiet day, and I was able to attend to routine office work at Palitana. For some time, I had been receiving information that gambling dens were running at a village called Dhola, located 65 km away, which in fact is an OP of Umrala police station. During the British period it was one of many non-salute states in Gohilwad *prant* (province) on the Saurashtra peninsula, comprising of only the village. It was a principality paying tribute to the Gaikwars and Junagadh[2]. It has also been a railway junction since the time of Bhavnagar State Railways, which functioned in the princely state of Bhavnagar in British India. All gambling dens wherever they existed did so due to police patronage. During those days the police had two main sources of regular illicit income: that being prohibition (of liquor) and gambling. In both cases a supervising officer like an SDPO can never rely on the support, loyalty, and integrity of the local police station staff, should he choose to do his duty diligently and curb that activity. The only option open is to arrive at these dens suddenly and virtually catch them, as they say, red-handed.

So it was that I took a spot decision to raid the gambling dens at Dhola. I departed Palitana at 5:30 PM and what followed that day is best described by an extract of my weekly diary dated 3rd of July.

> *Attended office routine. Left Palitana at 17:30 hours & reached Dhola at 18:30 hours. 65 kms. Carried out a raid u/s 12 Gambling Act and arrested Ramaniklal Harilal & Koli Magan Nagji. At 18:45 hours carried out second raid u/s 12 Gambling Act. Accused are Dhirajlal Sakarlal and Babu Valji. At 19:00 hours carried out a third raid u/s 12 Gambling Act. Accused are Umesh Lalji and Bala Kesbu. All the three offences are registered vide Umrala Police Station C. R. No. 44/79, 45/79, 46/79. Total amount recovered is Rs. 177-55 paisa.*
>
> *Also carried out a raid u/s 4-5 Gambling Act and arrested 1. Patel Shamji Mohan 2. Patel Shamji Ghanshyam 3. Rajput Shamji Keshav 4. Chandubhai Jagjivan 5.*

*Bhikha Daya 6. Popat Bawa 7. Govind Chana. Total amount recovered Rs. 505-15 paisa.*

*Left Dhola at 19:50 hours and reached Umrala at 20:05 hours. Carried out two raids u/s 4-5 Gambling Act. Accused arrested are Pravin Kalidas, Jika Dahya, Rahim Hussain, Girirajsinh Balwantsinh, Shanitlal Bhutha in one case and Abdul Rajak in another case. Total amount recovered was Rs. 164-80 paise in the first raid & Rs. 166-80 paise in the second raid.*

Clarification is required regarding the sections of law applied. Section 4 makes it an offence if any person opens, keeps, or uses any house, room, or place, for the purpose of a common gaming house. Advancing money for the purpose of gaming to persons frequenting any such house, room or place has also been made penal. For those who are found in any common gaming-house, gaming or present for the purpose of gaming, section 5 is applied. Sections 4 and 5 of Bombay Prevention of Gambling Act are cognizable offences, which means that the police can arrest without any warrant and are bailable. Any person found in a common gaming-house during any gaming shall be presumed, until the contrary is proved, to have been there for the purpose of gambling. Under the provisions of section 12 of the Act, a police officer may apprehend and search without warrant any person found gaming or reasonably suspected to be gaming, in any public street, thoroughfare or in any place to which the public have access including a race-course.

It was clear that such widespread gambling activities within the limits of the police station existed because of the patronage extended by the officer-in-charge of the police station. This is usually always done after paying bribe money to the police. In local parlance it is called *hafta*. The instalment is paid monthly and generally any person who runs a gambling den ensures that connections have been established not only with the local police but also with the special squads created at the district level for prevention of gambling. This was an occasion to give a proper dressing down to the SHO, which I proceeded to do, cautioning him of serious action against him if in future I found such illegal activities in his area. But I also took this opportunity to severely reprimand the accused persons warning them of dire consequences, should they decide to go back to such illegal activities. Suffice it would be to say here, that the kingpin amongst them was dealt with in a robust manner.

I was finally able to depart Umrala, the police station where we had brought all the accused, at 15 minutes past midnight. My diary records that on reaching Palitana at 0130 hours, I performed and checked men on night round till 03:00 hours. A PSI was doing night round duty in plainclothes. When questioned he replied that it was not always necessary to wear uniform during the night round. He was of course wrong and was merely covering the fact that he was absent from this prescribed duty assuming that the SDPO was out of headquarters and unlikely to return late in the night. It was safe to assume that he rushed out on learning that I had arrived. He had not made any station diary entry, a prescribed procedure which all must follow, before proceeding for town patrolling during the night. Before going home, I visited the police station and made an entry in the Station Diary regarding the unprofessional conduct of this officer. This generates a record for future reference and acts as a reminder to the officer-in-charge to ensure that such intransigence is not repeated.

Prevention of gambling was important not only for the police station but also for the supervisory ranks. Studies show that though people participate in gambling as a form of recreation or to earn an income, it can become a behavioural addiction. Such an infliction comes with all the negative consequences in a person's life, similar to issues faced by people who compulsively engage in drug and alcohol abuse. Hence it was identified as a social evil and made a crime. In fact, in 1927, an order was issued by the government directing public prosecutors, then known as police prosecutors, to press for deterrent sentences in cases of gambling, particularly those in which bucket shops[3] are involved. Directly recruited Assistant or Deputy Superintendents of Police were expected to take a keen interest in this work, and details of personal gambling raids were required to be attached to the weekly diaries in the form of a separate statement before dispatch to superior officers.

> *Yudhishthira slowly slips into a gambler's frenzy, blind to the consequences, forgetting himself. He hears only the clatter of the rolling dice, followed by Shakuni's chant, 'Won!' and cheers from the Kauravas' side. He begins to lose and lose consistently. By the end of round ten, halfway through the game, he has lost pearls, gold, his finely caparisoned chariot, a thousand elephants, choice horses, male and female slaves, and an army of chariots and charioteers.*[4]

The above extract from the book 'The Difficulty of Being Good' explains why gaming is evil. To be rich quickly without any labour is the dream of all sinners. That is the foundation of gambling, and the attraction is entertainment and the love of money. Both are very addictive strongholds of Satan. The victims are lazy, covetous, foolish, and ambitious at the same time. That combination is deadly. Gambling is a scheme to escape labour. and is a trait that can destroy life and livelihoods.

Several months later I had to visit Dhola Junction again, this time for the annual inspection of the police OP there. After finishing the days' work, I returned to the Rest House, located on the outskirts of the village, for wash and change, and then set out for a walk. It was almost dusk and near the railway station there were several handcarts selling fruits and vegetables. As I approached further, suddenly one person selling fruits from a handcart waved at me and then came across. I recognized him as the kingpin of the gambling dens which I had raided the previous year. He was all smiles when he informed me that since that day, he had turned a new leaf and had acquired a legitimate line of business. He had gained the respect of his family and friends. He expressed his gratitude for being dealt with "in a robust manner". I wished him well and asked him to stay on the right path.

In all the above cases charge-sheets had been filed in the courts of competent jurisdiction. One case, which pertained to running a gaming house, came up for trial. I deposed in the court as a witness and felt quite sure that the prosecution will secure a conviction. Few weeks later while camping at Sihor, the Judicial Magistrate First Class (JMFC), who was also the Circuit Judge and at the same location that day, sent word that he wanted to meet me. He was a young man perhaps a few years older than me and appeared to be in an apologetic frame of mind. The reason was obvious. He conveyed that he had acquitted all the accused, in the case wherein I had rendered evidence, on technical grounds. This was upsetting as I had personally ensured that the FIR is recorded properly, the case properly investigated, and a charge-sheet submitted to a court of competent jurisdiction well in time. The JMFC explained that there was no warrant issued to authorise police entry into a gaming house and carrying out the raid. He was referring to a provision contained in section 6 of the Bombay Prevention of Gambling Act, 1887 which empowers a SP or an ASP or a DySP to issue a special warrant to any officer not below the rank of a Police Sub- Inspector to enter any house which is used as a common gaming house. The latter term includes any house, or place where gambling takes place, and where instruments of gaming are kept and used for gambling.

I was nonplussed and for a good reason. As a Sub-Divisional Police Officer in the rank of an Assistant Superintendent of Police, I was a competent authority under the law to issue a special warrant to subordinate ranks. A bare reading of the relevant provision of the law did not allow for an inference that such a competent authority, should it decide to conduct the raid itself, was required to issue a warrant unto itself. I had cited myself as a witness and rendered evidence during the trial. It did not appear logical and nobody either during indoor training at the academy or while undergoing practical training in the field had ever mentioned this. Thus, absence of a piece of paper in the form of a special warrant came in handy for the defence counsel to persuade the court and obtain an acquittal on technical grounds. I do not believe that the acquittal was challenged in the higher court because the process is long and tedious, and there are too many other important cases which are required to be taken up before a higher judicial forum by the way of appeal. This, despite the fact that the police manual specifically directed that even in cases where punishment awarded, upon conviction, is less than minimum provided by the law, a report was required to be sent by the officer-in-charge of the police station through the SP as to whether it was a fit case for appeal or not. The only satisfaction that I could derive was the knowledge that some individuals, having gone through the grind of a trial, would now stay away from such addiction.

CHAPTER 11

# PRIME CRIME OFFICER

*A* vital duty entrusted to a Sub-Divisional Police Officer is the control and supervision of crime in his sub-division. To that end, he was required to maintain a crime register for each police station under his charge where details of crime recorded at that police station were regularly entered. It was the only record which kept him informed of the progress done by the police station officers in the investigation of crime registered at that police station. If he did not write them up regularly from day to day, he will not be able to know how many offences are reported in his sub-division, how they are investigated, and the progress made in each case. District Superintendents of Police would impress upon the SDPOs, and particularly the Assistant Superintendents of Police serving under them, the importance of making entries in the crime registers regularly. Such was the importance accorded to this document that the district police chief was required by the provisions of the police manual to check them out periodically and bring to the notice of the Inspector-General of Police- the head of state police force, cases of negligence on the part of the SDPOs in writing up these registers. Deputy Inspectors-General of Police in charge of ranges were under instructions to pay special attention to this matter during their annual inspections.

Palitana sub-division, as mentioned earlier, constituted of eleven police stations. Therefore, the same number of crime registers had to be maintained in the office and regularly written up. Each SDPO was supplied an aid in the rank of a police sub-inspector designated as Reader PSI. He played a critical role in aiding the SDPO in scrutiny of case diaries, weekly diaries and other papers of investigation that came to the sent regularly to the office. Entries in crime registers were made, by the Reader, based on case diaries received from the concerned police station. These case diaries, maintained under the provision of section 172 CrPC, are a true record, written in their own handwriting, of day-to-day investigation carried out by the concerned investigating officer, in cognizable cases and in inquiries under section 174 CrPC. A fair copy of the case diary is to be sent daily to the SDPO. On holidays as well as on other days, every case diary must be written up in the evening of the day of the enquiries or, if the enquiries have been prolonged into the night, the first thing the following morning, and a copy thereof was required to be despatched during the morning of the day following the day or night of enquiry, by the officer-in-charge of the police station to the sub-divisional officer. It gave an account of the time at which the information reached the investigating officer, the time at which he began and closed his investigation, the places visited by him, and a statement of the circumstances ascertained in the investigation. The case diary should show how the case progresses during investigation. It must also reflect the mind of the investigating officer. It is incumbent on the sub-divisional officers to see that diaries are properly written in accordance with the instructions.

Mansinh Dabhi, an experienced PSI of about fifteen years of service, was the Reader. He had a good grip not only on investigation of crime but also a thorough understanding of the crime-related records that are maintained at the police station level. A tall man, his sluggish disposition belied a sharp mind. Normally, the post of a Reader is not a sought-after assignment as most police officers would prefer to work in the field. Such was not the position earlier. The designation itself owes its origin to the requirement of British officers who needed somebody to "read" and translate from the vernacular to the English-language. In those days this was a preferred assignment as it allowed for proximity to the ruling class. Over a period, the post acquired considerable importance within the police hierarchy and generally seasoned officers were picked up. This became more important when the SDPO happened to be a freshly recruited member of the IPS doing his mandatory tenure in the subdivision. Back then, Readers were expected to know the details of every undetected case under discussions with the Deputy Inspector-General during the latter's annual inspection, who in turn was expected to try and find out why the offences were not detected, and then make his remarks thereon.

The office also maintained a register in which details of all crimes which had been visited by the SDPO were entered. The instructions were that these will be personally entered in his own handwriting by the incumbent officer. A diligent sub-divisional officer would have recorded intelligent notes concerning crime and made a mention about previous convictions, names of investigating officer, and other relevant details. Thus, it was my duty not only to write this register personally, making entries based on case diaries received but also to make sure that Reader PSI Dabhi did likewise for the eleven crime registers that he was required to maintain. The latter also contained entries when extension of investigation beyond the prescribed time limit had been granted by the SDPO, and the reasons thereof. It thus became a critical instrument of supervision in the days when the digital world of today had not been conceived or imagined.

*Discretion to abstain from investigation*

Section 157 (1) (b) CrPC allows the officer-in-charge of a police station who receives information of the commission of a cognizable offence, to use his discretion to abstain from investigating such information, if it appears to him that there is no sufficient ground for investigation. The discretion and the responsibility for the proper exercise of the same, lay with the officer-in-charge of the police station. This discretion should ordinarily be exercised when complaints or information of altogether unimportant offences or frivolous, vexatious, mistaken, or manifestly untrue complaints are received. In that event, an entry into the General Diary, statutorily required to be maintained at each police station, is mandatory. Since a copy of this is despatched to the office of the SDPO on daily basis, the latter, through their readers, make entries of such cases in their crime registers.

There is always a possibility that the discretion to decline investigation may be misused for the purpose of minimising crime or for favouring somebody, usually for less than honourable reasons. Sub-divisional officers during their tours of inspection were expected to make it a point of satisfying themselves that officers in charge of the police stations have intelligently grasped the purport and principles underlying the discretion vested in them. They were expected to keep a watchful eye on their working and, by constant and effective supervision, while encouraging the exercise of sound discretion, check any tendency towards negligence and laziness, such as might result in refusal to investigate for improper reasons or on inadequate grounds, or burking[1] of complaints of cognizable offences.

However, during the eighteen months that I functioned as SDPO Palitana Sub-Division, I did not come across a single instance where discretion to refuse investigation under section 157 had been exercised. Non-registration of crime is resorted to in diverse ways. The method that I had adopted for checking minimisation of crime was to scrutinise, during the annual inspection of the police station, the Non-Cognizable Crime Register. When a complainant approaches a police station and provides information about a crime, the police have the power of investigating only those cases of which according to the law they can take cognizance of. The law in this regard is contained in section 155 CrPC directing that when information is given to an officer-in-charge of a police station of the commission, within the limits of such station, of a non-cognizable offence, he shall enter the substance of the information in a book and refer the informant to the judicial magistrate. During inspections, I would make it a point of scrutinising every single complaint mentioned in that register and discover often that a cognizable offence had been minimised and converted into a non-cognizable one. I would then, regardless of how long back the complainant had approached the police station, get the offence registered and direct a speedy investigation. This I would reflect in the inspection note as well.

## Importance of visitation

Supervision of serious crime was a key result area for all sub-divisional officers. This took priority over every other aspect of an SDPO's functioning. Absence on casual leave was not a valid excuse for not visiting a scene of a serious offence, the proper course being to return at once or before proceeding on leave, to arrange for another officer to visit such a scene. Police Station Officer would send to his Sub-Divisional Officer, with a copy to his Superintendent of Police, a special report by the quickest means. In the earlier days telegram was a means of quick communication and for this purpose a separate category called "Special Police" telegrams was created. They took precedence even over the Express telegrams. Serious crime included all cases of murder, attempt to murder, culpable homicide, dacoity, train robbery, highway robbery between sunset and sunrise, robberies, and attempted robberies in which a firearm had been used, house-breaking with theft involving property of Rs. 5,000 or more, serious riots, serious motor accidents involving loss of life, and any case in which a police officer was accused of an offence, provided a complaint had been registered. These offences came to be known as *visitable offences* since the SDPO was expected to reach the scene of crime without any delay and supervise the investigation. In Gujarat, as mentioned earlier, death of a woman within seven years of marriage was also made visitable.

The SDPO, during visitation, are expected to identify themselves with the police enquiry in such serious cases. Though not as a rule in a position to take up the threads of an investigation, they could, under the provisions of section 36 CrPC, assume the position of an investigating officer whenever the occasion warranted such a step. Their presence during an investigation had to be brought out in the papers of the case, whenever possible, either by signing *panchnamas* or by recording statements of witnesses in the case. They were expected to personally go through the case papers, case diaries and *panchnamas* already prepared, question the persons concerned and verify their statements. To show that they have done so, they were expected to initial the case papers and attest the statements of witnesses with their dated signatures. Before an officer departed on conclusion of the visitation, in cases which remain undetected, it was expected that he would arrive at some definite conclusion and give suitable instructions to his subordinates.

The visitation of a serious crime was never a formality. On the contrary it institutionalised thorough and methodical working style which should be the hallmark of any police work. In the interest of the detection and prevention of serious crime in a district or on a railway and of police efficiency generally, this personal enquiry into crime by the SDPO was treated as a most important duty. A mere formal flying visit to the scene of an offence, with a halt there of a few hours only, cannot, in difficult and undetected cases, be expected to be productive of any appreciable results towards the detection of the case, and affords no sufficient guarantee that the subordinate police officers will proceed with their investigation regularly and correctly.

The presence, however, during an investigation for a reasonable time, the encouragement he can give to his subordinates, his supervision over their enquiries and the part he can himself play in the investigation would, of course, go far towards ensuring proper investigation. The occurrence of another serious offence, unless it were of a very grave nature clearly demanding the sub-divisional officer's presence, would not be sufficient justification for cutting short a visit. The full details of the part played by the visiting officer in the investigation and the results of their visits to the scene of crime would be reflected day by day in their weekly diaries[2]. By associating himself more closely with the subordinate police in their enquiries and by personally investigating or supervising the investigation of as many cases as possible, a sub-divisional police officer can do much to improve the tone, morale, and efficiency of the force. There is no better way of acquiring useful information about his charge, or of getting to know his men.

I took the mores and practices of a visiting officer seriously. Ordinarily the SDPO is required to spend at least one night at the scene of offence. If the offence was undetected, prevalent police manual instructions required camping there for at least five nights, unless detected earlier. It was further mandated that the place of camp should be within a radius of eight kilometres from the scene of crime. I recall a visitation concerning an undetected murder case in a village under Umrala police station where there was absolutely no accommodation available in any form including a rest house. But the village had a school consisting of two rooms. Summer vacations were on and consequently, I encamped in one of the classrooms whereas the investigating officer, who was the officer-in-charge of the police station, along with his men occupied the other. However, a toilet was not available, and for answering the call of nature early morning, one walked into the woods.

I remember a circular issued by the Inspector-General of Police, Bombay Presidency in 1937, directing sub-divisional officers to assist any case visited by him by putting themselves down as a witness to strengthen the prosecutor's evidence, when such a course is necessary. These assertions were valid more than four decades later and would reveal the seriousness attached to the role of a superior officer in ensuring quality investigation. Although the discretion was left to the officers in this respect, I exercised the same in favour of it on a few occasions. These salutary expectations from supervisory ranks found resonance in the provisions of the Bombay Police Act enacted in 1951, to amalgamate the District and Greater Bombay Police Forces and the Police Forces of the Saurashtra, Kutch, and Hyderabad areas, and of the Vidarbha regions, of the State of Bombay into one common police force, and to introduce uniform methods regarding the working and control of the said force throughout the State. Section 97 provided that a Police officer of a rank superior to that of a constable could perform any duty assigned by law or by a lawful order to any officer subordinate to him. In case of any duty imposed on such subordinate, a superior where it shall appear to him necessary, could aid, supplement, supersede or prevent any action of such subordinate by his own action, or that of any person lawfully acting under his command or authority, whenever the same appeared necessary or expedient for giving more complete or convenient effect to the law or for avoiding an infringement thereof. An excellent enactment which, while statutorily empowering a superior officer, also at the same time brought home the role that the legislature expected him to play in discharge of his responsibilities. I have always maintained that this particular provision far surpassed in clarity as well as in impact an analogous provision contained in section 36 CrPC[3].

## Administration of crime

The duties of a Sub-Divisional Police Officer are multifaceted as far as administration of crime is concerned. It is widely believed that a person in police custody will not be accessible to his defence counsel. If such an access was granted, it was attributed to the largess of an investigating officer rather than to a procedure described. This however is not true and even here the SDPO has a role to play. All applications from pleaders or other members of the legal profession, for interviews of accused in police custody, for the purpose of defence, could be preferred, and the officer-in-charge of the police station was expected to, if there were no valid objections, facilitate the same and appoint a suitable time. If there were valid objections, the officer-in-charge of the police station had to forward the application without any delay to the SDPO with an endorsement stating what the objections are, and the latter could take a decision to allow such a meeting or otherwise. Another important function was to grant permission in those cases where one of the accused persons was allowed to become an approver. With a view to obtain the evidence of a person supposed to have been directly or indirectly concerned in or privy to the offence, pardon can be tendered to such a person on condition of his making a full and true disclosure of the whole of the circumstances within his knowledge relative to the offence and about every other person concerned, whether as principal or as abettor, in the commission thereof. The investigating officer, whenever he finds it necessary to make an accused person an approver, could obtain the permission of his sub-divisional officer.

It is the duty of the SDPO to see that investigations are promptly and vigorously conducted by officers-in-charge of the police stations. In no case should the latter fail to submit a charge-sheet or a final report within fourteen days of registration of the FIR, without satisfying the former that there is sufficient cause for further delay, and in no case must the completion of the investigation be delayed beyond one month from the date of the recording the FIR. Assistant or Deputy Superintendent of Police were tasked to carefully go through the papers and exercise adequate control and supervision, through their orders, over the progress of the enquiries by obtaining explanation where such seems necessary, giving orders calculated to further the investigation and to elucidate points, and stimulating the investigation. Final reports submitted by the SHO or the investigating officer when there is no sufficient evidence to justify the forwarding of the accused to a judicial magistrate, had to be properly scrutinised by the SDPO. This became relevant for crimes registered with the police station, other than serious offences. The latter category in any case received proper attention from the supervisory ranks due to the institutional arrangements enumerated above. In the remaining cases, which were in large numbers, sometimes a closure report was filed by the investigating officer without having made proper efforts to either arrest the accused or seize the stolen property. A sub-divisional officer is not bound to forward a final report to the JMFC immediately. He may of his own motion direct further enquiry, or he may for special reasons, permit a case to remain pending under investigation.

*Maliciously false complaints*

Sub-Divisional Police Officers have a vital role to play when maliciously false complaints are lodged with the police by any individual. While the forwarding a closure report to the JMFC at the end of investigation, the SDPO is expected to consider the question of prosecuting the complainant under section 211 of the Indian Penal Code. This legal provision is for those who institute any criminal proceeding, with the intention of causing injury against anybody, knowing that there is no just or lawful ground for a charge against that person. If the SDPO decides in favour of a prosecution, he should, while forwarding the final report, make a separate report to the magistrate concerned, giving details of the case, and requesting him for reasons shown to lodge a complaint in writing in the court of competent jurisdiction. There is yet another analogous provision in the Indian Penal Code contained in section 182. This is regarding giving false information, with intent to cause public servant to use his lawful power to the injury of another person. Back then as a young officer, I could not fathom the difference between the two but grasped the same some years later.

An important supervisory tool that facilitates the SDPO to oversee his charge efficiently, is the Station Diary. In other provinces of the country, it is called the General Diary. Maintained at every police station, the main object of the station diary is to safeguard the interests of the public by chronicling briefly, at the time they take place, all important occurrences affecting the police and the public. A further object of the diary is to keep superior police officers informed of such occurrences. The diary is to be written up as from midnight to midnight, and the entries therein, are to be made chronologically hour by hour, as the occurrences they record become known to the SHO, the exact time being shown against each entry. It records the receipt of information regarding local occurrences of importance, such as fires, accidents, strikes, fairs, processions, public meetings, unlawful assemblies, epidemics, wandering gangs, the time of registration of all cognizable and non-cognizable cases, showing the sections of law under which recorded. It also mentions the discharge or release on bail by the police of arrested persons, departure from the police station of arrested persons for enquiries or for courts, quoting the buckle numbers policemen in charge of each prisoner, time of departure and the name of the court to which sent, time of return of prisoners from courts, or from enquiries with results, action taken on broadcast messages relating to missing motor cars, murders, riots- noting the date and serial number of the wireless message, affrays between civilians and members of the armed forces, misconduct of police officers and men calling for disciplinary action, visits paid by superior officers and other high government officials.

The Station Diary also recorded the performance of departmental duties by the Station House Officer, such as parades and inspection held or attended, attendance at courts, town patrols, night rounds, assistance to officers of other police stations. It was thus a critical document received in the office of the SDPO in original, submitted early on the day following that for which it was written up, the carbon copy being retained in the police station as an office copy. My office would receive eleven station diaries, for those were the number of police stations under my charge and it was the duty of the Reader PSI Dabhi to scrutinise them and then put them up to me, with his comments if any. In those days, means of transmission were competent but not quick. Consequently, I would get to see the Station Diary of far-flung police stations after two or three days, sent sometimes by post, or sometimes by a special messenger who would be arriving at the sub-divisional headquarters for some other work as well. On occasions when I was camping outside my headquarters, which was at least two or three weeks in a month, the Station Diary would be sent along with the other letters and mail that my office would have received.

Crime charts, graphs, and maps played a significant role. The SDPO office maintains crime charts in respect of cognizable crime, month by month, for each police station and for the whole subdivision. I must however admit, that after the initial enthusiasm of having the charts and maps displayed in my office, I lost interest in the same primarily because of the extensive travel that I had to do while attending to my multifarious duties as a sub-divisional officer. In any case during my entire tenure neither the Superintendent of Police, Bhavnagar District nor the Deputy Inspector General of Police, Rajkot Range visited my headquarters. Therefore, interest or impetus at the senior level was also absent.

CHAPTER 12

# IN A FIT OF ANGER

*I*t was a Tuesday in July 1979 and monsoon had set in vigorously. I had arrived at Sihor the previous evening after having carried out a successful raid under the Bombay Gambling Act, 1887, at village Jithri, for worli matka gambling and an unsuccessful raid under the Bombay Prohibition Act[1], 1949, at village Ambla, for opium. The purpose of the visit was to conduct the annual inspection of the police station, and this was a detailed procedure which entailed inspection of all crime records, writing up service sheets of the men, and evaluating them for both physical fitness and grasp of police work. Police manual rules mandated that this ought to be done over a period of four days in a detailed manner, and I commenced work in right earnest. Sometime later in the evening, I received a telephonic message from Vallabhipur police station about the death of a married woman and hence departed for that location. Visitation of serious crime was always accorded top priority.

Vallabhipur, is an ancient city located in the Saurashtra peninsula of Gujarat, near Bhavnagar in western India. It was the capital of the *suryavanshi maitraka* dynasty who ruled in this area from

470 AD to 788 AD. Over the centuries, not much development had taken place, the economy being agrarian, and it was now a taluka headquarter. On arrival, I was met by PSI Gangabhai Laxmanbhai Khunti, the officer-in-charge of Vallabhipur police station. He apprised me of the facts of the case which in brief was, that one Jasuben, wife of Talshi Bijal Koli had been immolated the previous evening, at the residence of her husband where both were residing with the latter's parents. The incident had occurred at Chamardi, a village located 7 km south of the police station. However, neither the inquest could be held, nor the post-mortem done because the relatives had cremated the body during the night itself. Khunti learnt about the incident after Talshi and his mother Kunverben were admitted in the government hospital at Vallabhipur for treatment of burns, and an accidental death case had been registered. He had already been to the scene of incident, drawn up a *panchnama*, examined some witnesses and had concluded that there was something fishy about the whole incident. However, nobody had come forward with any untoward claim.

Although it was past 9 PM and there was no electricity in the village, I decided to proceed to the village and speak with a few witnesses. The arrival of the police in substantial numbers in two police jeeps after sunset was not a small event in the village in those days, and this lent a certain gravity to the enquiries that I was about to undertake along with PSI Khunti. The latter himself was a directly recruited Sub- Inspector of Police having joined the police in the same year and month that I had, July 1976. In his outward demeanour he appeared timid but in fact he was methodical in his approach even if cautious. He was no more experienced than I was as far as police work was concerned. Nevertheless, between the two of us we succeeded in establishing what had happened. Jasuben, the deceased, was married to Talshi Bijal and had come to live at village Chamardi where her husband lived along with his parents, his younger brother, and the latter's wife. The deceased was a lively person and soon found the confines of the village suffocating. It did not help that she did not get on well with her mother-in-law and soon found that the husband also tended to be dissatisfied with whatever she had to say or do. Consequently, the resultant brawls would frequently end up by her leaving for her parental home in another town nearby. Her father-in-law and mother-in-law also disapproved of her going to her parental home in such manner.

India has been a patriarchal society with the male members dominating most rituals and customs. Marriage is the only occasion when the woman gets prominence in manifold ways. The preparation for marriage, the wedding celebration, the procurement of new clothes and jewellery for the bride, lends a great degree of importance to her and builds up a sense of enthusiasm and euphoria for her future home, where she will go after her marriage. In the songs sung on the occasion and in the reference made to her during the discussions in the run-up to, and shortly after the marriage, she is often compared with Goddesses Lakshmi, Sarasvati, or with Sita. However, the anti-climax sets in early, within weeks sometimes days. In most middle or lower-class homes, a daughter-in-law carries the entire burden of household chores. The drudgery can be excruciating especially when the young woman is aware of the transformation taking place in the society, in the context of the space women occupy, during interactions at school or through the medium of newspapers. In those days there was no television in rural areas. For the freshly minted bride, the transmission to a new home which is going to be hers for the rest of her life is not easy. That is why there is a custom in accordance with which the brother comes after couple of days of the marriage to bring the bride back to her parents' home for few days. She returns when the groom comes over to fetch her. The intent here is to help her settle in while conveying that her parental home is always there as a backup. Of course, this also is symbolic as in most families the prevailing sentiment is, that regardless of the situation, she should remain at her husband's home.

Jasuben was soon disappointed with her surroundings. Before marriage, her parental home was Sihor, a town with a municipality located along the river Gautami. This erstwhile capital of the Gohil rajputs, surrounded by hills, is situated about 20 km. from Bhavnagar. Known as 'Saraswatpur' during the Mahabharat period, it is often regarded as 'Chhote Kashi' also. This is due to the religious activities associated with the several temples and *shivalayas* in and around this medium-sized town. The town exhibits a definite texture and architecture connected to its ancient temples and buildings. On the other hand, the majority of Chamardi's workforce was employed in the agricultural sector. Apart from a primary school, and there was nothing else of any interest within 20 km radius of the village, except cultivated or barren agricultural land. Those who desired to educate themselves beyond the primary level, did so by travelling to Vallabhipur. For those who desired university education, the only option was to move to Bhavnagar, which was the district headquarters.

On the day of the incident, Jasuben's parents had come to Chamardi for a social purpose and having learnt of the same, she had sent word to her parents that she would like to go back with them when they commence their return journey back home. Her husband and his parents were not in agreement with this, and a massive row erupted at the residence. Foul language was used on both sides, albeit the prominent aggressor was the husband. The neighbours were already aware of the discord between the husband and wife and being a man of sensitive disposition, the latter used to be embarrassed at the ruckus that fights with his wife caused within the earshot of the neighbours. At some point of time, in a fit of rage, Talshi, the husband, picked up a can of kerosene and poured it over his wife. Continuing to sense defiance, he lit a match and set her on fire. While this was happening both his parents stood cursing Jasuben. The unbearable pain made the latter cry out loudly and she attempted to run out of the room. Both Talshi and his mother tried to stop her. But the flames were so fierce that both suffered burn injuries. In the meantime, Jasuben collapsed, and it was her father-in-law and another person called Koli Mohan Uka, a neighbour, who carried her indoors. A hospital van was sent for to convey the former to the hospital. Just as the members of the *koli* community began to collect at the residence, Jasuben passed away. Consequently, the hospital van when it arrived, was sent away. It is a measure of how lowly placed the life of a daughter-in-law is, in the eyes of the elders of the community, that it was decided to hush up the matter. The time was now past 11 PM and as per the custom amongst the Hindus, no cremation takes place at that hour. Contrary to all norms, without performing any ritual[2] which are customarily done before the body is taken to the burning ghat, Jasuben's mortal remains were consigned to the flames.

The above facts were established after inspecting the scene of offence and speaking with three witnesses despite the late hour. The room where the deceased was set on fire was also used as kitchen and that is the reason why the deceased's husband was able to lay his hands on a can of kerosene immediately. In the *panchnama* drawn by PSI Khunti earlier in the day, a bottle containing the inflammable liquid usually used in a stove for cooking purposes, had been seized. This room-kitchen was bordered by a veranda on one side which could be entered through a door and that is where the deceased had collapsed, after she ran out in flames. The latter's sister-in-law Vasantben Manji revealed substantial details. She was in the house when the incident happened. She heard loudly spoken abuses hurled between the husband and his wife Jasuben, and the cursing of the father-in-law and the mother-in-law. Her position as a younger daughter-in-law did not allow her to intervene so she came out and sat on the veranda. She stated that the fight was always because of the insistence of Jasuben to go to Sihor, where the latter's parents lived. An important input that this witness provided was that the deceased had been held both by her father-in-law and mother-in-law, as the husband was dousing her with kerosene. She stated that Jasuben ran out of the room all ablaze even as the husband and the mother-in-law tried to prevent her from going out. After the former collapsed on the floor just outside the house, she was carried inside by the father-in-law Bijal Jiva, and Mohan Uka. After her death, the deceased was taken away during the night for cremation. She deposed that the deceased did not like to stay with the husband and frequently quarrelled when she was not allowed to go to Sihor.

The next witness to be spoken to was Katuben Jina. She was a neighbour and ran out of her home when she heard the cries of a woman- "Help, Help, I have been burned". She saw the deceased in flames, even as the latter's husband tried to stop her and flung her to the ground. According to this witness, the deceased had then said- "those who have done this to me will also suffer." The incident so much unnerved this witness, that she ran back inside her house.

PSI Khunti's men located one Pushottam Raghav, who also lived near the scene of offence. He was a *waghari* by caste, and thus would owe no communal loyalty to the *kolis*. He revealed that he had just returned home when he heard the deceased cry out "Help, Help, I have been burned". He ran towards the house of the deceased and found her lying on the ground. Bijal Jiva and Mohan Uka carried her to the veranda of the house and then inside. Later, he learnt that the husband of the deceased had set her on fire. A vital information he provided was the names of twelve persons from amongst the *koli* community who took away the dead body of Jasuben for cremation, and amongst them was Manji Bijal, the brother-in-law of the deceased and husband of witness Vasantben. The importance of this witness can be realised from the fact that Vasantben, the younger daughter-in-law was a member of the family and could at any time before or during the trial be influenced upon to retract from the statement recorded by the police. Pushottam on the other hand, not being from the same community, could be relied upon to speak the truth.

Earlier in the day, HC Jani had recorded the statement of Talshi Bijal and his mother Kunvarben at the government hospital at Vallabhipur, where they had been admitted, during which time they declared that they had suffered burns because a petromax had burst. Together they made no mention of the deceased or about any incident pertaining to her. Jani, as a part of this enquiry, had visited Chamardi and discovered that in the same house Jasuben had also suffered burns and later expired. This had resulted in registration of an accidental death case, the special report regarding which had triggered my visit. Two hours of work late in the night had now established that this was no case of accidental burning but that of homicide. Accordingly, an offence of murder was registered well past midnight, along with relevant section of law pertaining to causing disappearance of evidence of an offence by disposing of the body through cremation, in violation of all norms. PSI Khunti took over investigation of the case.

Since the following day I had scheduled inspection parade of police personnel posted at Sihor police station, I decided to return there to attend the parade. The distance was only 25 km, and I did not want to inconvenience the police staff over there by remaining away as they would have made detailed preparation for the event. I recall reaching Sihor at 2.15 am. Less than five hours later at 7 am, I commenced annual inspection of the police station beginning with reviewing the parade of the men and checking the condition of kit issued to them. Fortunately, despite the fact that the monsoon had set in, it did not rain and I was able to assess the men for their ability in handling a .303 rifle, and their virtuosity with the lathi. Then, directly from the parade ground I departed for village Chamardi at 11 am.

On reaching the village, the first task I undertook was to verify the *panchnama* of the scene of offence drawn up by the investigating officer earlier, when the incident was treated as a case of accidental death. Although I had visited the previous night, it was important to look at it in again in detail during the day to ensure that all facts had been included, and all parameters covered. Seven more witnesses were located, and their statements recorded. Amongst them were the wife, son, and daughter-in-law of Purshottam whose statement had been recorded the previous day. Two other witnesses, namely Pushottam Mitha and Ghugha Dayal had visited the house of the deceased where the father-in-law Bijal Jina had told them that his son was responsible for setting the former on fire. It must be borne in mind that villagers are cautious in their approach, and nobody comes forward to volunteer information unless they are identified by reason of their proximity to the scene of crime or to the dramatis personae, and then questioned.

Both Bijal and his younger son Manji were interrogated and placed under arrest. They confessed to the role they had played. The cremation ground was also inspected, and the bones of the deceased collected under a "*discovery panchnama.*" This is a document prepared by the investigating officer under section 27 of the Evidence Act, 1872. It is founded on the principle that if the confession of the accused is supported by the discovery of fact it may be presumed to be true and not to have been extracted. It comes into operation only when certain facts are deposed to as discovered in consequence of information received from an accused person in police custody, and that information relates distinctly to a fact discovered. This is the only exception to the provisions of the law that confessions made before a police officer is not admissible in evidence. This is to rule out any possibility of an accused person making an admission of guilt under inducement, threat or promise by a police officer. And this exception was on the premise that if a fact is discovered as a consequence of information given, some guarantee is afforded thereby that the information was true and therefore can be safely allowed to be admitted in evidence during the trial.

As mentioned earlier in this book, confessional statements made to police officers are admissible in evidence under section 27 but only that portion of the confession which is absolutely necessary to lead to the discovery of property or other relevant fact, is admissible. The words "fact discovered" in the section are not to be treated as equivalent to the object or article produced; the fact discovered embraces the place from which the object is produced and the knowledge of the accused about its existence at that place and the information given must relate distinctly to this fact. Information as to past user or the history of the object produced is not related to its discovery in the setting in which it is discovered. There may be cases in which the object produced by an accused person may not in itself be of an incriminating nature and its production would be irrelevant in the absence of any evidence to connect the article with the offence in question, apart from the accused's confession. However, the difficulty, insuperable as it may be, of proving that a fact discovered on information supplied by the accused is a relevant fact can be no justification for reading into the section something which is not there and for admitting in evidence a confession barred by section 26. The latter section states categorically that no confession made by a person whilst he is in the custody of a police officer shall be proved as against such person.

It is not as if the bones recovered from the cremation pyre could have been found anywhere else. And yet, newly minted police officers that we were, both Khunti and I decided to "discover" them as per the provision of section 27. During the trial, the slightest attempt on the part of the defence to prove any circumstance vitiating a confession is usually sufficient to render the confession irrelevant and inadmissible. Even when relevant, it is at best a very flimsy and, by its very nature, unreliable piece of evidence. We knew that it could not be regarded as an end to itself, but merely as a basis for working out the case by procuring evidence to verify and support it. It is only when corroborated by such independent evidence in material particulars that a confession acquires some evidentiary value as against the person making it. The cremation of the deceased was done late in the night in the presence of twelve people who were to be charged with abetment in destroying evidence. All of them knew Jasuben had been set on fire by her husband and killed. All of them were either related to each other as a part of the extended family or belonged to the same community. Whatever legal safeguards were available to strengthen the case, they had to be deployed.

Four witnesses, including one relative who lived in the village, also had learnt that the deceased had been done away with. One of them, Purshottam Mitha, had arrived at the scene of offence and had assisted with moving the deceased to inside the house. None of them had volunteered to inform the police about the crime, though it was apparent by now that the whole village knew, and none of them withheld any information when questioned by the police. The village also knew about the severe incompatibility between the husband and the wife. I next made inquiries about the parents of the deceased, Kalubhai Kanji and Mithiben Kalubhai who lived at Sihor. Both happened to be at village Chamardi on the day of the mishap. Along with the investigating officer, I went to Sihor and met them at their residence. The former revealed that he also belonged to Chamardi and had relocated to Sihor several years ago. On the day of the incident, he was there along with his wife Mithi as his brother had passed away. The latter had departed after attending to the important rituals connected with the demise of her brother-in-law whereas he had stayed back at his ancestral home. Late in the evening Bijal had come to him to inform that Jasuben had suffered burns. He went along and met his daughter who was lying prostrate on the floor. She told him that she was severely burnt, had been set on fire by her husband and needs to be conveyed to the hospital as nobody was doing that so far. He further revealed that he cursed his daughter's in-laws, especially the husband, and departed. Later in the night Bijal came again to inform him that his daughter had passed away and they were taking the body for cremation. The former asked him to join at which point of time Kalubhai told him that this could not be done as women were not cremated in the night. He later learnt that they had gone ahead and had cremated his daughter regardless.

Mithiben the mother of the deceased confirmed the details provided by her husband. Statements of both were recorded. There revelations were startling and in some non-official capacity, were upsetting for me. They had chosen not to report the crime or even take-up the matter with the community elders. Nothing in ones understanding of familial ties or upbringing would allow one to believe that a parent would do nothing on learning about the atrocity that their offspring had suffered, resulting in death. Both had stated that their daughter was not happy as she was being ill-treated at her husband's home. It was a measure of the societal pressures that operate on the parents of a married daughter in conservative and rural settings, at least in those days.

I returned to Chamardi, and set about the task of questioning, and then detaining all those who had participated in the funeral of the deceased. By late evening of that day, we had arrested seven persons. Manji Bijal, the brother-in-law of the deceased, who had led the funeral procession, had already been arrested earlier in the day. Under questioning all the accused admitted that they were aware of the circumstances that caused the death of Jasuben but had decided to take away the body for cremation as that was the consensus within the local *koli* community. They confirmed that they did this to avoid legal complications, should anybody alert the police. In fact, Bijal, the father-in-law, was insistent that the body be taken away at the earliest.

Next day efforts were made at village Chamardi to locate the remaining accused, and we succeeded in locating two more who had taken the body of the deceased to the burning ghat. Both confessed to their involvement and were placed under arrest. It was now time to question the husband Talshi and his mother Kunwarben who were admitted as indoor patients at the government hospital at Vallabhipur and were reportedly stable. The burn injuries that they had received while attempting to prevent the deceased from running out after she had been set aflame, were not serious. During questioning, both confessed to have sprinkled kerosene on Jasuben resulting in her death. The investigating officer was instructed to place them under arrest as soon as the mother and son were released from the hospital. A police guard was posted, in the meantime, to ensure that they did not go away anywhere on their own volition. A written communication was given to the Medical Officer to provide prior information about the discharge of both the patients.

I was ready to conclude the visitation of this serious crime. Except for two accused who were yet to be arrested for being part of the funeral procession which carried the deceased's body for cremation, all the other culprits had been arrested and accounted for. My parting instructions to PSI Khunti was to send the bones of the deceased which had been earlier recovered from the cremation ground to the medical authority at Jamnagar; arrest the remaining two accused at the earliest; get the map of the scene of offence prepared; and charge-sheet the case, after getting the draft approved by me, in the court of competent jurisdiction within the prescribed time limit.

CHAPTER 13

# THE WEEKLY DIARY

*T*here is no document that encapsulates the work done by a Sub-Divisional Police Officer as well as the Weekly Dairy. Every Assistant and Deputy Superintendents of Police is expected to maintain and write up day by day as the facts come to be known, in their own handwriting for each week commencing on Sunday and ending on Saturday, a diary in a bound book stamped, paged, and endorsed by the Superintendent of Police, details of their movements and proceedings. Its importance can be gauged from the fact that a SP whilst holding temporary charge of a sub-divisional officer on leave, was also under obligation to write the latter's weekly diary.

All cases of serious crime which were made visitable for an SDPO and all cases which he or she personally enquired into, are required to be reflected. When sub-divisional officers visit the scene of crime in any of these cases and make personal investigation, they must enter day by day their proceedings, setting forth briefly the places visited by them in the course of their investigation, the persons examined and facts ascertained through their investigation. In fact, the SDPO's diaries regarding any personal investigation into an offence should *mutatis mutandis*, though in less detail, contain very much what a sub-inspector is required to record in his case diary, which he writes in his capacity as the investigating officer. In special report cases not visited by the SDPO, the entries in the diaries had to be based on the details available from the case diaries submitted by the investigating officers.

How much importance was placed on effective supervision of crime by the SDPO can be judged from the following extract of a circular issued by the Inspector-General of Police, Bombay Presidency in 1896.

> *The town, the police station and the taluka, the nature and the date of crime, the name of the complainant and the amount of loss are to be given at the head. After giving the above, the Sub-Divisional Officer should invariably give some account of the circumstances of the case. It is not sufficient to know, for instance that a certain house was broken into, Rs. 4,000 stolen, and that enquiries are being made. A short precis of such particulars as have been learnt from the Sub-Inspector's reports should be given.*[1]

Inspection of a police station and an OP or other offices, including a reference to any grave irregularity of which the higher authority should be informed, or which is likely to be the subject of special investigation, and visits to and inspections of shops of licensed manufacturers under the Arms Act, were directed to be reported in the sub-divisional officer's diary. In fact, the SDPO is expected to inspect the shop, stock and accounts of every licenced manufacturer or vendor within their respective charges at least once a year and report the result to the district magistrate.

In cases of tours, the distance in kilometres has to be given, if journeys are performed by road or by water in a country craft. In addition to the name of the village at which the camp was located, the name of the taluka was required to be mentioned. The place of camp is, as a rule, the place where the officer is at midnight. If the officer is outside the district at that hour, it is irregular to enter as his camp the place where his office or tents might have been during that time. Time of arrival and departure, and vehicle used, was also entered by all Assistant and Deputy Superintendents of Police in their weekly diaries in respect of all journeys undertaken by them, especially that pertaining to the scene of crime or place where any personal investigation was conducted. Similarly, the time of beginning and ending night rounds had also to be shown in the diaries.

Reproduced below, by the way of illustration, is the weekly dairy for the week-ending 14th July 1979.

*Weekly diary of Shri K N Sharma, SDPO Palitana Division for the week ending 14-7-79*

| Date | Camp | No. of Returns | Proceedings |
| --- | --- | --- | --- |
| 8-7-79 Sunday | Palitana | 62/1 79 | Received special report of Sihor PS AD No. 16/79 at 0815 hours. Left Palitana at 1000 hrs. & reached Mota Surka at 1100 hrs. 40 Kms. Worked as per Crime Memo No.1 of 62/79. Left Sihor at 1400 hrs. and reached Bhavnagar at 1430 hrs. 25 kms. Left Bhavnagar at 1745 hrs and reached Mota Surka at 1820 hrs. Left Mota Surka at 1945 hrs. & reached Madhada at 2100 hrs. Left Madhada at 2215 hrs. and reached Sihor at 2315 hrs. 50 Kms. Between 1900 hrs. & 1930 hrs. did investigation of Sihor P.S. vide C.R. No. 76/79 u/s IPC 457, 380. Worked as per case diary No. 6. |

| | | | |
|---|---|---|---|
| 9-7-79 Monday | Sihor | 63/1 79 | Received special report of Songadh PS CR No. IPC 304A, 279, MVA 116, 112 at 0900 hrs. Left Sihor at 1100 hrs. and reached Songadh at 1115 hrs. Worked as per Crime Memo No. 1 of 63/79. In this connection left Songadh at 1130 hrs. and reached Piprala at 1145 hrs. Left Piprala at 1230 hrs. & reached Songadh at 1245 hrs. Carried out a raid u/s 4-5 Gambling Act and arrested one Khatubha Karsanji at 1630 hrs. Amount seized Rs. 149.50 ps. Nagji Ghusa and Ghusa Bhagwan were also arrested in the same raid. Left Songadh at 1745 hrs. and reached Jithri at 1750 hrs. 3 kms. Carried out raid u/s 12 of Gambling Act. Arrested Bhupatsinh Bahadursinh and Malubha Vajubha. Left Jithri at 1810 hrs. & reached Sihor at 1850 hrs. Carried out Tonga checking. Left Sihor at 1930 hrs. and reached Songadh at 1945 hrs. Left Songadh at 2015 hrs. & reached Sihor at 2025 hrs. |
| 10-7-79 Tuesday | Sihor | 64/1 79 | Commenced inspection of Sihor P. Station. Left Sihor at 1500 hrs. and reached Bhavnagar at 1530 hrs. Met D.S.P. Left Bhavnagar at 1645 hrs. & reached Sihor at 1715 hrs. Received a telephonic message of Vallabhipur PS AD NO. 6/79 u/s 174 Cr.P.C. at 21:00 hrs. Left Sihor at 2145 hrs. & reached Chamardi at 2200 hrs. Worked as per Crime Memo No. 1 of 64/79. |

| | | | |
|---|---|---|---|
| 11-7-79 Wednesday | Chamardi | P/1 64/2 79 | Left Chamardi at 0115 hrs. and reached Vallabhipur at 0130 hrs. Left Vallabhipur at 0145 hrs. & reached Sihor at 0215 hrs. Held inspection parade and Kit inspection between 0700 hrs. and 1015 hrs. Left Sihor at 1100 hrs. and reached Chamardi at 1115 hrs. Worked as per Crime Memo No. 2 of 64/79. Left Chamardi at 1845 hrs. & reached Sihor at 1900 hrs. Left Sihor at 2145 hrs. & reached Chamardi at 2200 hrs. Left Chamardi at 2345 hrs. & reached Vallabhipur at 2400 hrs. |
| 12-7-79 Thursday | Vallabhipur | N/1 64/3 79 66/1 79 | Left Vallbhipur at 0100 hrs and reached Songadh at 0145 hrs. Supervised Jagran Bandobast. Left Songadh at 0200 hrs and reached Sihor at 0215 hrs. Supervised Jagran Bandobast. Held departmental proceeding of UPC Balvantsinh Ladhubha. Examined PI A K Patel. Next date fixed on 15-7-79. Also conducted D.P. of UPC Ghanshyamsinh Hathisinh. Recorded his preliminary statement. Next date fixed on 19-7-79. Left Sihor at 1230 hrs. & reached Vallabhipur at 1300 hrs. Worked as per Crime Memo No. 3 of 64/79. Concluded visitation. Left Vallabhipur at 1900 hrs. and reached Sihor at 1930 hrs. Held Sheet remarks of police station staff. Meanwhile received a special report of Songadh P.S. AD No. 10/79 u/s 174 Cr.P.C. Left Sihor at 2100 hrs and reached Ramdhari at 2130 hrs. 22 Kms. Left Ramdhari at 2300 hrs. and reached Songadh at 2315 hrs. Worked as per Crime Memo No. 1 of 66/79. |

| 13-7-79 Friday | Songadh | 66/2 79 | Continued visitation and worked as per Crime Memo No. 2 of 66/79. In this connection left Songadh at 1000 hrs. & reached Ramdhari at 1015 hrs. Left Ramdhari at 1145 hrs and reached Songadh at 1200 hrs. Concluded visitation at 1640 hrs. Left Songadh at 1640 hrs. and reached Sihor at 1700 hrs. Held Sheet Remarks of remaining HC & PC. Also held local leader meeting. Received telephonic message at 2335 hrs. that since SDPO Mahuva who was visiting C.R. No. 95/79 of Gadhada P.S had been called away to Talaja, hence efforts should be made to trace remaining accused. Left Sihor at 2345 hrs. for Gadhada. |
|---|---|---|---|
| 14-7-79 Saturday | Gadhada | | Reached Gadhada at 0100 hrs. Today made efforts to trace the remaining accused. In this connection left Gadhada at 1200 hrs. & reached Vavdi at 1230 hrs. Made enquiries about the absconding accused. Left Vavdi at 1300 hrs. & reached Gadhada at 1315 hrs. Three more accused were arrested today. Since the rest of the accused are Kathis and hence contacted one Bhanbhai who is their leader. He assured that that he will produce the others tomorrow afternoon. Instructed CPI Botad to pursue the matter. Left Gadhada at 1900 hrs. & reached Paliyad at 2000 hrs. 45 Kms. Paid a surprise visit to the police station. Left Paliyad at 2200 hrs. & reached Sihor at 2400 hrs. 98 Kms. -in order to continue with the inspection. |

Both the content and the hours of work put in, was typical of the work-schedule of a SDPO in those days. I used to write in the prescribed bound book in my own handwriting which later was typed by a clerk assigned to my office. Copies were sent the District

Superintendent of Police, the District Magistrate, the Range Deputy Inspector-General of Police and the Deputy Inspector-General of Police, Criminal Investigation Department. For the benefit of the last-mentioned functionary, a crime statement was attached giving details of all offences falling under the heads, and having been reported during the week, of coinage and currency notes, administering of poison or drug for gain, thefts involving loss of property worth Rs. 2,000 or more, robberies involving loss of property worth Rs. 500 or more, criminal breach of trust involving loss of property worth Rs. 2000 or more, and housebreakings with thefts involving loss of property worth Rs. 1,000 or more. This brings out the procedure followed to keep the superior hierarchy informed and their expected involvement in the control of crime.

A vital attachment of the weekly diary was the Crime Memo. This was written in the personal handwriting of the SDPO for all cases of serious crime that he had visited. The first page of this document had a prescribed format consisting of sixteen items providing details of the crime and included such matters as the date and time of receiving a special report, the date and time of departing for the scene of crime, and the reasons for delay if any. Under the standing orders, a sub-divisional officer was required to proceed as soon as possible, upon receiving the special report, and in any case within two hours. After conveying the details of the crime under the heading "Brief Facts" and describing the scene of offence, the crime memo was a true account, recorded for each day of the visitation of the work done by the SDPO. This would include places visited, witnesses examined, suspects questioned, arrests made, case papers initialled, and instructions given to the investigating officer. The narrative here should bring out vividly the keen interest taken by the supervising officer that would make it clear that the visit was not a mere formality or perfunctory. I have always maintained that out of all the documents and diaries that are mandated in the police department for the control and management of crime, the Crime Memo is the least valued for reasons which I have never understood. If I may attempt an explanation, it could be because the whole emphasis is on the Case Diary written up by the investigating officer and required to be maintained statutorily under section 172 of the CrPC, whereas the Crime Memo lacks that status. I have never come across a single case where this document was asked to be produced in a court of law to resolve any issue or dispute of facts during a trial.

A regular source of corruption for the police is the monthly instalment of bribe money that is collected from prohibition and gambling dens. SDPOs were directed to be particularly vigilant and encouraged to conduct personal raids in this regard. Cases of gambling that I made out on 9th July within the limits of Songadh police station were in that context. The details of these raids had to be sent with the weekly diary as a separate attachment under the head, "Gambling & Prohibition raids carried out by the SDPO Palitana for the W. E. 14-7-79". Since a successful raid allows for the presumption that the den was running with the connivance of the local police staff, the next logical step was to call for the explanation of the police officer in-charge of the police station. This certainly acted as a deterrent.

The junior clerk posted to my office was Chittranjan Vasantrai Vaishnav. In his late forties, he belonged to the old school- those who attended to their duties diligently and lived a simple life.

## The Weekly Diary

Affectionately addressed as Chittabhai, he was never absent, never late and was well-meaning in the advice that he proffered. He had joined the police department as a junior clerk and had remained as one even after two decades of service. I remember him mentioning once- "Sir, I am not too bright." I did not share his opinion of himself as I found him to be trustworthy and reliable. It was not an easy task for him to type out, week after week, crime memos and weekly diaries that I regularly wrote and gave to him. He was also responsible for receiving mail in my office and putting it up to me. Since I was out of my headquarters most of the month, he would dispatch the same with a special messenger to wherever I was camping. Chittabhai also assisted with departmental proceedings entrusted to me as an Inquiry Officer. I was new to the job and beginning to acquire a grip on criminal law but possessed little knowledge of service matters. On the other hand, he had helped my predecessors, many of whom in the rank of DySP, were far more experienced. On some occasions departmental proceedings were scheduled to be held at a different location for the convenience of witnesses and all concerned. Chittabhai would travel with me or if I was already out of headquarters on a visitation and was to proceed to that location directly, he would travel there in a State Transport Corporation bus with the relevant papers. Thus, on that Thursday, 12th July, Chittabhai had arrived at Sihor in the morning with the papers concerning UPC Balvantsinh Ladhubha and UPC Ghanshyamsinh Hathisinh. The acronym DP, as mentioned in the extract of the weekly diary reproduced above, is widely used to denote departmental proceeding.

*Jagran Bandobast* mentioned in the diary needs to be explained. Jaya Parvati *vrat*, is a Hindu festival, lasting five days, that is observed in *Ashada Maas* (month of July) by unmarried girls and married women in Gujarat and some other parts of western India. The story or legend of Jaya Parvati *vrat* (or fast) is associated with a Brahmin woman who observed this *vrat* to secure the life of her husband who had become unconscious after being bitten by a snake. The divine couple, Shiva and Parvati, are worshipped during this time. Worship of the latter is also known as Gauri *vrat*. Unmarried women observe this fast for securing good husbands whereas married women observe this fast for marital bliss and for their husband's long life. On the last day, the women who have fasted have to remain awake the whole night. This is called *jagran*. During this time, women and young girls throng the marketplace late into the night wearing embroidered clothes and jewellery. There is a festive atmosphere in the town, and carts bearing various articles and trinkets are allowed to remain on the main thoroughfare throughout the night. Consequently, proper arrangements are made by deploying more men to ensure law and order. A component of the district armed reserve is also kept in readiness to be deployed should the occasion demand. The special arrangements created to maintain public order for the occasion is, in the local parlance, referred to as *bandobast*. Although supervision of crime was a key result area for a SDPO, maintenance of public order was also a top priority. As a matter of fact, police manual regulations provided that higher supervisory officers, such as the SDPO and the SP, should invariably be present on the scene of the apprehended trouble and should not leave the matter to be dealt with by subordinates. That is the reason why despite being busy with a visitation of a serious offence at village

Chamardi under Vallabhipur police station, I made it a point to check the efficacy of the arrangements. Such visits by senior officers go a long way in ensuring proper compliance.

Surprise check was also encouraged to improve the efficiency and responsiveness of police stations. During the time when I functioned as a sub-divisional officer, this duty was insisted upon to keep the police staff on their toes. My own visit to Paliyad police station on that Saturday of 14$^{th}$ July, was primarily to catch red-handed the SHO who was notorious for being under the influence of alcohol. As it turned out, he was sober, and I spent two hours there pouring over various records with the objective of satisfying myself that they were maintained properly.

Such were the details that were recorded in the weekly diary. The importance and relevance of this document can be discerned from the fact that the district magistrate, who was one of the recipients of this diary, was under instructions, after due scrutiny, to report to the government points requiring immediate attention. In that case he was to mark copies of such reports to the Inspector General of Police. The intense and hectic schedule seen in the contents of the week reproduced above was by no means an exception. On the contrary all throughout my tenure, I had to function much in the same way for that was the only manner one could keep one's charge under proper control. Those days means of communication were limited and even primitive. Telephone lines did not have a dialling facility and one had to go through the telephone exchange operator to be connected elsewhere. Wireless communication in the form of High Frequency and Very High Frequency wireless sets were available but these were utilised for specific laid down purposes, mainly to do with maintenance of public order. Thus, personal visits through frequent travel, were found to be the most effective way of supervision.

The officers to whom copies of the weekly diary are sent, are expected to scrutinize the diary, and make such remarks and issue such instructions as they deemed necessary in relation to the scope of the control which they exercised over the work of the SDPO. Of the four superior functionaries to whom copies of these diaries were dispatched, only two, namely the District Superintendent of Police, Bhavnagar on a regular basis and the Deputy Inspector-General of Police, Rajkot Range occasionally, issued checks on the weekly diaries. The issues raised would mostly be about certain mandatory duties that a SDPO had to perform. So, if one had not attended a single parade during the week, a query would be raised about the same and if no night-round was performed, you were expected to explain the reason why. The district police chief, Zulfikar Ali Saiyed, was an experienced officer with a good grip on crime work. He, particularly, went through the crime memos that were attached to the weekly diary and would regularly convey his observations. He was inclined towards legal work and since mine was the only weekly diary, which was written in the English language, the other two SDPOs wrote in Gujarati, I would receive comments pertaining to, for instance, the dying declaration or the scene of crime or similar matters. I must admit at being a trifle sensitive when such observations were received by me assuming some-times that it was a fault-finding move. The truth was that these checks on the weekly diary were generally at the initiative of the staff officers, designated as Readers, of those superior functionaries, and they too were under obligation to issue them as that part of their functioning was a key result area for the post that they held.

# MISTAKE OF CASTE– A TRAGEDY

*H*indu society is usually described as divided into several castes, the boundaries of which are maintained by the rule of caste endogamy. There is enormous literature on these caste divisions from about the middle of the 19th century which includes census reports, gazetteers, castes-and-tribes volumes, ethnographic notes and monographs, and scholarly treatises by eminent scholars and anthropologists. A breakdown of the population of Gujarat into major religious, caste and tribal groups according to the census of 1931 indicated that the upper caste which included the brahmins, banias and the rajputs, formed a mere 13% of the population of which the rajputs contributed 4.85%. Forty-eight years later, in 1979, the situation was no different.

The word *Rajput* literally means son of a king in the Sanskrit language. It was extended to cover any Hindu clan that ruled in western India. The regions that now form Gujarat have at various times been ruled by a few dynasties, all which from the 10th century onwards, claimed to be Rajputs. The last major Rajput clan to settle in Gujarat were the Jadejas, who had arrived from Sindh. In addition to being divided into clans, the Rajputs are divided into two categories, the Rajput proper and the *garasia*, who are known as *darbar* in Saurashtra and as Rajput in Kachchh. In addition, there are also various allied groups such as the Gujjar, Nadoda, Jinkara, Purbiya, Maiya, Khant, and Vantia.

The Rajputs in theory are divided into thirty-six clans, but in practice the number varies from region to region. The term "Rajput" denotes a cluster of castes, clans, and lineages. It is a vaguely defined term, and there is no universal consensus on which clans make up the Rajput community. In medieval Rajasthan and its neighbouring areas, the word Rajput came to be restricted to certain specific clans, based on patrilineal descent and intermarriages. In Gujarat, the main clans are the Bhati, Chauhan, Chavda, Chudasama, Dahima, Darad, Devda, Gohil, Rathod, Sindhav, Raizada, Rehvar, Padhiyar, Sanol, Jadeja, Jethwa, Parmar, Solanki, Vaghela, Vala, Vadher, and Zankant. The Rajputs are endogamous, with the clans being exogamous. Thus, there is no intermarriage amongst the clans of Sarvaiyya, Chudasama, Rana, and Raizada since they claim descent from a common ancestor.

The dramatis personae of the of the suicide that I was required to visit belonged to the Garasiya and Karadiya Rajput communities.

Earlier that first week of October 1979, I had returned after availing a spell of earned leave. Seven months of intensive functioning as a sub-divisional police officer called for a break. I had spent most of my leave in Ahmedabad and some in Delhi. It was a welcome respite, and I was ready now for the next phase of my work as an SDPO. In striking similarity to when I first joined duties at Palitana sub-division in February that year, when I rejoined duties after availing of my leave, the very first special report that I received pertained to the suicide committed by a married woman.

The incident had occurred at Umrala which was also a police station headquartered town. I was met by PSI J M Thakar, who was the officer-in-charge of the police station. The facts indicated that the deceased was one Pravinaben, wife of Jaimalbhai Ramjibhai. Before her marriage she lived in Ahmedabad along with her parents who were *garasiya* Rajputs, and about eight months ago she had been married to Jaimal. On arriving at her marital home, she noticed that she was to be part of a joint family consisting of her father-in-law, mother-in-law, and sister-in-law. Although this was the norm in most such cases in those days, Pravina who came from an urban center like Ahmedabad would have wished it different. She, however, accepted it with good grace as she developed a comfortable and happy relationship with her husband. Therefore, sometime later when she discovered a more serious matter, she made the decision to accept the reality and make the most of her marriage. The serious matter was that while finalizing the arranged marriage, her husband's family had wrongly represented that they were *garasiya* Rajputs when in fact there were *karadiyas*.

The Rajputs claim to be Kshatriyas or descendants of Kshatriyas, but their actual status varies greatly, ranging from princely lineages to common cultivators. There are several major subdivisions of Rajputs, known as *vansh* who claim descent from various sources. Rajputs are generally considered to be divided into three primary *vansh*: Suryavanshi denotes descent from the solar deity *Surya*, Chandravanshi from the lunar deity *Chandra*, and Agnivanshi from the fire deity *Agni*.

On the other hand, *karadiyas*, although they consider themselves to be rajputs, the upper strata of the latter did not accord them such a status and so there were no intermarriages between them. The term *karadiya* dates to the Muslim invasion of India; those rajputs who agreed to pay taxes- known colloquially as *kar*- to the rulers, obtained the title of *karadiya*- *diya* meaning to give, colloquially. They are currently classified as Socially and Educationally Backward Classes (SEBC)[1].

Pravina was a well brought up city-educated girl. Umrala where she arrived after her marriage was 173 kilometers away from her parental home and located in a rural tradition-bound part of Saurashtra. Her husband worked in a small capacity. Before he got married to the deceased, he would, as per the practice and custom of most joint families, give the salary that he would earn to his father. However, after the marriage he refrained from doing so, although they continued to stay in the same home. This resulted in frequent quarrels with his father. The family also had a sense that Pravina displayed a condescending attitude towards them because of the caste factor. Such notions may have been exaggerated although in rural settings they do play a significant role. Her parents, while reconciled to the fact that the marriage had taken place, were never comfortable and hence had limited interaction with the family of their son-in-law.

Three days prior to the incident there was a furious quarrel between the father and the son. The cause of disagreement was the desire of Pravina to go to Ahmedabad with Jaimal. The latter's father did not want them to do so. That day both the deceased and her husband left the house and went to live with a neighbour. The following day the couple moved to the house of Jaimal's uncle, Jivubhai Ghughabhai. Both came to the house after all the adult members had departed for work, leaving behind two small children.. While there, they had a brief discussion amongst themselves, and Jaimal set out to arrange for money to enable them to go to Ahmedabad. Pravina was familiar with the house as she had come here on a few occasions earlier. It transpired that the fact of her marriage below her caste status, the internecine feud at her marital home and the prospect of returning to her parental home under such as unhappy circumstances along with her husband, had taken their toll on her mental equilibrium. Disgusted that she was, she walked into the kitchen, poured kerosene on her body, and set herself on fire. As the flames leapt up, the excruciating pain made her run out of the house, through the premises of a factory located opposite, and then collapse on a lane near the house. Jaimal heard the commotion in the market nearby and rushed towards her. He quickly put out the flames. Since his wife had suffered burn injuries, he arranged for her to be shifted to the civil hospital at Bhavnagar. While under treatment, Pravina passed away.

After apprising myself of all the facts, I visited the scene of the incident. This was a typical village home consisting of a courtyard, a single room, a verandah, and a kitchen. I checked and found that the *panchnama* had been drawn up properly by the investigating officer. Before Pravina passed away, her dying declaration was recorded by the executive magistrate. When I perused this document, I found that she had admitted that she had set herself on fire, but she also stated that she feared one Bhura Ghugha. This was the younger brother of her father-in-law.

## Dying Declaration

Dying Declaration are admissible in evidence in a court of law under section 32 of the Indian Evidence Act. Whenever a person whose evidence in a case is likely to be relevant as to the incidents or the circumstances which could eventually result in his or her death, it is advisable to record their dying declaration. Even if such a declaration is made to a police officer, it is admissible in evidence and its use is not barred by section 162 CrPC. This is a general provision which prohibits in the normal course any statement recorded by the police to be used for any purpose connected with any inquiry or trial in respect of any offence under investigation at the time when such statement was made. In the normal course dying declarations should ordinarily be recorded by the executive magistrates and if possible, in the presence of the accused, and the judicial magistrates should be approached only when the executive magistrates are not available. In case it is not practical to get the declaration recorded either by an executive magistrate or a judicial magistrate in time, an investigating officer can himself record it, preferably in the presence of the *panch* witnesses. Even if it has been made orally in the presence of any person, it may be proved in court by the oral evidence of that person.

The declaration becomes admissible if the declarant later dies. If he survives, it will be useful, if made before a magistrate, only to corroborate his oral evidence as a witness in Court. If it was made before a Police officer, it will be treated only as a statement covered by section 162 CrPC.

The declaration must be complete by itself. If the declarant dies before he has finished it or if it has any sign that he intended to change or add to it, it will not be of any evidentiary value. The person making the declaration must be a competent witness and must be speaking from personal knowledge of the facts. If reduced in to writing by the police, the declaration should, as far as possible, be in the form of questions and answers and in the very words of the declarant. If practicable, the declarant should be asked to sign it, and the *panch* witness and the police officer should attest it. Signs made before the death, explaining the cause of death, can be a statement under section 162 CrPC and is admissible as a dying declaration. This is based on section 119 of the Evidence Act which makes provision for examining dumb witnesses in a court of law. A witness who is unable to speak can give evidence in any other manner that he or she can make intelligible. This can be by signs or in writing. Evidence so given is treated as oral evidence. That apart, the FIR given by a complainant can be treated as dying declaration if he or she subsequently dies and is not available for examination.

Pravina was a married woman. Dying declaration of a married woman committing suicide should not be recorded in the presence of her mother-in-law, father-in-law, husband, or any other influential person in the family of the husband. As far as practicable, a well-respected, non-partisan social worker, if immediately available, should be invited as a *'panch'* when such a dying declaration is recorded. I therefore enquired with PSI

Thakar whether the legal requirements had been followed and he replied in the affirmative.

A total of thirteen witnesses were examined. Close relatives are a category in themselves and must be questioned carefully. Shantuben Govindbhai was the mother-in-law of the deceased who said that she was not at home but returned immediately on learning about the incident. She went with the deceased to the hospital at Bhavnagar and confirmed the cause of friction between the couple and her husband. Her daughter Jayaben was also questioned. She reported that at the time of the incident she was away and working at a local school. She corroborates her mother on the point of the reasons of tension prevailing in their house. Next Manglaben Jivubhai was examined. She was the young daughter of Jivubhai to whose house the deceased and her husband had shifted on the day of the incident. She testified that she was playing outside the house with her friends when suddenly, she saw the deceased run out of the house, her clothes inflamed. At that time there was nobody else at home and could not say why the deceased set herself on fire.

A relevant account came from witness Himmatbhai Jivabhai, who was the owner of a lathe factory located opposite the house of Jivubhai. He said that at the time of the incident he was at work along with Bhupatbhai Vithalbhai and Hussainbhai Mohammadbhai. Suddenly he saw the deceased running out of the house located opposite his factory, her clothes on fire, enter the premises through one door and then exit through the door on the other side. They were shocked and ran behind Pravinaben. The latter had collapsed in a lane. He confirmed that it was known in the village that the father-in-law of the deceased was asking the young couple to move out of the house as Jaimal was not contributing his earnings. The statement of this witness was corroborated in material terms by the other two witnesses present within the factory premises. These individuals are in the category of what may be called impartial and disconnected witnesses. Their testimony helps with obtaining a dispassionate account of the circumstances leading to the incident or a crime under investigation. In keeping with this practice, witness Bhilabhai Gurabhai, a neighbour, was also examined. According to this witness, at the time of the incident he was at home, he did not suspect any foul play and that his impression was that the deceased and her husband were on the best of terms.

Jivubhai, at whose house the incident took place, and his wife Shardaben were also examined. They had left early in the morning for work in a nearby agricultural land and did not know when the deceased and her husband would arrive at their house. Though close relatives, Jaimal is the nephew of Jivubhai, they both claimed they had no idea why the deceased committed suicide and reiterated that they only heard about the incident later.

In the dying declaration recorded, the deceased had mentioned the name of Bhura Ghugha as one who she feared. That document did not reveal the reasons for such apprehensions. Consequently, Bhura was questioned in detail. He is the younger brother of Pravina's father-in-law and stated that three days before the incident he was summoned to the house by his older brother as his nephew Jaimal was quarrelling with his father. According to this witness, he had left after pacifying them and does not know why the deceased in her deposition before the executive magistrate conveyed apprehensions about him. On this point the husband of the deceased, Jaimal, was questioned and he corroborated the statement of the former.

In the meantime, the parents of the deceased had arrived from Ahmedabad. Both said that they did not suspect any foul play. The deceased in her last letter to them had conveyed that she was happy. Both however confirmed that their son-in-law's family had been less than honest about their actual caste and had they known that they were *karadiya* rajputs, they would not have gone ahead with the matrimonial alliance.

This clearly appeared to be a case of suicide caused by the anguish of a Rajput woman who was brought up in a traditional household which cherished and spoke about the superiority of their clan and generated pride for their lineage. They grow up listening to the stories of Rajput valour. 'Courage flows in our blood' is what they are told. Often the women seemed to be comfortable being locked up inside the four walls of domesticity. 'It is a man's duty to go out, earn and protect his family. It is the duty of the woman to take care of his heir and home,' are the rules they had been brought up to believe in. Pravina had been married for less than a year and realised that it was impossible to change the situation. She must have suffered specific humiliation when on the day prior to her suicide she had to leave her in-law's house and stay, along with her husband, at a neighbour's home. Rural societies can be very judgmental and whatever may be the exalted status of one's caste, the circumstances in which the deceased was placed, is considered abhorrent.

I concluded visitation after initializing the case papers, case diaries, *panchnama* and instructing the investigating officer to include the post-mortem report before sending the case papers to the Sub-Divisional Magistrate for disposal.

CHAPTER 15

# CORRECTION, INSTRUCTION, STIMULATION

*I*nspection of the police station is easily one of the most important supervisory functions that a Sub-Divisional Police Officer performs. Done diligently and sincerely, it can go a long way in making the police force efficient and result oriented. An SDPO must inspect every police station in his subdivision once in a year along with its out-posts. Palitana sub-division consisted of eleven police stations namely, Palitana Town, Palitana Rural, Songadh, Sihor, Gariadhar, Gadhada, Vallabhipur, Umrala, Botad, Paliyad and Velavadar Bhal.

On 8th October, a Monday in 1979, I commenced inspection of Palitana Rural police station. Depending on the strength of the police station, minimum number of days were prescribed for this work[1]. Thus, I would be spending the next five days on this assignment. The object of inspection is not merely criticism or the correction of faults. It should be treated as an opportunity of ascertaining what is wrong and giving instruction as to better methods. In the first place, the inspecting officer is responsible for the administration of his charge, and he can obtain satisfactory results only by making the best possible use of the material at his disposal. Inspection is a means to this end and should not be looked upon as a routine or the satisfying of a statistical test for the purpose of his annual report. No officer can administer his charge properly until he knows his men and the conditions under which they live and work. Therefore, the sooner he inspects the better it is for both, the supervisor and the supervised. The maintenance of law and order, and the prevention and detection of crimes depend largely on the efficiency of the subordinate ranks, and consequently it is necessary to see that, as far as possible, every man is in the right place. An officer is dependent for his success upon his subordinates, and he cannot run all over the subdivision, attending to every individual case himself. During the British period, the district officers were under instructions to spend the touring season doing inspections. The philosophy behind this practice is best summarised in three words- correction, instruction, and stimulation.

There is a well laid down procedure to be followed. On arriving at the police station, I was met by PSI H S Bodat. I began by looking at the general statistics, dividing them into detected cases, undetected cases, pending cases, special crimes, and preventive actions. The figures are always useful not only for the testing of a subordinate's work, but as a basis on which general reorganization requirements can be figured out. Bodat was an experienced hand, having joined the force as a police constable and risen to the rank of a sub-inspector. He gave mostly satisfactory answers while explaining the increase in a certain category of crime.

Palitana taluka consisted of Palitana town, which was a municipality, with a separate police station, and Palitana Rural police station consisting of ninety-three villages within its jurisdiction. The villages were allotted to three out-posts and one central beat known as the *sadar* beat. The latter is that unit consisting of villages of which a head constable is in-charge and who is headquartered in the same town where the police station is located. This is distinct from the villages that are part of an OP. That afternoon I visited two villages Mota Jaliya and Adpar, both class 'A' villages of the *sadar* beat. The work done during such a visit and the logic behind classification of the villages has been discussed later in this chapter.

Later that night at 10 PM, I received a special report concerning the death of a married woman by burning at the village Ratanpar under Vallabhipur police station. Although inspection of the police station is a particularly important aspect of an SDPO's duties, special report crimes always took precedence. I therefore departed at 11 PM and was able to return on the following day by 9 PM, having examined 16 witnesses including the parents of the deceased woman, the conclusion being that her clothes had caught fire accidentally while cooking.

On the second day, inspection begins with a parade at 7 AM. Accordingly, I arrived at an open ground where men of Palitana Rural police station stood in platoon formation. Bodat, the SHO stood in front in command of the parade. He was dressed in a tunic, trousers, cross-belt, and a peak cap. This is called the ceremonial dress and is known colloquially, as the First Dress. In his right hand he held a ceremonial sword. After the general salute, the parade commander escorts the reviewing officer towards the platoon. This walk is done at a normal pace. However, on reaching on the right side of the assembled men, both the reviewing officer and the parade commander switch to a slow march which enables proper scrutiny of the turnout of the police station personnel. I used to pay special attention to the wearing of the fatigue cap, the shine of polish on the shoes, the proper shaving of the face, the cleanliness of the .303 rifle that each man held in his left arm and disapproved when I found anyone wearing a chain around their neck, or having their fingers adorned with a ring.

After scrutiny of men, the reviewing officer walks back to the podium and then watches as the parade commander leads his men in a march past in front of him. Noteworthy is the fact that a SDPO is required by police manual regulations to have mastery over ceremonial drill, company drill, musketry, dacoit operation, riot drill, methods of training, guards and escorts and all other important forms of drill. Police station personnel are required to be tested in their handling of weapons, their knowledge of the lathi drill, tear-smoke ammunition and bayonet fighting. In compliance with these directions, I proceeded to test PSI Bodat on his ability to take squad drill. I had some mastery over the subject as right from my days as a trainee officer at the Sardar Vallabhbhai Patel National Police Academy, Hyderabad, I was fond of and took keen interest in all forms of drill including ceremonial parade. Bodat did not have an impressive voice, but he knew his drill and was able to put his men through the motions without faltering. There are many who wonder about the relevance of such exercises in modern days of policing. What squad drill does is to make it clear, to all men forming part of the platoon, that the voice that emanates from their commander is the one that they must respect and always obey. This fosters discipline and so long as police forces choose to wear a uniform with weapons and other accoutrements, squad drill and parades will remain an important component of the work procedure.

While inspecting the officers and men in various items of drill including the ceremonial drill, the reviewing officer is expected to give due weight to precision of movement, timing and bearing of the squad collectively. He should see that regimentation is minimised and that everyone in the squad has attained individual proficiency. The tendency to perform these exercises as a form of collective drill was frowned upon and emphasis laid on development of individual capacity and prowess. I checked each man for their ability in musketry, reserving the test of bayonet fighting for those men who belonged to the armed branch of the police station. The latter needs explanation. In Gujarat and Maharashtra, both part of the former bilingual Bombay state, recruitment for the constabulary is done separately for the Unarmed Branch and the Armed Branch. The former are those who, after training, are posted to a police station to assist with crime control and investigation of crime. Essentially, this was the component that dealt with law and order. The latter on the other hand, were deployed for escort and guard duties and for maintenance of public order. There was a presumption that the unarmed Branch required educated constabulary as they had to assist the investigating officer, handle case papers, and participate in court procedure. Therefore, the level of education for recruitment was higher than that prescribed for the armed branch.

Drill, musketry, and kit inspection are tests of general discipline and supervision. I was expected to ascertain the knowledge of PSI Bodat, and the head constables of the drill laid down, including fire control, physical training, and the use of the lathi, before writing their service sheets. Particular attention should be paid to the condition of all firearms.

Kit Inspection consisted of a physical examination of the uniform articles, including clothing, and other accoutrements issued to the constabulary. After the ceremonial parade and the individual testing of their proficiency in squad drill and musketry was completed, a 15- minute break was given for the men to lay out their kit which was brought along to the parade ground in a large black steel trunk. The latter was also a government issue and were ubiquitous in those days. I inspected each such kit, accompanied by Chittabhai, the junior clerk from my office, who had also reported for the inspection parade. In addition to recording immediate requirements, the inspecting officer was expected to make a note of the general condition of the clothing and accoutrements, with a view to the preparation of an economical indent for the district. Those items that needed replacement were noted, and for the purpose of the official record, categorised as condemned. This would become part of the inspection note, copy of which is sent to the Superintendent of Police. It is in the latter's office where action would be taken to replace the kit items so condemned.

It was well past 11 AM when the parade and the outdoor part of the annual inspection was completed. After a break of one hour all men were asked to reassemble at the police station where Orderly Room was scheduled. This is a uniquely named function where the inspecting officer meets individually all men who have a representation to make and needed redressal of any grievance. The head of the state police force, then in the rank of Inspector General of Police (IGP), the Range Deputy Inspector General of Police (DIG) and the Superintendent of Police (SP) were also mandated by the police manual regulations to hold Orderly Room. For such a purpose, an Orderly Room register is maintained and the SDPO was expected to take the same along with him on tour to facilitate suitable entries when camping in far-flung areas of his jurisdiction. The Station House Officer would sometimes produce an erring policeman in the Orderly Room and depending on the gravity of the misconduct, a decision would be recorded as to the next course of action.

Service Sheet was an important document kept individually for each constable, head constable and *jamadar*. The last-named rank is now redesignated as Assistant Sub-Inspector. All details of the individual from the date of his joining the police force and till the date of retirement, whether pertaining to transfer, promotion, rewards, punishment or any other service matter, were faithfully recorded. When an SDPO decides the date of the commencement of the inspection of a police station, the service sheets of all men of that police station are sent with a special messenger by the office of the SP. The service records must be carefully checked and written up after the men have been personally examined in general work, law, and efficiency by a written test of an informal nature. I proceeded to meet each man individually, and scrutinized the performance based on work done in the last one year. Such details were kept ready for perusal by the SHO, and I would verify their authenticity by asking a few questions. I would then make a brief entry of the work done and grade that individual as either very good, good, average, or below average. In the case of head constables, inspecting officers had to pay attention to assessing their knowledge of the drill laid down, including fire control, physical training, and the use of the lathi, before writing their sheets. Chittabhai would be at hand assisting with this work. Each man had to be examined in conjunction with his patrol book, with a view to estimating his efficiency. The entries recorded during such sheet remarks session would be utilized later for evaluating their fitness for a promotion or for the release of the higher scale of their salary band. In retrospect, I realize that the method of such evaluation was rather arbitrary. In those days there was no redressal for any adverse entry recorded in the service sheets and it was very rarely that the SP changed what was entered by the SDPO.

The following day was spent on the detailed examination of the crime recorded at the police station and the way the same had been dealt with. Special attention was paid to the various mandatory registers and records kept for this purpose. Registers relating to crime such as First Information Book, Cognizable Crime Register, Non-Cognizable Crime Register, Case diaries, Station diaries, village crime records, other confidential records had to be thoroughly scrutinized. Those were the days when neither the internet, nor a computer or any other digital platform had been invented. Everything was manual and on the integrity of the maintenance of these records, rested the foundations of a sound criminal justice system.

Next, I checked case-papers and details of detected cases. An intelligent scrutiny of such cases can reveal who did good work, who is responsible for failures or wrong registration, and whether activity or slackness was displayed and what methods of investigation were employed by the SHO and his subordinates. Particular attention was paid to delay in visiting the scenes of offences and to ascertaining whether the SHO went himself or sent a head constable, and whether he was justified in so doing. A perusal of the case papers would show how far detection depended upon confessions, in how many cases property was recovered by searches, how house-breakings were committed, and how the different methods can be classified, and consequently who was responsible for them. The inspecting officer also must check whether sufficient attention is being paid to the preparation of the sketches of the scenes of offences and to the use of photography.

Epidemics of special forms of crime, such as dacoities and robberies on highways or elsewhere, and riots, required organized efforts directed either by the SP or the SDPO. An analysis of these were made and meticulously recorded in the inspection note. This police station had no such issues and I therefore moved on to house-breaking, a common and objectionable form of crime which specially requires collective treatment.

When examining cases sent for trial, particular attention was paid to the reasons for cases ending in acquittal or discharge; a perusal of the judgment was often found helpful. The office of the SDPO was required maintain an Acquittal Register where details of all cases that did not end up in a conviction were entered. I found it more convenient to peruse the acquittal judgements while at the police station during inspection, and then make the required entries in the register as against doing that in my office. However, I must admit that it was not always possible to do so and Dabhi, the Reader Sub-Inspector in my office often went through judgements and made the required entries in the register.

Preventive action is most important and, in this connection special attention and efforts had to be directed towards resident criminals, wandering gangs, professional criminals and receivers of stolen property. I had grasped early that whether due attention had been paid to preventive action or not, would be revealed by the thoroughness with which the SHO has written up his village crime records, the uses he has made of the provisions of Chapter VIII[2] of the Criminal Procedure Code, his knowledge of the movements of notorious criminals after their release from jail and the efforts he has made to arrest absconding offenders. I used to personally go through registers concerning criminal matters and leave my remarks, especially on the history sheets; registers maintained under the Habitual Offenders Act; in the Village Crime Note-Book; and the Absconders' Register. During the inspection of this particular police station, I found that the SHO and his men were not up to date so far as absconders and known criminals were concerned.

With a view to obviating the opportunities of acceptance of illegal gratifications in cases of offering bail, the SDPOs, while inspecting a police station under their charge, are expected to make it a point to examine a few cases of refusal of bail by the police and find out, if necessary, by personal enquiry with the persons concerned, whether the refusal of bail was or was not justified. This provision of the police manual brings out vividly the importance of a thorough inspection of a police station. I do not recall now if I checked on this. Probably, I did not.

Palitana Rural police station had three out-posts, namely Dam, Noghanvadhar and Bodana Nes. An out-post is a sub-unit of the police station and includes in its jurisdiction twenty to thirty villages. It is headed by a police officer of the rank of an assistant sub-inspector or a head constable. Two police constables are assigned for supporting the in-charge. They serve the purpose of displaying police presence in far-flung areas and make it convenient for the citizens to seek help especially in the earlier days when the means of transportation were limited, and the police station located quite far.

On the third day of my inspection, a Wednesday, I proceeded to Dam out-post. The premises consisted of precisely one small room which the in-charge head constable had spruced up suitably. Records that are to be scrutinised are limited but the most important amongst them is the Occurrence Book. Although a complainant usually proceeds directly to the police station for lodging a cognizable complaint, sometimes they may approach the OP. It is then in this book that their complaint is recorded, and a copy forwarded immediately to the police station for registering a FIR. It should be noted that the latter has statutory sanction under section 154 CrPC. On the other hand, the existence of the Occurrence Book is through an administrative order issued by the IGP and ratified by the government in the home department. Another point of scrutiny is whether the SHO has visited the OP from time to time and inspected the kit, dead stock, and after carefully examining the registers of the out-post, recorded his findings in the Inspection Book. All serious irregularities coming to light in the course of an SHO's inspection had to be reported at once to the SP or the Sub-Divisional Officer, so that the officer in question may take such notice of them as may appear to him to be necessary.

I also visited two class 'A' villages falling under the jurisdiction of this out-post, namely Thadach and Rajasthali. All villages under a police station including those under the out-posts, are divided into three classes- Class A: (important villages), Class B: (unimportant villages) and Class C: (deserted villages). The officer in-charge of the OP is required to visit and camp for the night at each 'A' class village at least once a month. He is also required to visit each 'B' class village once in three months, and a 'C' class village once in six months. During the inspection of this OP, I checked whether this requirement had been met. During my own visit to these villages, it is customary to meet the village head man or the *sarpanch,* the police patel and prominent citizens residing therein. I asked them about their general well-being and whether they had any specific issue to mention and from the responses received, I would make some sense of the performance of the local police. After this meeting, I proceeded to the *harijan vaas.* This was that segment of the village where the so-called "untouchables" resided. Rural India then was caste dominated and there was no social intermixing between the upper castes and the lower castes. Often the latter were subjected to discrimination and for that reason it was decided that when a senior officer visited a village, he will go to that area and ascertain their well-being. I must have spent about 30 minutes amongst them meeting a few available residents. They are usually quiet, not very expressive, and during this visit, my experience was no different.

Dam OP had been so named because it was located near a dam built on Shatrunjaya river. I decided to stay the night at the guesthouse located on the dam. The following day I had to proceed to Botad, a police station located 100 kilometres away where I had been asked to conduct an enquiry against a PSI who had been charged with late registration of a murder offence. The inspection had to be suspended for the duration. On completion of the work at Botad, I proceeded directly to Noghanvadhar outpost, reaching there after sunset. Since no work could be done at that time and, it would inconvenience the citizens should I ask to meet them, I decided to camp at the OP. The following day, just as with Dam OP, I held a local leader meeting and visited the *harijan vaas*. I then proceeded to village Kumbhan, an 'A' class village of this OP and similarly reached out to the local leaders and visited the *harijan vaas* of this village as well.

Back at the police station, I continued with the scrutiny of crime records, this time concentrating on accidental deaths registered during the year. I also inspected the *muddamal* room containing articles, jewellery or cash seized during the investigation of a crime and cross-checked them with the entries in the Muddamal Register. That same day I also proceeded to Bodana Nes, an OP located at a distance of 25 km, and inspected the same. Two 'A' class villages namely, Junapadar and Morchupana were also visited where I met with the local head men, other citizens, and the *harijans* in their residential localities. The existence of factions or ill feeling in respect of lands, temples, processions, festivals, women, religious or communal disputes or the occurrence of stone throwing are likely to give rise to riots or other crime, and it is in these meetings that one gets a true picture of the local situation. On completion of my work late that evening, I camped at the out-post.

The following morning, Saturday, was the last day of inspection. At the police station I held what is called a "note reading". Reader PSI Dabhi who had remained at the police station throughout the time when I was inspecting out-posts, had drafted a detailed inspection note which I proceeded to read out to PSI Bodat. This was a solemn occasion primarily because it signalled the end of the inspection, and I am certain that Bodat must have heaved a sigh of relief. A typed copy of the note would follow later, containing directions, admonishments, and advice. The SHO would be expected to report compliance within a month.

CHAPTER 16

# THE SCOURGE OF CASTE

The period between seventh and twelfth century witnessed gradual rise of several new royal-lineages in Rajasthan, Gujarat, Madhya Pradesh, and Uttar Pradesh which came to constitute a social-political category known as Rajputs. In Rajasthan, a single warrior group evolved called rajput (rajaputra-son of kings), they rarely engaged in farming, considering it beneath them as tilling of land was for their peasant subjects.[1] In Rajasthan, the Guhilot rajputs ruled the princely states of Banswara, Dungarpur, Mewar, Pratapgarh and Shahpura. In Gujarat, they are generally referred to as Gohil and have once ruled the princely states of Bhavnagar, Palitana, Lathi and Vala. Thus, Gohilwad as a major portion of present day Bhavnagar district was once ruled by Gohil rajputs.

The Gohils were also entrusted with the responsibilities of principalities as also of landholdings as *zamindars*. In the local social milieu, they are referred to as *darbar*, which roughly translates to mean somebody from the ruling class. Since they were related to the royal houses, they enjoyed tremendous influence in the rural areas. In 1979, thirty-two years after India became independent, I came across instances of supercilious and arrogant behaviour by few members of the rajput community in their dealings with the other communities. Although the trend was receding fast, it manifested itself in the form of social misbehaviour, and sometimes resulted in a crime. An example of the former, which I recall visiting in a village in Bhavnagar taluka, was a rajput thrashing a villager for not bowing to him in salutation as they passed each other in the main bazaar! Sometimes a rajput ran a flourishing business in gambling and liquor, and the local police would not do anything lest it might invite his wrath. However, most members of the community are known for good etiquette and polished manners. Overall, their presence had a subduing effect on the other communities in a social gathering, especially in rural settings, and this instilled, in some misguided souls, a sense of immunity.

Several members of the rajput community formed the bulk of the constabulary in Bhavnagar district. I was often reminded by old-timers in the district that if the Station House Officer of a particular police station was a non-rajput, it was difficult for him to function efficiently. Personally, I came across some fine officers and men of the Rajput community who were proud of the uniform they wore, and their lineage only added to their sense of self-worth. Arrogance and a demand for subjugation is a trait that human beings display when they are in a position of domination, and this has little to do with ethnic background and more to do with human nature. Consequently, there were several instances, many of them unreported, of rude behaviour demanding submission from members of other communities, especially when that person was neither a government servant, nor a person of some social standing.

Madhuvan is a village located within the limits of Datha police station. The district headquarter, Bhavnagar, was 70 km away while Talaja, the taluka headquarter was 18 km away. Located near the sea-coast, it was a small village consisting of about 120 houses. The main occupation of the residents then was farming with the majority landholdings vested in the rajputs. The latter in turn employed people from the *koli* community to work as labourers on their land. Koli Bhagwan Rambhai, lived in the village along with his wife and son. His younger brother Bhimabhai also stayed with him in the same house along with his wife and their son. This young man had been named Tulshi by his parents. He had acquired some degree of formal education and was a person of independent disposition. He was quite aware that the social disparity around him did not have the sanction of law in independent India. His parents did not have the means to educate him further and therefore for the last couple of years he began doing odd jobs to supplement the family income. Now aged 20 years, he was working in a candy factory at Pithalpur, a village located 6 km away.

Tulshi's father, Bhimabhai had entered into an agreement with one Mahipatsinh, a rajput, of a nearby village Janjmer to till the latter's land. According to the arrangements, the former would get 25% of the produce from that land annually. The rest would accrue to the landlord, who was also responsible for bearing the cost of the seeds needed to sow the land, procure fertilizers, and other incidental expenditures. This was a normal practice in rural Gujarat. When the land has been cultivated and the crop is standing, particular care is taken to ensure that herbivores animals do not enter the agricultural field and damage the produce. Many villagers and landlords also owned cattle, and herds of sheep and goats which were graminivores, commonly referred to as grazers. Most would take them for grazing to open land owned by the government, commonly called *gauchar* or sometimes with permission of the cultivators, into that piece of agriculture plot, where the crop had been taken down and moved out for sale as well as for home consumption.

The region had seen good monsoon that year, and the farmers were quite happy with the crop that had grown. Certain members of the *darbar* community, not wanting to bother going to the *gauchar* land, decided to enter the agriculture plot which was being tilled and taken care of by Bhimabhai so as to enable their cattle to graze. This was objected to by the latter, but nobody took notice of him and there was not much he could do, given the fear and the awe with which the *kolis* looked upon the *darbars*. However, he reported the incursion to one Navalsinh who had interest in the land. The latter accompanied by Bahadursinh, a relative, came to Madhuvan and chastised the intruders. Enraged at the audacity of Bhimabhai to tattletale against them, the local *darbars* arrived at the residence of the elder brother Bhagwanbhai and beat up the family, including Tulshi's cousin brother Mohan Bhagwanbhai, in the presence of the womenfolk.

Tulshi was not at home and when he learnt about the incident, he was indignant. Socially, economically, or physically it was beyond his capacity to take on the *darbars* of his village. His resentment simmered within as he knew that neither the village elders, nor the government functionaries, including the police, would take any serious notice of this fracas. After all nobody was seriously injured, and historically the backward classes were used to such domineering behaviour of the ruling class in Saurashtra. The young man, growing up in independent India, could not accept such brazen illegality nor could he bear the social stigma which follows when the family is assaulted, and the fact is known to the whole village.

*Navratri* is one of the most significant and auspicious festivals in Hindu culture which is celebrated with much joy, enthusiasm, and fervor. It is a nine day festival, during which the devotees offer their prayers and worship the nine different forms of Goddess Amba. Similar celebrations take place in West Bengal where Goddess Durga is worshipped. In Gujarat, the most visible manifestation is the group dance called *garba* accompanied by live orchestra, seasonal raga, or devotional songs. It is a folk dance where people of different background and skills join and form concentric circles. The circles can grow or shrink, reaching sizes of hundreds or thousands of people, dancing and clapping in circular moves in their traditional attire. The garba dance includes *dandiyas* (sticks), coordinated movements and the striking of sticks between the dancers. Post dancing, the group and the audience socialize, and feast together.

In the last week of September, about a month after the incident at Bhagwanbhai's house, during the *navratri* festival, Tulshi stayed back at Pithalpur to take part in the festivities. Two young man from the *darbar* community of Madhuvan were also in the village having arrived to participate in the *garba*. Virubha Hanubha was 21 years old and Sahadevsinh Ghanubha was 20 years old. Both had taken part in the assault on Tulshi's family and this fact was known to the latter. Resentment still prevailed within the persona of the Tulshi and he accosted both, asking why they had misbehaved with members of his family including his father and uncle. Not accustomed to being questioned like this by any member of the *koli* community, Virubha attempted to brush aside Tulshi disdainfully. The latter stood his ground in full public view and abused the former. For both the *darbar* young men this was unheard of, and they were deeply embarrassed and angry. They were not on home territory, the composition of the population at Pithalpur was in favour of the other backward classes, and therefore there was not much they could have done by way of retaliation. Tulshi, on the other hand, worked in the village and had several friends and acquaintances. Virubha decided to bide his time.

Two weeks later, on 11th October, and about ten days before Diwali that year, Tulshi requested permission of his employer Manishankar Revashnakar to return home early as he wanted to visit his ailing brother at Madhuvan. He decided to walk home and as he approached the outskirts of his village, he was spotted by Virubha who by that extraordinary hand that fate plays, happened to be in that area. Seized by an irrational urge to seek revenge for the purported humiliation that he had to undergo earlier at Pithalpur during the *navratri* festivities, Virubha who had a *lathi*, a long heavy bamboo stick with him, stealthily came up behind Tulshi. He delivered a powerful blow to the latter's head with such force and impact, that Tulshi simply collapsed on the ground without a whimper. The path to the village was alongside a partially empty canal, and Ranubha Jilubha, a *darbar*, was tending to his buffaloes, in there. He told Virubha to stop at once but the latter ignored this and asked him to go away.

Ranubha, aware of the nature of the assailant's temper, ran away from the spot. This crime was also witnessed by Bogha Pata, another villager who was working in the adjacent agricultural field, who simply kept quiet.

Virubha dragged the body of the now deceased Tulshi about fifty feet away to that part of the canal where there was water. He dumped the body there and placed a heavy large stone on the chest to prevent it from being swept away. He next proceeded to the farm of Sahadevsinh and informed him about his having taken revenge and killing Tulshi. Both returned to the canal with ropes and wooden sticks, using which they trussed up the body and carried it towards a large swathe of marshy land which nobody normally visited. There were no farmhouses or cultivated agricultural land nearby, and both the accused placed the body of the deceased behind a clump of shrubs so that it was not visible to anybody outside. Access to the area became difficult because of the ankle-deep water in that area throughout the year. By now darkness had descended and both returned to their respective homes.

It was a measure of the power of the *darbar* community that despite the murder taking place in broad daylight and seen by two people, nobody either spoke about it openly or reported it to the police. However, whispers in the village began to make the rounds. On the day following the murder, Jasubhai Revashankar the younger brother of the deceased's employer who also worked at the same factory at Pithalpur was informed by a stranger passing by, that Tulshi had been assaulted by some *darbars* of his village. He conveyed this to his elder brother Manishankar. When the deceased did not turn up for work the second consecutive day, the latter visited village Madhuvan and contacted the deceased's family. Mohan, the cousin of Tulshi was at home, who informed his father Bhagvanbhai, and they were surprised, having presumed that the deceased was probably staying over at the factory after work. This was another extraordinary dimension of life in rural India that while the rumour of the assault that had taken place just outside the village, had reached the employer of the deceased in another village, his own family were kept isolated, perhaps because of the fear of consequences of caste dynamics. Understandably the deceased's father, uncle, and cousin started searching for him. When the family and friends could not trace Tulshi, they finally, on 14$^{th}$ October, approached the local police station for help.

PSI D K Patel was the Station House Officer of Datha police station. He recorded a Station Diary entry before he proceeded to make inquiries about the missing person. By nightfall PSI Patel became aware of a rumour that a dead body had been noticed in the vicinity of the deceased's village, but nobody was able to show the exact location. It is to the credit of this young officer that he pursued the information relentlessly and scoured the surrounding areas throughout the night. By 9 AM of the following day, four days after the murder, Tulshi's body was discovered.

The body had decayed and there was a foul smell emanating from the area. In fact, it was this fortuitous but unfortunate event that led the police party to wade through the swamp and examine the bushes behind which the body was found. In any case under investigation in which a person has met with his death, the SHO or a police officer not lower than a sub-inspector empowered by section 174 (3) CrPC, is required to send the body to the nearest civil surgeon or other qualified medical man for post-mortem examination. It was not possible to transport the body to the hospital. If that was done, there was a distinct possibility that vital evidence would be lost sight of in such surroundings. Therefore, a government doctor was summoned to the spot who after examination opined "No definite opinion as to the cause of death can be given as the body is decomposed to a greater extent." It was noted that the body was found naked. Despite the lack of clear medical opinion, PSI Patel went ahead and registered an offence of murder, and of causing disappearance of evidence, under section 302 and 201 IPC. The deceased's uncle Bhagwanbhai, filed the complaint.

Earlier that week, on a Sunday, I had begun inspection of Botad police station. The previous night from 0:30 AM to 3 AM, I had performed night round in Botad town. During the day as I continued examination of crime records at the police station, I was looking forward to an uninterrupted next four days to complete this important work. However, that was not to be. On the third day, just as I was about to begin the inspection parade at 6.30 AM, I received a special report about the murder of Tulshi. Datha police station where the offence was registered was part of Mahuva sub-division. The incumbent SDPO was busy visiting another serious crime and therefore I received instructions from the SP's office to proceed to the scene of crime immediately. Soon after concluding the parade, I left at 0900 hours, and after travelling 183 km, reached village Madhuvan by 1415 hours.

My first port of call was the place where the offence was committed. This was on the outskirts of the village, as mentioned earlier, and I went ahead and verified the *panchnama* of the scene of offence. Signs of a heavy object being dragged, from the place where the deceased was hit to the canal where his body was first dumped, were even now visible and duly recorded in the document. It was also possible to make out the place from where the accused Virubha had lifted a heavy stone and placed it on the chest of the deceased. The investigating officer PSI Patel had recovered and duly attached three coins of five *paisa* denomination and one charm worn around the neck of the deceased. Blood-soaked sample of mud was also taken for forensic examination.

I visited the place from where the dead body was recovered. As mentioned earlier the area was covered with ankle-deep water and the body was found thrown behind a clump of shrubs. Two pairs of trousers, one torn shirt, one handkerchief and one belt were recovered at some distance from where the body was lying. Coins worth ₹ 4 and 15 paise were also recovered. The investigating officer had attached them under a *panchnama*.

Thereafter I proceeded to verify the statements of witnesses that Patel had so far recorded. This included the father and the cousin of the deceased. Statements of witnesses who were aware of the dispute arising out of land trespass were also taken on record.

The statement of witness Navalsinh Bhagwansinh of village Janjmer to whom the accused Virubha had made an extra-judicial confession, was verified. The latter had conveyed to the former that the deceased had been done away with as he had been abusive. Extra-judicial confession is a weak piece of evidence, and the police must ensure that it is corroborated by other prosecution evidence. To accept extra-judicial confession, it must be voluntary and must inspire confidence. If the court is satisfied that the extra-judicial confession is voluntary, it can be acted upon to base a conviction. Mahipatsinh Rupsinh, the owner of the land that Bhimabhai, the father of the deceased was cultivating, testified about the dispute, and confirmed that Navalsing along with one Bahadursinh Ratansinh had, prior to the murder, contacted the trespassers amongst their *darbar* community in Madhuvan and conveyed their displeasure. Their testimony was important to establish a motive.

Two critical eyewitnesses were Ranubha Jilubha and Bhoga Patha. Both confirmed their presence and of having witnessed the crime. The latter stated that since he was busy working, he did not pay much attention till he heard the Ranubha calling out the accused whereupon he peered over the hedge and found Virubha standing with *lathi* in his hand whereas the deceased was not visible as he was lying prostrate on the ground.

Questioning both the accused, Virubha and Sahadevsinh revealed a certain facet of our societal composition. Both were friends, belonged to the same community, brought up in the same village with almost identical community values, and both were present at the village Pithalpur during the *navaratri* celebrations earlier that year, and yet, it was Virubha who nursed the grievance that how dare the deceased, a *koli*, stand up to a *darbar*. Both the accused as well as the victim were of the same age group and exposed to an identical form of governance, right from their birth. They could easily have been friends or if not, could have maintained cordial relations as is the practice in most villages across the state of Gujarat. It was not as if the deceased's family had, after the incident of land trespass, picked up quarrel with the *darbars*. They had merely reported the incident, which in fact it was their duty to do, to the landowners who were themselves of the same community as the trespassers. Virubha admitted that he had killed Tulshi, and Sahdev confessed to have helped the former in removing the body from the scene of offence with the aim of concealing the crime. In most families, pride is inculcated in a child by the mother specifically about their lineage, the anecdotes of valour of their ancestors and the superiority of the caste if they belong to the upper crust. The male members support such an upbringing primarily with the good intention of ensuring that their progeny take pride in their roots. This is the case with most castes and communities in all societies. And yet the downturn is that some individuals do not recognise that societal norms cannot transgress the law of the land. Both the accused were not criminals in the sense of being robbers, dacoits, or fraudsters. And yet they had committed the heinous crime of killing another human being and had subjected themselves to be forever branded as one.

The *lathi* and rope used in the commission of crime had been recovered under a discovery *panchnama*, and I verified the same.

I spent the night at Datha and the following day headed for Mahuva, the sub-divisional headquarters, with both the accused to get their confession recorded under section 164 CrPC. The JMFC accepted them in judicial custody and fixed the date for recording their confession to two weeks later. We had taken along Ranubha and Bogha Patha, the two eyewitnesses to have their statements recorded by the JMFC which was duly done. This last action is particularly important because there was every possibility that these witnesses, either due to threat or inducement, could turn hostile while tendering evidence in a court of law. Such statements cannot be used as evidence by themselves, as they have been made behind the back of the accused. The only object in recording such statements is to obtain a hold over the witnesses.

My next destination was Pithalpur for verifying the statements of the employer of the deceased and his younger brother, who confirmed the facts given earlier in the narration. Individuals who saw the public spat that took place between the deceased and the accused Virubha during the *navaratri* celebrations were also located, and their statements recorded. Later that evening, I returned to Datha and camped for the night over there.

It was necessary to put in place a mechanism for preventive action. This included deploying a police party of armed policemen in the village to prevent any altercation between the *kolis* and the *darbars*. The latter were more likely to be the aggressor as two of their kin had been detained. I instructed the Station House Officer to initiate action under section 107 CRPC against ten *darbars* for ensuring good behaviour and keeping peace. Proceedings under this section are an effective means for preventing a breach of peace or a disturbance of public tranquility which is reasonably apprehended in connection with religious processions, festivals, fairs, elections, or any political movement. It is not always essential in every case that there need be two parties fighting against each other. It must, however, be clear that a breach of the peace is imminent, unless averted by proceedings under the section. For proceedings to commence, the police have to collect evidence, oral and documentary, of persons acquainted with the circumstances of the case regarding the specific occasion on which the breach of the peace is anticipated, the existence of a cause, quarrel or other circumstances which is likely to lead to the breach, and the period of its duration. Further, the declarations of the parties indicating their determination to carry out any action or to prevent certain things in connection with the subject-matter of the quarrel, the strength and the following of the party or parties, and attempts made for conciliation, with their results, have to be ascertained. Although it was not necessary to record elaborate statements of witnesses, short notes being sufficient, I instructed PSI Patel to choose the first option in the interest of fairness and thoroughness.

Care had to be taken to see that action under this preventive section is taken against the party who is about to play an aggressive part calculated to lead to a breach of the peace and not against a person who is acting within his rights, though a breach of peace may be apprehended as a result of the activities of a person or persons who may feel aggrieved by the lawful exercise of such rights. In some exceptional cases, it may be difficult to decide who is acting beyond his rights and it may be desirable on account of some peculiar circumstances to proceed against both the parties, but these would certainly be rare.

Following morning, I went through the post-mortem report which had just been received and noted that the medical officer had added nothing of value and merely repeated the preliminary opinion that he had rendered after conducting post-mortem *in situ*. Since the work in the capacity of a visiting officer had been completed and since the normal and regular supervision of this crime would be the duty of the incumbent SDPO of that subdivision, I concluded visitation and departed for Palitana.

CHAPTER 17

# THE OFFENCE OF RAPE

*R*ape, before medieval times, was never viewed as a crime against the victim. It was viewed as a crime against property, and the property in question were women who were supposed to belong to their husbands or fathers. The term rape originates from the Latin *rapere* (supine stem raptum), "to snatch, to grab, to carry off". In Roman law, the carrying off, of a woman by force, with or without intercourse, constituted "raptus". In medieval English law the same term could refer to either kidnapping or rape in the modern sense of "sexual violation". Rape is a type of sexual assault usually involving sexual intercourse or other forms of sexual penetration against a person without their consent. The act may be carried out by physical force, coercion, abuse of authority, or against a person who is incapable of giving valid consent, such as one who is unconscious, incapacitated, has an intellectual disability, or is below the legal age of consent. The term rape is sometimes used interchangeably with the term sexual assault.

As a crime, rape is defined in section 375 of the Indian Penal Code, 1860. Prior to the latest amendments, it provided for a maximum punishment of 10 years imprisonment. Intercourse with a female, with or without consent, if she was below the age of 12 years, was rape. It is worth noting that committing rape on a wife was also recognized provided she was below the age of 12 years and made punishable with two years of imprisonment. The age limits were revised upwards to 16 years for women in general and 15 years, if she was the wife in 1940. The Criminal Law (Amendment) Act of 1983 inserted clause (5) the purpose of which was to protect and safeguard the interests of a woman who consents to sexual intercourse without knowing the nature or consequences of the act because she is mentally ill or under the influence of a stupefying or unwholesome substance.

On December 16, 2012, a physiotherapy intern was brutally gang-raped in a moving bus in Delhi. Later she was thrown out of the bus and eventually after a few days succumbed to her injuries. This was the Nirbhaya gang rape case which shook the entire country because of the barbaric nature of the crime. In January 2018, in Kathua district of Jammu and Kashmir, an 8-year-old girl was raped and killed by a group of men. The main accused was a priest at a temple where the rape had taken place. This shocking case led to national protests and a demand for stricter laws. In the backdrop of Jammu and Kashmir where political changes were taking place, this case was heavily politicized on communal lines.

Both the above cases of violation led to major amendment of the law. The 2013 criminal amendment widened the definition of rape and increased, for the first time after 1860, the punishment of rape by a person in a position of trust or authority towards the woman, to rigorous imprisonment for a term which shall not be less than twenty years, but which may extend to imprisonment for life, which shall mean imprisonment for the remainder of that person's natural life, or with death. New crimes like the offenses of stalking, voyeurism, and acid attacks were added. It also provided for death penalty in cases where the victim was killed or left in a vegetative state and increased the age of consent from 16 years to 18 years. The Kathua case led to the 2018 Criminal Amendment Act, which mainly changed the Protection of Children from Sexual Offences Act, 2012 as the rape was against a child, and made death penalty possible for the offense of the rape of a minor under 12 years.

Forty-four years ago, in October 1979, a 15-year-old girl was raped and murdered in a brutal manner. There was however no outcry of the kind noticed for the Nirbhaya or the Kathua case. Nonetheless, the narrative below will bring out the painstaking and sincere efforts made to trace the criminal. That the efforts failed in achieving its objective is a testimony of the frustrations that a police officer suffers.

It was a busy week as usual. I had commenced inspection of Botad police station on Sunday, checked men doing night rounds, visited two class A villages, proceeded to supervise a murder case in the neighbouring Mahuva sub-division- as my counterpart was on leave-, attended a meeting at Bhavnagar in the office of District Magistrate and Collector regarding elections, and carried out a prohibition raid that resulted in the seizure of opium. That Friday, I received a special report regarding the rape and murder of a young girl at village Parvala under Umrala police station.

On arrival at the scene of the offence, I was met by Police Sub-inspector J M Thakar. The victim Manju (name changed) lived with her parents, two sisters, a brother and the latter's wife. They belonged to the darbar sub-caste of the Patel community whose main occupation traditionally was agriculture. The night before the discovery of the body, at about 8 PM, Manju had asked her sister-in-law, Vasant, whether she would like to go to answer the call of nature. The latter is a euphemism for a toilet as in those days in the villages as a rule, citizens had to go out in the open to defecate. Since drainage system had not yet been introduced in rural India, there was no question of toilets being constructed in a house. It was especially difficult for women who had to either perform these bodily functions before dawn early in the morning or later in the evening after nightfall. Little girls are accompanied by their mothers or an elderly female relative and it was customary for women to go out in pairs or threes' or more, in the interest of safety and security. Vasant having declined, Manju checked with other female members, but all seemed to be preoccupied. She therefore ventured out alone, carrying a torch with her. When Manju did not return after half an hour, her mother Kashiben got worried. She asked her other daughter, Labhu, who did not know anything. Therefore, the father, Purshottambhai Vashram was informed and he along with his son Premji, went looking for his missing daughter. No headway could be made that night and the pair returned confused and perplexed as such an event was not normal.

After acquainting myself with the facts of the case, I decided to take over personal investigation. As mentioned earlier in this book, directly recruited Assistant Superintendents of Police were expected to investigate six cases in a year. The first port of call was the scene of offence where the dead body was discovered. This was a piece of agricultural land belonging to one Purshottam Chaggan Waghari. It transpired that two young girls aged 9 and 14 years had gone over there to cut the grass. It was the younger of the two, who came across the dead body of Manju, and started screaming. She had a good reason to do so. The body was found lying on its back with the legs drawn up and thighs wide apart. Her petticoat was thrown over her waist, thus exposing her private parts. Incised wounds were noticed on the stomach, neck, and hands. A whitish fluid was discovered on her vulva and the inner portion of the thigh.

Earlier in the day the body had been sent for post-mortem. However, my inspection revealed that there was a standing cotton crop in that agricultural field, and it was between two rows of this crop that the body was located. PSI Thaker informed me that the cotton crop was found intact and that there was no sign of struggle. I scrutinized the *panchmama* of the scene of offence and noted that blood-soaked mud and control sample had been attached.

Two kolis, Talsi Mohan and Thoban Gopal lived on the same plot of agricultural land and worked there as labourers. It was a customary practice for hired labour to stay on the land which had to be tilled, usually in small one-room huts. The former resided therein with his family and during questioning stated that no sound or commotion was heard by him during the night. The latter, who occupied an adjoining hut, said the same thing. Next, I proceeded to question one Naranbhai Dhanji who stayed at some distance from the scene of offence. He revealed that during the previous night at about 10 PM, Premji, the brother of the deceased, had come over to enquire after his sister. This witness had no knowledge and therefore replied accordingly. He claimed to have learnt about the death of the deceased only the following day. Similar responses were received, upon questioning, from two other witnesses including a police patel who lived in the vicinity.

After examining the scene of offence and questioning witnesses located nearby, I returned to the village and to the house of the deceased. Speaking in detail with the family was important although I was quite aware of the shock that they were in. The father, the mother, the brother, the sisters, and the sister-in-law of the deceased were all present. Labhu, the sister of the deceased, remembered that the latter had come home at about 8 PM and requested the ladies of the house to accompany her. Since nobody was inclined, Manju proceeded to collect some water in a container and went out in the dark. Collectively, they could contribute nothing further to the facts that I had already learnt and individually they could not come up with any theory or suspicion regarding the perpetrator. Although a delicate subject, romantic interest of the victim, if any, had to be probed and the surest information would come from the female members of the family. Gently, I made inquiries about the general temperament of the deceased, about her friends, her education, and her interests. Beyond the natural curiosity and the tentative attraction for the other sex commonly seen in teenagers, there was nothing out of the ordinary as far as the deceased was concerned.

Extended family in investigation of cases such as this can also provide valuable inputs, especially so in rural settings in India where everyone is into everyone's lives. Premji Kalyan was the uncle of the father of the deceased and his house was located opposite the house of the latter. Nobody approached him during the previous evening, and it was only the following morning that he learnt that Manju, his niece, was missing. Although an elderly gentleman, he proceeded to search for her and by the time he arrived near the agricultural field of Purshottam Chaggan, the dead body of the deceased had already been discovered. He could not provide any information which could lead to the detection of the crime. Next to be questioned was Narain Manji, a cousin. He stated that the previous evening he had gone in search of the deceased and returned late at night without any success, after which he had gone to sleep. The following day he had learned that his cousin had been killed. This witness was in the same age group as the deceased and appeared to be worldly-wise. I therefore attempted to make inquiries about any romantic connections of Manju. The outcome was the same as with the intimate family- the deceased was neither known for any such connections nor was she ever found moving about in the village just to pass time. This was a simple well-behaved daughter commonly seen in villages, in those days.

Keshav Vashram was the paternal uncle of the deceased. He stated that during the night when the crime was committed, he was at his *wadi*. The latter term approximates to a farmhouse. He mentioned that Premji, the brother, accompanied by one Nanji Harji came to him around 1 AM to convey that Manju was missing and he had immediately proceeded to the residence of the deceased. Thereafter he searched the area around the village where women normally converged to answer the call of nature, but he did not find anybody there. In the morning at about 5:30

AM he sent men in all directions, but to no avail. Later in the day, he learned that the body of the deceased had been located. This witness could provide no clues regarding the identity of the accused.

I decided to camp for the night in the vicinity and selected for this purpose a nearby village Ranghola. A practical reason for doing this was that there was a makeshift night camping facility there and since it was located nearby, I would be better able to control the investigation efforts that were underway. Circle Police Inspector J M Patel had joined during the day and he along with PSI Thaker were dispatched to meet residents of nearby villages for any information that they could provide. In fact, two teams were formed under the leadership of these two officers. The culprit had left virtually no clues at all. I also separately summoned the Sarpanch, the village headman, his deputy, and the police patel at my place of camp for a discussion which would lead to some definitive line of investigation.

The following day I visited the scene of crime again, and along with some fifteen persons, including policemen and villagers, searched the area in a radius of 3 km, walking through cultivated and uncultivated agriculture land. However, nothing of importance was discovered. From the body of the deceased, under an inquest *panchnama*, one pair of silver anklets, one pink coloured saree, one yellow blouse, one petticoat, four plastic bangles, and one *tulsi* beaded necklace had been seized. During my further questioning of witnesses and residents in the village, I made inquiries regarding any old enmity which would have motivated the crime. In this connection three theories emerged:

A. The elder sister of the deceased was married to one Himmat Keshav of village Gadhula and later divorced. Since this sister's marriage was again fixed at another place, the former husband and his family could have committed the crime to seek revenge.

B. The brother of the deceased, Premji Vashram, had a fight with one Lakha Rambhai of village Ranghola. The latter was an Ahir by caste and was known for his strong ways and bad behaviour. Could it be that he committed the crime out of pique?

C. It was rumoured that Premji had molested or had attempted to molest the sister of one Babubhai Nanji, another local bad character, about a year ago. Hence, the latter could have committed the crime as revenge.

After discussions with the Circle Inspector and the investigating officer, theory C looked most probable. Consequently, Babubhai Nanji was interrogated. He stoutly denied any involvement, nor could we produce any collaborative piece of evidence that could even obliquely point to his alleged culpability.

There were certain earmarked locations in the village in the open, where women converged either before sunrise or after sunset, to discharge their toiletry functions. This, as noted earlier, was the practice across the state in rural areas. Two houses were located near this area, residents of both belonging to the Bharwad community, a pastoral caste. They are primarily into herding goats and sheep, and although considered a nomadic community, they are also among the most urbanized having occupied a niche position in the supply of milk, which forms their main source of income. This has enabled them to improve their traditional social position. One house was occupied by an elderly couple who confirmed that village women did come to the area behind their house for relieving themselves but during the night that the deceased went missing, they heard nothing. The other house occupants were a young couple and on detailed questioning they too could provide no information that could help with the detection excepting confirming that the woman of the locality used the area behind the house, arriving in groups of three or more, for discharging their toiletry requirements.

Located near the house of the deceased was a diamond polishing and cutting factory which employed about twenty-five young men. Over ninety percent of the world's diamonds are cut and polished in India, and at the heart of this industry lies the city of Surat, a metropolis in the south of Gujarat. Major workforce comes from Saurashtra and the Patidars, who from times immemorial were agriculturists, had taken to this trade in a big way. Those employed in such factories have more liquidity on hand than those who work in an agricultural field, and consequently were smartly turned out as compared to other village lads, and ambitious. Five of these boys were selected for questioning to establish firstly, whether anyone of them had befriended the deceased and secondly, whether they had any information that would lead, even remotely, to the detection of the crime. All of them claimed no knowledge about any activities regarding the victim. This was not a surprise because by now I had realized that the mother of Manju was a strict lady who kept a sharp vigil over her daughters. This was also borne out by the fact that when the deceased did not return home after an appropriate time, it was Kashiben, the mother, who noticed it immediately and sent out her son, Premji, to look for Manju.

Up till now no clue had been obtained which could lead to the detection of the offence. I assembled the local community leaders and exhorted them to assist the police. Plainclothes men were deputed to make discreet enquiries. We continued to question other residents of the village but located nobody who saw the deceased walk out of the house or return to it. Later that night, I returned to the village Ranghola to camp there for the night.

Next morning, I began by questioning nine more workers from the diamond factory mentioned earlier. They, like their colleagues the previous day, denied any knowledge about the crime or even about the personal life of the deceased. All of them stated that they learnt about the murder only in the later part of the day after the body was discovered.

The post-mortem (PM) on the dead body had been conducted by the medical officer at Vallabhipur, a taluka headquarter town located 25 km away. The PM note had not been received and I proceeded to Vallabhipur to expedite the same and discuss certain aspects of the crime. On arrival I was informed that the note would be ready in an hour's time, which in fact is what happened. The cause of death was given as "shock due to anti-mortem serious injury." Other notable features of the PM note revealed that hymen of the deceased was intact. White discharge was present over the vulva and faecal matter was seen in the anus. The left shoulder bone was broken. Significantly no external injury was found on the external or internal genital organs. The doctors confirmed that the accused while attempting rape, failed in penetration. From the sociological point of view, the medical officer opined, that the deceased was a virgin.

The PM note did not clarify what was the white discharge noticed on the external genital organs of the deceased. The doctor orally conveyed that it was semen, which opinion he had based on the smell of the fluid. A glaring error was that neither he in his capacity as medical officer nor the investigating officer had bothered to take a sample of this white discharge to conclusively establish that it was indeed semen. Careful examination of a rape victim is critical. Resistance offered by victims in violent crimes always brings out certain clues like hair of the accused clutched by victims or pubic hairs found matted with semen on the genitals of the assailants and victims. Hair clotted and matted with blood on cutting or biting, are frequently found at the scene of crime. It is the duty of the medical officer, in case of rape, bestiality or sodomy, to remove foreign hair found on the genitals of the victims for examination and comparison if the accused is known or arrested later. Often marks made by the teeth may be found on the skin of the victim in rape and sex murder cases. In those days DNA had not been discovered or at least it was not known to investigating officers within the police force. Today the semen sample can link the perpetrator conclusively by comparing this polymer which is the main constituent of chromosomes.

On return to the village, I decided to meet the two young girls who had chanced upon the body of the deceased the day after the murder. Madhu, at 14 years, was just a year younger than the victim. I went across to her home and spoke with her in the presence of her parents. She, along with her younger cousin, Kanchan, aged 9 years, had gone to fetch grass from the land owned by Purshottam Waghari. It is here where the younger girl first came across the body, and they were both so shocked that they ran away screaming and frightened. At that time on the terrace of a nearby home three persons were standing, and she identified two of them, namely Naran Dhanji and Bhikha Meghji. Enquiries revealed that the younger girl was so traumatised that she was in no position to be questioned. It was decided not to insist meeting her for the moment.

In the meantime, the teams set up under the leadership of Inspector Patel and PSI Thaker returned and reported no progress. Plainclothes men deployed in the village and the surrounding areas had fared no better. Discussion amongst us lead to the conclusion that the place where the dead body was discovered was not the scene of crime. The reasons for such a conclusion were the following:

A. There was no sign of struggle at the place where the body was found. In fact, the body was placed neatly between two rows of standing cotton crops.

B. Assuming that Manju was kidnapped from the place where she went to answer the call of nature, it would not have been possible for her to have carried both her slippers, torch as well as the mug for carrying water. In the process of forcing her away, one or more of these articles would have fallen on the way. However, all these were found intact around her body as she lay mutilated and violated in that agricultural field.

C. Her house from where she left was surrounded by other houses and the time was such that no person would have attempted to molest or kidnap her without fearing exposure. By and large, a sensible person would not make such an attempt.

In rural settings, when even some cattle are lost, the entire village is made aware of. In this case only close relatives were informed, the rest of the residents of the village learnt about the incident after the body was discovered. In certain communities, illicit relations including incestuous once are not unknown. Many a times if a girl becomes pregnant out of wedlock, she is liquidated to save the family honour. We had completed three days of intense investigation and Parvala village had never seen such vigorous police activity. It was decided to withdraw camp for one night and return the following day and continue the investigation. Such action sometimes encourages the reticent amongst the villagers to come out and speak. That night I returned to Palitana, while Patel and Thaker returned to Botad and Umrala, respectively.

When we converged at the village the following afternoon, informants reported that the talk in the village was that something had happened to Manju at her home. As happens in cases like this, one source considered the deceased to be a girl of loose morals whereas others claimed that she possessed a flawless reputation. None of this was of any help, and we decided to continue with the examination of other relevant witnesses.

Kanchan, the younger of the pair which had discovered the body was now mentally and physically prepared to be questioned. As gently as we could, we spoke with her at her home. She corroborated in specific details the statement given by Madhu, her elder cousin. The examination of witnesses was now extended to questioning visitors to the home of the deceased in the last one month. Primarily these were friends and acquaintances of the father and the brother of the deceased. The list also included distant relatives who came from other villages and towns.

Both Madhu and Kanchan had spoken about sighting three persons on the terrace of the house located near the place where the dead body was found. They had identified two and we were able to locate the third person, Jayram Mavji. On questioning, he revealed that on the night the deceased went missing, her brother Premji had come to his house and told him that his sister could not be found. The efforts made in the night yielded no result and the following morning he along with Naran Dhanji and Bhikha Meghji had climbed to the terrace of the house and were looking around towards the extended agricultural land in the hope that they could locate Manju. It was at that time when they heard both the young girls who had discovered the body screaming and running away from an adjoining plot. Bhikha was also questioned, and he corroborated the substance of the statement given by the earlier witness.

Thereafter PSI Thaker was dispatched to the village Ranghola to locate Lakhu Ahir. He was the same person with whom Premji Vashram had a fight and was known for his strong ways and bad behaviour. Thaker returned to report that Lakha was away at Amreli for the last two weeks, and it was unlikely that he was involved.

Manju had three close friends in the village, namely, Lakshmi, Anju, and her namesake, Manju. They were also examined but nothing useful was forthcoming. Earlier a lady police head constable had been asked to join the investigation from Botad. She had been camping in the village mixing with the womenfolk. She too had drawn a blank.

In the meantime, PSI Thaker proceeded to locate and question certain *wagharies* residing at Dhola junction. On his return he reported that he had questioned four individuals who perhaps could have provided some information but in fact knew nothing about the crime we were investigating.

After another night halt at Ranghola, extensive questioning was taken up of even peripheral witnesses in the hope that some clue could be forthcoming. By now almost all the elders in the village had been examined. I also proceeded to village Gadhula where Himmat Karsan, the former husband of the elder sister of the deceased now lived with his second wife. He denied any involvement, stating that it was he who divorced his first wife on the ground that she was not allowing him conjugal rights and therefore he had no interest in the former wife's family. The question of revenge killing, or rape did not arise. The divorce had taken effect more than a year ago and having married again, why would he like to indulge in such an act!

I had now put in six days of sustained efforts to trace the offence. Ideally, one should have detected the case and that would have given me tremendous satisfaction as it was the first case of rape and murder that I was investigating. Practically all theories were exhausted, all the leads checked, and every possible witness examined. As a sub-divisional officer my primary duty was supervision and ensuring compliances with police procedure across the eleven police stations of my subdivision. I could not have continued with the investigation with the same kind of focus and time and therefore handed over investigation to J M

Patel, who as the CPI was mandated by the standing instructions of the Inspector General of Police to make all possible efforts to trace such undetected crime and who, more importantly, would have both the time and experience to do so.

CHAPTER 18

# PROHIBITION IN THE BI-LINGUAL BOMBAY STATE

*T*he surest way of destroying a reputation was to let it be known that a person was in the habit of consuming alcohol. In those days in Gujarat this was taken very seriously and if that person happened to be a civil servant, specifically a police officer, it would damage his career substantially. Such was the importance attached that the registration of an offence under the Bombay Prohibition Act, 1949 against a police officer was treated as a special report crime and therefore made visitable by a SDPO. The statute was concerning the promotion and enforcement of alcohol prohibition in the erstwhile Bombay State, of which both Gujarat and Maharashtra were part of. Under the Act a permit is mandatory to purchase, possess, consume, or serve liquor. It empowers the police to arrest a person for purchasing, consuming, or serving alcohol without a permit with punishment ranging from three months to five years in prison.

In ancient times some classes of society used to drink intoxicants called *somras*. Yet India has nurtured the hope of eradicating the evil of alcoholic drinks. In the year 1878, during the British Raj, the Bombay Excise Act was implemented resulting in financial benefit for the government through imposition of duty on various alcoholic products. This resulted in the creation of the Excise department.

Mahatma Gandhi came to India from South Africa in 1915, and he noticed that the condition of the people was miserable, and a large section of the population was living in poverty. One of the reasons for this poverty of the people was the evil of alcoholic drinks and drugs. Mahatma Gandhi formulated a four-pronged program at that time to gain freedom from foreign rule. One of these was the anti-drug policy. Prohibition is one of the most important principles of Gandhian philosophy. The Mahatma had unequivocal views on alcohol consumption. In 1927, he had said:

"I would rather have India reduced to a state of pauperism than have thousands of drunkards in our midst. I would rather have India without education if that is the price to be paid for making it dry."

Provincial government system was introduced in India as a result of the Government of India Act, 1935 and when the Congress came to power in 1937, the Bombay state at that time decided to implement the liquor ban policy in phases, inspired by the ideas of Mahatma Gandhi. The government lasted till October 1939, when it resigned protesting India's involvement in the Second World War. During that time, the policy of drug prohibition was abandoned, and prohibition suffered a setback. However, after independence in 1947, the Bombay Prohibition Act came into effect on June 16, 1949. From that date, the Excise Act of 1878 enacted by the British Government was repealed. On 26th January 1950, the Constitution of India came into force, and it adopted the Prohibition Act of 1949 without any changes. The prohibition of alcohol was introduced in the constitution as a directive principle of state policy. Article 47 directs- "The state shall regard the raising of the level of nutrition and the standard of living of its people and the improvement of public health as among the primary duties and, in particular, the state shall endeavour to bring about prohibition of the consumption, except for medicinal purposes, of intoxicating drinks and of drugs which are injurious to health."

Since the introduction of complete prohibition in the State from 1st April 1950, the former department of Excise came to be designated as the Prohibition and Excise department. The police department was made the chief agency to deal with detection, investigation, and prosecution of offences under the Prohibition Act. Though officers of the Prohibition and Excise department of and above the rank of inspector had been invested with powers to investigate offences, these officers generally passed on information of the commission of offences and handed over the cases detected by them to the police for investigation. The home guards also assisted the police in this work. Under section 133, officers and servants of local authorities are bound to assist any police officer or person authorized to carry out the provisions of the Act. Under section 134 of the Prohibition Act, village officers, officers of other departments of the State Government, and officers and servants of the local authorities were bound not only to give information to the police of the breaches of the provisions of the Act which may come to their knowledge, but also to prevent the commission of such offences. Under section 135, occupiers of lands and buildings, landlords of estates, owners of vehicles, are bound to give notice of any illicit tapping of trees or manufacture of any liquor or intoxicating drug to a magistrate or to a prohibition officer or to a police officer, as soon as it comes to their knowledge.

All revenue officers of and above the rank of Mamlatdar (Tehsildar) or Mahalkar, all magistrates, and all officers of the department of Prohibition and Excise of and above the rank of sub-inspector had been authorized, under section 123 of the Prohibition Act, within the limits of their respective jurisdictions, to arrest without a warrant any person whom they had reason to believe to be guilty of an offence under the Act, and to seize and detain any article or contraband. The officer so authorized, when he arrests any person or seizes and detains any articles, was expected to forward such a person or the article, without unnecessary delay, to the officer-in-charge of the nearest police station.

As Chief Minister of the erstwhile Bombay state from 1952 to 1956, Morarji Desai with a single-minded devotion insisted on enforcement of the dry law with ruthless persistence, resulting in the entire state going dry. Although the Prohibition and Excise department was in existence to regulate alcohol products and molasses by issuing licenses, permits, or passes of various prohibited substances, the responsibility of enforcing the dry law came upon the police force. With a view to eradicating the evil of corruption and bribery and for a more effective implementation of prohibition policy, the Anti-Corruption and Prohibition

Intelligence Bureau was set-up to be headed by a Director, who was an officer of the rank of Deputy Inspector General of Police. The latter was declared head of department and would function under the administrative control and supervision of the Home Department. In every district, at least one sub-inspector of police of this bureau was stationed. Corresponding to the six ranges in the mofussil, there were six units with headquarters at Rajkot, Ahmedabad, Bombay, Poona, Aurangabad, and Nagpur, each in charge of a DySP. The Greater Bombay unit was placed under a Superintendent of Police.

Such was the importance placed on this new legislation, that it was included in the law paper which a directly recruited officer of the IPS had to pass as a part of departmental examination. In pursuance of sub rule (1) of Rule 6 of the IPS (Pay) Rules, 1954, the Government of Bombay had prescribed a period of two years from the date of his joining the State of Bombay within which directly recruited Assistant Superintendents of Police were required to take the examination, failing which they were not allowed to draw increments on the due dates. Similar conditions were stipulated for directly recruited sub-inspectors of police while undergoing basic courses at the Police Training School, Nashik. A thorough study of the Bombay Prohibition Act, 1949 was included in the second paper on law. It was also part of the syllabus for head constables qualifying for promotion as sub-inspector.

It was clear that more than the members of the public, civil servants were expected to abide by the dry law scrupulously. Therefore, through a Government Resolution issued in July 1954, offences committed by government servants under the Bombay

Prohibition Act were directed to be treated as involving moral turpitude and accordingly, persons found guilty either by courts of law or in departmental proceedings, were to be dismissed from service. Separately the IGP directed that at each police station, two separate Registers, viz. "Known Criminals Register", and "Surveillance Register" in respect of persons convicted for offences under the Prohibition Act, and for those committing the offences of distilling, selling, and smuggling, had to be maintained. It was further directed that each police station will maintain a separate register known as the "General Conviction Register" for the prohibition offences in which the names of all the prohibition offenders had to be entered.

Certain safeguards were introduced by the government in 1957 to prevent undue harassment to police officers who diligently enforced the dry law. Whereas, in other cases, a magisterial enquiry was mandatory regardless of whether an instance of police firing resulted in injury or loss of life, no such procedure was required to be followed, if the police opened fire in self-defense, during prohibition raids against illicit distillers who attacked the police. Persons convicted of an offence under the Bombay Prohibition Act and Bombay Opium Smoking Act were held ineligible for being given contracts or licenses at the discretion of the Government, provided the grant or issue of which was not regulated by any Act.

Under section 165 CrPC, police officers are authorized to search only if there are reasonable and sufficient grounds, and they must keep a record of the same. Whenever a question arises as to whether there were reasonable grounds or not, it can be decided only from the record made about the grounds that existed at that time. The best way of keeping such a record is to mention them in the FIR itself, whenever it is convenient to do so. In other cases, the grounds should be mentioned in the case diary. However, through an order issued in 1959, the IGP directed that, especially for prohibition cases, the words to the effect "on receipt of reliable information" would suffice, thereby facilitating frequent searches by the police seeking to enforce the prohibition law. To judge whether sincere efforts were being made to enforce prohibition, the monthly crime review was required to include information on prohibition cases to enable the IGP to assess the quality of work done by the district police in the enforcement of the Prohibition Act. Further, graphs for prohibition offences were to be maintained in the offices of the Superintendents of Police separately on a yearly and monthly basis, indicating the classification and disposal of cases. Such was the focus of the senior police hierarchy which in turn was because of the state governments' insistence on scrupulous enforcement.

A year earlier in 1958, the village police patels had also been roped in. They were expected to be aware of the illicit distillation going on in their villages and it was their duty to inform the police about the commission of such offences promptly to enable the latter to take necessary action. The IGP conveyed that the government desired that the police patels should be dealt with severely if they were found to be conniving at prohibition offences in their jurisdiction. The SHOs were directed to bring to the notice of the SP any omission on the part of the police patels. The new law required a change in the police philosophy. Persons giving information about offences under the excise laws and prohibition orders had to be treated as informants and not complainants.

Care similarly had to be taken to see that the strictest possible secrecy about their names was maintained. Immediate action was necessary on information received from members of the District Prohibition Committee, who were provided with badges in token of their identity. Since Goa, Daman and Diu were Portuguese territories, borders where they existed needed extra vigilance and strict watch.

All district police chiefs were told that if a person who is arrested in a prohibition case and released on bail, resorts to the same activities and is rearrested, his bail application should be opposed. Police prosecutor would bring such cases to the notice of the trying magistrate and insist that bail be denied. In suitable cases, the court may be moved for the cancellation of the bail. To focus attention on the known bootleggers and distillers, a list of such people was also maintained.

The involvement of the government in ensuring enforcement of the dry law continued relentlessly even towards the end of the first decade since the enactment of the law. In 1959, it was conveyed that whenever cases involving important public personalities or substantial haul of illicit liquor or rounding up of gangs of smugglers or such other important information for the breach of the Bombay Prohibition Act, 1949, was detected, the Superintendents of Police should immediately submit reports regarding the seizure or arrests of persons to the Secretary to the Government of Bombay in the Revenue Department. Copies of such reports had to be sent to the Inspector-General of Police, the Director of Prohibition and Excise, the Commissioner of Police, Bombay and the Director, Anti-Corruption and Prohibition Intelligence, Bombay. Additionally, the District Superintendents of Police were directed to furnish a report every month to the Director, Anti-Corruption and Prohibition Intelligence, regarding the action taken during the preceding month in the matter with names of notorious distillers concentrated upon and made to stop their illegal activities, names of notorious bootleggers followed up and made to stop their illegal activities, areas where concerted efforts were made to stop the anti-prohibition activities and those that had been cleared up.

On bifurcation of the Bombay province, Gujarat and Maharashtra came into existence on 1 May 1960. Whereas Maharashtra relaxed prohibition gradually from 1963 onwards, Gujarat became the true inheritor of the culture developed for enforcement of the dry law in the bilingual Bombay state. As SDPO, it was my duty to not only to maintain the legacy but also ensure compliance in true spirit. Unfortunately, nearly 30 years of prohibition had turned the brewing and sale of illicit liquor into a booming underground business. Many a one-time thugs and smugglers switched livelihoods, sensing a more profitable opportunity. In metropolitan areas, the massive profits from the illicit liquor trade would act as the launchpad for a parallel economy with tentacles in everything from prostitution and gambling and, eventually, gun-running and terror. Gangs formed and allied with one another to protect their territories. Their grip on the city, their ruthless wars, and the deep inroads they made into local law enforcement would last decades. Regular bribes received from these dens became a major source of illegal income for the police department. It is common knowledge that the kingpins of the illicit liquor business operate under the canopy of political and police patronage. J. B. Kripalani, an ardent crusader for prohibition, had suggested in an article that effectively enforcing prohibition would necessitate a major overhaul of the existing police structure and the introduction of a cadre of honest policemen to enforce the new law. It would take a sincere and committed officer to ensure that his men walked the straight and narrow path while taking appropriate action to wipe out the menace.

It was therefore disappointing when late in the evening I received a special report about an offence registered against a police constable who was found under the influence of alcohol. It transpired that G S Ahuja, CPI Palitana, was patrolling in the town along with a PSI H S Bodat in connection with Eid ul-Adha, a festival celebrated by the Muslims to honour the willingness of Abraham (Ibrahim) to sacrifice his son Ishmael (Ismail) as an act of obedience to God's command. It is a customary duty of the police to patrol the streets on all days of major religious festivals for the maintenance of public order. Posted on duty on that day was Constable Chandbhai Mohammadbhai. The CPI noticed that he was not in proper uniform and approached him to question him in this regard. Chandbhai replied that he had gone out of town and had reported back in a hurry. However, his demeanour indicated that he was not normal and was found to be in a drunken condition. Ahuja, therefore, asked him if he had consumed liquor to which the accused replied in the affirmative. The constable was taken to the police station by PSI Bodat, an offence registered against him under the Prohibition Act, and he was placed under arrest. The CPI then came personally to inform me of the development.

As visitations go, this was a straightforward affair where both the complainant and witnesses are usually police officers themselves. In drunken cases, the accused must be sent for medical examination where a preliminary report about his condition is prepared. The medical officer would usually opine that- his breath is smelling of alcohol; that his speech is normal; and that the person forwarded as an accused, has consumed alcohol. He would also take a blood sample and send it to the Chemical Analyser to determine the content of the alcohol in the blood. After perusing the preliminary report of the medical officer, I proceeded to examine witnesses which consisted of PSI Bodat who had filed the complaint, CPI Ahuja who had found the accused in a drunken condition, Constable Prabhudas Damodardas who had taken the accused to the hospital for medical examination, and couple of other policemen who were present at the police station when the accused was brought in and had noticed that he was drunk.

The following day I visited the spot to which the accused had been detailed for *bandobast* duty. This was opposite a cinema, and I was able to locate an employee who confirmed that Chandbhai appeared to be under the influence of alcohol, when he reported for duty the previous day. I also located two other witnesses who were present there with their handcarts, selling food and sundry articles, when the CPI accosted the accused. They corroborated in substance the charge against the delinquent.

There were standing orders in place that the submission of charge-sheet should not be delayed in prohibition cases. Section 173 CrPC provides that the investigations into the offences should be conducted by the police without unnecessary delay, and the charge-sheet submitted as soon as the investigation is completed. So before concluding the visitation, I directed the investigating officer to ensure that the report from the Chemical Analyser is received at the earliest to facilitate submission of the case papers to the court for trial. Separately, a set of preliminary enquiry papers were prepared which would be sent to the SP, who was the disciplinary authority, for initiating departmental proceedings against Chandbhai.

In 1949, the then Inspector General of Police, Bombay State had issued a circular conveying the following:

> *Detection and prevention of prohibition offences is as much a part of the duty of the Police as any other duty in regard to crime. All Police officers and men must put forth their best efforts for the proper discharge of this duty and take suitable measures to suppress excise crime, if it exists in any part of their charge. They must be fully conversant with the various orders and notifications issued by Government from time to time under the Prohibition Act and also allied enactments. They must work in full co-operation with the Excise Department and the Local Prohibition Committees. If it is found that any Police officer does not take sufficient interest in this important branch of his duties, it will be noted as a factor to his discredit and disciplinary action taken.*

One month later, CPI Ahuja was instrumental in registering an offence of drunken misbehaviour against another police constable, Nanu Kalu. In Palitana town, policemen were deployed for maintaining order during Muharram, a period of fasting, prayers, and austerity. Muslims usually get together on this day to mourn the death of Imam Hussein, and to honour his martyrdom, they express sadness and grief in many ways. As the Tajiya (replica of the mausoleum of Imam Hussain) procession, arrived in Bhairavnath Chowk, the accused constable, gave his .303 rifle to his colleague PC Balashankar, joined the procession, and started dancing. This was an unusual happening and a crowd collected. Sensing that this could become a potential trouble spot, Ahuja, who was present nearby supervising the bandobast, came at once only to discover that the constable was under the influence of alcohol. When the CPI along with a head constable tried to hold the latter, he pushed them away and himself fell on the road. Nanu was taken to the police station whereupon he took off his shirt and belt, threw it on the table, and started abusing everybody. He declared that he cared little for his job. An offence was registered not only under the Prohibition Act, but also under section 110 of the Bombay Police Act which was regarding behaving indecently in public or in a disorderly manner in any office or station house. The sense of importance given to such incidents can be gauged by the fact that the CPI himself became the complainant on behalf of the state. As in the manner of the earlier case narrated above, it was a special report case, and I visited the same in my capacity as a Sub-Divisional Officer. Nanu Kala was arrested, placed under suspension, and prosecuted. Departmental proceedings were also initiated against him.

Seventy-three years later, in contemporary times the enforcement of prohibition has taken a backseat. Senior police officers no longer devote quality time for its enforcement and the government of the day have no interest beyond making cosmetic noises by the way of placating public opinion.

CHAPTER 19

# AN ELEVEN-YEAR-OLD ENMITY

*R*ajput Karsan Kala was a dynamic man who resided in the village Navaniya located 12 km north of Vallabhipur police station, and 52 km away from the district headquarters, Bhavnagar. Although he was not educated, he was well-known as a public figure and was liked by many for his helpful nature. Then in his late forties, he was President of the Kanpar Cooperative Society and, of the Vallabhipur *Kharid-Vechan Sangh*. He was also Director in the District Cooperative Bank and the District *Sahakari Sangh*. Having contested the panchayat elections, he was a member of Vallabhipur taluka panchayat. Consequently, Karsan Kala exercised meaningful influence over public affairs in the area. Not unnaturally, this brought him into conflict with certain sections of the village as they resented his interference in the village affairs.

Spread over 736 hectares, the village had a population of about nine hundred with the largest groups being that of patels, kolis and *darbars*. There were a few houses of *karadiya* rajputs as well, a community to which Karsan Kala belonged. Patels, predominantly found in the state of Gujarat, were a community of land-owning farmers and later, with the advent of the British East India Company, of businessmen and merchants. The term derives from the word Patidar, literally "one who holds (owned) pieces of land called patis", implying a higher economic status than that of the landless. Their two main subcastes are *leuva* patels and *kadva* patels. The former are extensively found in Saurashtra, and it was this subcaste that resided in village Navaniya. The two prominent groups within them were those having the surname Sakariya and Bhojani. Since 1968, due to certain societal reasons, friction existed between the two and Karsan Kala at that time had sided with the sakariya patels. The feud had resulted in two offences being registered, one against the sakariyas for causing grievous hurt and the second, a cross complaint, against the bhojanis for causing simple hurt. The *darbars* had sided with the latter, and one of their own, Bharatsinh Dipsinh was grievously injured. The former believed that the fracas at that point of time was instigated by Karsan Kala, and this had left a bitter feeling amongst them. Over the years the hardened attitudes on both sides manifested themselves in altercations, but these were not serious enough for the police to intervene.

Sunday, 4th November 1979, was a rather pleasant day and I was looking forward to a relaxed schedule. The previous week had been hectic, my duties requiring me to travel extensively. Around noon, I received a telephone call from the Superintendent of Police, Bhavnagar directing me to proceed immediately to Vallabhipur in order to ascertain facts about the whereabouts of Karsan Kala. Apparently, the SP had received information that something untoward had happened in the village. Shortly after this conversation, I received a message from the police station indicating that the Karsan's body had been found and an accidental death case, registered. By the time I reached Navaniya, the accidental death case was converted into a full-fledged murder investigation as it was clear from the injuries inflicted on the body, that the deceased had been killed.

I was met by PSI G L Khunti, the SHO of Vallabhipur police station who apprised me of the facts of the case. Two days ago, on a Friday, Karsan had left the village in the afternoon and proceeded towards Ratanpar to purchase an oil engine. Since a wheel of his motorcycle developed a puncture, he had stopped to get the same repaired. He then proceeded towards village Melana where the wheel again sustained a puncture. After attending to the same, he came to Vallabhipur and spent the night at the government rest-house, called Pathik Ashram. The following day, Saturday, he proceeded towards village Navaniya to return home. Next day, at 6:30 AM, his brother Bhura Kala was proceeding towards village Kanpar to purchase cotton on his bicycle when he came across his brother's motorcycle lying on the side of the road. Surprised by this, he stopped to look around when he discovered his brother's body lying in a shallow pit in the nearby bushes. He immediately returned to Navaniya to inform his family and sent one Bachu Dharamshi to inform the police. Khunti also told me that on receipt of this information he had registered an accidental death case but after he visited the scene of offence and examined the body, it was clear that Karsan had been killed. He therefore registered an offence of murder and himself filed a complaint on behalf of the state.

## An Eleven-Year-Old Enmity

I visited the scene of offence, which was located near a small canal, called a *nala* in the local language, on the south of which there was a ditch containing stagnant greenish water. The road to village Navaniya was twenty feet broad and not metalled. On both the sides of the road which ran from east to west are thorny bushes, colloquially called *bawal*. The distance between the point where the deceased was killed and where his body was dumped, was twenty-one feet. The *nala* was located fifty-two feet away. At forty-seven feet, one shoe was found along with a towel and a turban belonging to the victim. Also discovered was a green-coloured ball-point pen with a red refill. I examined the *panchnama* of the scene of offence and discovered that Rs. 2629/- found on the body of the deceased had also been recovered. The victim had been carrying a diary and some documents which were also seized. Blood-soaked mud along with a control sample, for forensic analysis, had also been attached.

As is usually done in such cases, I began by speaking with the wife, son, and daughter of the deceased. All the three confirmed that Karsan had left for the village Ratanpar, last Friday after which there was no communication with him. It was on Sunday morning that they learned about his death. They could convey no other details and neither did they suspect anybody. I also questioned his brother Bhura, who merely confirmed what Khunti had already told me. He too did not suspect anybody. Just to make sure that there was no discrepancy in his statement, I also questioned his wife Anuben. This was important because he was the first person to see the body in the morning and the veracity of his statement needed to be corroborated to rule out any ulterior motives.

Chhaganbhai Kalyanbhai was a business partner of Karsan Kala and lived in Vallbhipur. On hearing about the death of the latter he had come to Navaniya. He revealed that on the previous day, Saturday, the deceased had met him at about 6 PM in the evening and they had parted after discussions regarding their business activities. He could not point towards a possible motive for the killing. The next witness to be questioned was Punabhai Ratanbhai who owned a *pan-bidi* shop at Vallabhipur. His testimony confirmed that the deceased was in town late in the evening, since around 9:15 PM, he had come to the shop of this witness and purchased a Taj cigarette. This was corroborated by Narain Bhikha who was present there and both he and the deceased had exchanged pleasantries.

In the meantime, Dimple, the German Shepherd, who I had first encountered at village Jalalpur during the investigation of an undetected robbery case, had arrived from Bhavnagar along with her handler. These canines can cover miles and miles of forest looking for a lost hiker or someone buried after an avalanche and can even locate the bodies of drowned victims underwater in oceans and lakes. The ability of dogs to cover large areas in a relatively brief period of time supplies a great resource when looking for victims or accused. Although human searchers play a key role that cannot be replaced, search and rescue dogs are able to get the job done with unique precision. Dimple was taken to the scene of offence and made to smell articles of clothing and other surroundings but could not make any headway.

Meanwhile discreet enquiries revealed that Karsan was a man with a glad eye and was reportedly having liaisons with several women. Further enquiries revealed that there was a *koli* woman, a vegetable vendor, who was rumoured to be in touch with him. PSI Khunti deployed plainclothes men to check on this angle. Having arrived in the late afternoon, apart from visiting the scene of crime, I had by now examined and questioned as many as thirteen witnesses. It was dark and I therefore decided to return to Vallabhipur for the night.

Next day I spent about two hours at the police station poring over past records to trace any enmity or motive connected with Karsan Kala. In doing so, I was following a guideline contained in the Gujarat Police Manual Volume III, which suggested that as soon as the crime is reported, the investigating officer should first consider the facts of the case thoroughly and should consult the police station crime record, such as Village Crime Note-Book, Conviction Register, or Known Criminals Register. To deal effectively with crime, every police station was required to maintain a continuous record of the criminal history of individuals and localities. This was secured through five vital records for each village. Collectively called the Village Crime Note-Book, it consisted of Village Statistics (Part I), Village Crime Register (Part II), Village Conviction Register (Part III), Notes on Crime in Village (Part- IV) and the History Sheets (Part V). These registers were treated and marked as confidential so as to give them the status of "privileged documents". All entries in the notes on crime in village were directed to be made by the SHO in his own handwriting. Entries in "History Sheets" could be written up by them or at their dictation, by the writer head constable or constable and must in either case, be signed by the officer himself. Entries in other records could be made by subordinate police officers under the direction of the SHO, who will invariably initial them. Such was the importance attached to these records that the SP and the SDPO were expected to, at the time of their inspection, compare the entries in the registers maintained at the police out-post, the police station and the district office, and ensure their accuracy. The attention paid to preventive action by the SHO is revealed by the thoroughness with which he has written up his village crime records, his knowledge of the movements of notorious criminals, and the efforts he has made to arrest the absconding offenders.

The effort was worthwhile. While going through the records pertaining to the village Navania, I discovered that the existence of feud between the sakariya patels and the bhojani patels of eleven years ago had been duly recorded as also the bitterness amongst the *darbars.*

Kanpar was a village which the deceased passed by frequently on his way home, and I proceeded there to make further inquiries from his acquaintances. Two witnesses, Jivan Kalyan and Tribhuvan Mulji, who were sitting at the temple by the roadside, saw the deceased go by on Saturday at 9:30 PM on his motorcycle. There was nobody with him. Here I learnt of a subdued rumour floating around about the amorous relationship of Karsan with the wife of a former *talati,* a junior village revenue officer. There was nothing substantive to it. I next proceeded to village Pipal to question those who owned the farmland adjoining the scene of offence. Khunti, who was accompanying me, located three witnesses, one of whom Premji Khima confirmed that on many an occasion earlier, he had seen the deceased go by but on the fateful night he must have missed him as he was busy sowing cotton seeds.

In the meantime, I received word that SP Bhavnagar had arrived at village Navaniya. I therefore proceeded to the village to meet him and acquainted him with the facts of the case. Together we visited the scene of the crime, and I carefully noted his instructions regarding the further course of action required to be taken for the successful detection of the crime.

After the departure of the SP, questioning of several individuals in the village was undertaken. One person, Natubha Ravubha, a *darbar,* conveyed that he learned about the crime only in the morning when the body was discovered. What he said next was interesting. He said that he knew nothing about the deceased as the families were not on speaking terms due to a quarrel several years ago. Khunti was asked to check on this, and within an hour he reported that even as recently as about four days ago, an altercation had occurred between the deceased and the *darbars* on the occasion of *tulsi vivah*. This is a ceremonial wedding of the goddess Tulasi, a form of Lakshmi, with a *shaligram* or an *amla* branch, a personification of God Vishnu. The Tulasi wedding signifies the end of the monsoon, and the beginning of the wedding season. It transpired that on that occasion an altercation broke out between the sakariya children and the *darbar* children. After things had calmed down, on hearing of the dispute, the deceased arrived on the spot accompanied by a few sakariya patels and himself, carrying a lathi. He is reported to have uttered words to the effect that "all the *darbars* must be weeded out and done away with." He must have said this more for the impact his words would have on his support base, and less as an actual threat. We located a witness, Arjun Dharamshi, who was present on the occasion and heard these words. This witness also revealed that two *darbars*, namely, Prabhatsinh Jorubha and Andubha Dhirubha, were standing near the temple and witnessed this.

In the meantime, plainclothes men deputed at village Navaniya brought forward two witnesses, both sons of Premji Khima, who had been examined earlier in the day. The boys mentioned that, unlike their father, they were present on their farmland and at about 9:30 PM the previous night, had heard the motorcycle of the deceased pass by. They further revealed that the bike had stopped and when attempts were made to start it again, presumably by the deceased, it had not. Since it was of no consequence to them, they had finished their work and returned home. Neither of them had any further information as to what happened thereafter.

Investigation so far had not revealed any concrete motive for the commission of the crime nor was it pointing towards any individual as a likely suspect. During the day, we questioned the *koli* woman vendor from whom the deceased would buy vegetables, a witness Batukbhai Laxmiram, with whom the deceased dined the previous night while at Vallabhipur at Rajnikant's hotel, Rajnikant himself, and even the peon of Pathik Ashram where the deceased had spent the night. In fact, the last-mentioned witness was taken aside by PSI Khunti and quietly asked as to whether the deceased was accompanied by any woman. Beyond corroborating known facts, none had any idea as to how the victim had met his fate. To leave virtually no stone unturned, I directed Khunti to traverse the route taken by Karsan Kala around the same time as the day of his journey to Navaniya and question every person he met on the way. Late in the night the PSI returned having recorded the statements of four such persons which unfortunately could throw no further light that could lead to the detection of the offence.

Since additional manpower was required, I requisitioned the anti-theft squad of my subdivision to join the investigation. That night I decided to camp at village Navaniya, converting a room of the village school into a makeshift accommodation.

I begin the third day of our investigation early in the morning by first reviewing the work done so far by PSI Khunti. Next, I sent word to PSI J M Thaker, SHO of the neighbouring Umrala police station to join and help with the investigation. Several residents of the village were questioned about their movements around the time the deceased was returning to the village. Most of them knew nothing and all provided details of various activities they were busy with at the relevant time. In the meantime, PSI M M Parmar, SHO of Talaja police station of Mahuva sub-division, and who had earlier served in the area also reported for assisting with the detection of the crime.

One witness, Jorubha Dipsinh, worked as a security guard for the State Bank of India at Vallabhipur. He said that for the last eighteen years he was not on speaking terms with the deceased as the latter had declined to provide grass bundles at his doorstep. Apparently Karsan Kala at some point of time in the past was in this business. The witness, being a *darbar*, expected deference on the part of the deceased which was not forthcoming. The brother of this witness, Ravubha Dipsinh was also questioned. He provided details of the fracas that happened in 1968 between the sakariyas and the bhojanis and confirmed that the deceased had supported the former whereas his own community, the *darbars*, were with the other side. Regarding the incident on the day of the tulsi vivah, his nephew Prabhat Jorubha had conveyed to him the insulting utterances of the deceased regarding their community.

The mystery of the ownership of the pen recovered from the scene of crime had not yet been solved. Although plainclothes men detailed for the purpose moved around and made efforts in this direction, nothing came of it. In rural India it is generally believed that the barber knows everything about everybody in the village since he is constantly sought after by various patrons. Historically, barbershops were also places of social interaction and public discourse. They were the locations of open debates, voicing public concerns, and engaging citizens in discussions about contemporary issues. The village barber was therefore duly commissioned to find out all that he could, and in particular, establish the ownership of the pen recovered from the scene of offence. This may seem unusual in today's time but in the earlier years given the limited resources at the disposal of the police, both in terms of workforce and logistics support, every traditional method available for detection of crime was put to use.

By now I was beginning to sense that there were some people who knew about the crime, but there seemed to have descended *omertà* on the village for which reason witnesses were not forthcoming. We divided ourselves into four teams and spread out across the village including the farmlands to question every possible person who knew anything, even if remotely connected, with the crime. We shortlisted five persons who were not available in the village, with no ostensible reason known for their absence. PSI Khunti was assigned the task of locating two such missing Kolis and also visit village Ratanpar as it was reported that one Dharamshi Jivraj had said in public that a *karyakarta* (political worker) will be killed shortly. PSI Thakar was assigned the task of locating two other persons, and bringing them in for questioning. At the village as intensive inquiries continued to be made, we came across our first break-through in the form of a witness Bachubhai Sukhabhai. He revealed that the previous Saturday he passed by the farmland of one Amarshi Jivan which is adjoining to the scene of crime. As he was moving towards Navaniya after nightfall, he saw some people from his village moving in the opposite direction, and towards the scene of crime. He revealed the names of all the people, as they were from his own village, and further revealed that one of them Balvantsinh Dipsinh was carrying a *dhariya* (sickle) in his hand while the rest were armed with *lathis* (a long heavy bamboo stick).

Amarshi Jivan was summoned for questioning. He revealed that on the day of the offence, towards dusk eight people from his village, all *darbars,* had come and parked themselves on the *nala* near his farmland. They sat smoking *beedis* whereas he himself after finishing the work of cutting wood had departed for home. He identified them as Andubha Dhirubha, Navubha Jethubha, Natubha Ravubha, Jasubha Ravubha, Prabhatsinh Jorubha, Balvantsinh Dipsinh, Vajubha Dipsinh and Banubha Dhirubha. This witness also revealed that the pen found at some distance from the scene of the offence belonged to him and must have fallen while he was cutting wood. Himmat, the son of this witness who was assisting his father, corroborated what the latter had said.

The focus now shifted specifically on the above-named suspects and none of them were found in the village. Rigourous inquiries with their relatives, in particular their parents and siblings, regarding their whereabouts were undertaken. Two suspects namely, Navubha Jethubha and Andubha Dhirubha, were likely to have gone to the house of Ratubha Jethubha, the former's brother who resided in Bhavnagar. It was late in the evening by the time I reached the place of the suspects hideout in that town. Both the suspects were inside the house and attempted to hide themselves in adjoining rooms once they sensed that it was the police at the door. They were both picked up, taken to a nearby police chowkey and interrogated. In the meantime, witness Bharatsinh Dipsinh who had been previously injured during the 1968 feud was located and questioned. Apart from confirming the existence of enmity between the two suspects' families and the deceased, he revealed that Andubha, who was his nephew, had come to meet him last Sunday and revealed that he, along with seven others, had eliminated the victim, Karsan Kala.

At 10 PM that night, both the suspects were formally placed under arrest for the murder of Karsan Kala and taken to Vallabhipur and locked up. I returned to Navaniya for follow-up action. Police teams working at the village had located another witness to whom Navubha Jethubha had made an extra-judicial confession, much like Andubha. A witness who had seen Balwantsinh carrying a *dhariya,* and Natubha and Prabhatsinh, carrying *lathis* while returning to the village at 10 PM last Saturday, was located and questioned. The statements of both these witnesses were recorded. I also questioned Dhirubha whose two sons had participated in the crime. Andubha was in police custody as mentioned above whereas the second son Banubha had escaped to Surat, a city located 375 km in south Gujarat. Evidently both his sons had confessed to him about their involvement in the murder before they moved out of the village.

In the meantime, PSI G L Khunti and PSI J M Thakar, had returned to report on the tasks assigned to them. They had brought along some people who they were sent to find. There was no further requirement of them as in the meantime proper suspects had been located. When I recall this method of summoning witnesses or likely suspects for interrogation or questioning, one is embarrassed at the highhandedness involved. Back in 1979, although there was little awareness amongst the people about how the police should treat witnesses, there were already in existence salutary provisions in the police manual, laying down a proper course of action. One such mandate directed:

> *Witnesses should be treated with consideration and with full respect due to their position. Investigating Officers should, whenever possible, make a point of going to them instead of calling them away from their homes and work. Much of the difficulty experienced in obtaining evidence would be overcome, if Investigating Officers were uniformly considerate. As far as possible, a Head Constable or Constable should not be deputed to call witnesses and complainants to Police Stations. Written requests in very polite terms in letter form, mentioning the time and the place at which their presence is required, should be sent to the persons concerned.*

In a situation like this one, where a high-profile murder has taken place, most proprieties due to the members of the public are not observed even today. We had yet to arrest the remaining six accused and therefore all efforts were in those directions.

During the day, both Navubha and Andubha were interrogated, and their statement was recorded which brought out the manner in which Karsan Kala had been done away with. The initiative to eliminate the latter was taken by Natubha Ravubha. He collected the others involved in the crime and exhorted them that such utterances of the deceased as made on the day of tulsi vivah was unacceptable especially in view of their pre-eminent position in society as *darbars*. They had known that the deceased had left the village and would return the following evening. It would be best to intercept him on the way home, before he reached the village. Therefore, all the eight accused persons left Navaniya in the evening and set off towards Kanpar village and waited near the *nala* for the victim. Sometimes past 9 PM, the latter arrived on his motorcycle and as luck would have it, the bike stalled not far away from where all the accused were waiting. It was Natubha who rushed towards the deceased with his *lathi*. On seeing this, Karsan Kala moved away from the motorcycle with the intention of confronting the former. However, all the other assailants joined in and delivered grievous blows on his head, face, neck, and arms. Balwantsinh and Andubha were carrying *dhariya* (sickle) and *kodali* (axe) respectively, and this resulted in fatal injuries to the victim. Karsan Kala died on the spot. Thereafter, Banubha, Natubha, and Navubha dragged the deceased by his legs and threw him in a shallow pit amongst thorny bushes. With the completion of their objective of eliminating their arch enemy, they all headed home. In the process everybody forgot to do anything about the motorcycle of the deceased lying unattended on the road.

The PM note had been received and the cause of death was given as "due to the injury to vital organs- Brain." I camped for the second night at the village although there was no prospect of going to bed. With the sustained efforts of questioning relatives, searching houses, visiting neighbouring villages and in general putting pressure on the immediate families to persuade the remaining accused to come forward we finally, by early morning at 3 AM, succeeded in arresting five accused, namely, Natubha, Jasubha, Prabhatsinh, Balwantsinh and Vajubha. Their interrogation continued during the night, and they confessed to having murdered Karsan Kala. Their statements were recorded accordingly. Further, the weapons used by them for the commission of crime were seized under a discovery *panchnama* in compliance of the provisions of section 27 of the Evidence Act.

Andubha, who had used an axe, produced it in the presence of two witnesses. The weapon contained bloodstains. Since he had thoroughly washed his shirt and no bloodstains were found on it, the same was not attached. His mother deposed that on the day, Saturday, when the murder was committed, he had come home and told her about the same. Accused Vajubha, similarly produced a bloodstained shirt and a *lathi* used in the commission of the crime. His son Ganpatsinh deposed, that after committing the crime his father had returned home and told him that they had done away with a nuisance. Apart from drawing up a discovery *panchnama*, statements of all witnesses, mostly relatives, were recorded.

All the accused were produced before the JMFC at Sihor who remanded them to police custody till 13th November. This gave us five days to round up the remaining accused Banubha and collect all the required evidence for submission of a charge-sheet against the perpetrators.

As the day ended, I recalled that the instigator, now an accused, Natubha Ravubha, was questioned three days ago and had stoutly denied any involvement. We called his father Ravubha Dipsinh who stated that his son had not told him anything about the crime earlier but when the police summoned him on 5<sup>th</sup> November, on return he had told his father that he was indeed involved and mentioned names of the other accused. Like everybody else in the village and in that community, this witness too did not come forward to inform the police despite intense investigative activity going on in the village.

That night I camped at Vallabhipur at the government guest house and succeeded in getting a few hours of rest.

Next morning was the fifth day of my visit of this serious crime. Weapons of offence used in the crime by the remaining five accused were seized under a discovery *panchnama* along with bloodstained clothing. Jasubha and Natubha produced a *lathi* each which bore no bloodstains. Prabhatsinh led the investigating officer to his house from where a *lathi* was recovered bearing bloodstains. Similarly, Navubha produced a bloodstained pyjama which had been washed but the markings could be faintly seen. Sickle which was used to inflict injuries during the assault was recovered from the residence of Balwantsinh. It bore no bloodstains.

The statements of witnesses, relatives and others were recorded to collect supporting evidence. This included mothers, fathers, wives, daughters, sisters, brothers, sons, and neighbours of the accused. Although each one of them was now willing to come on record and state that their son or ward had confessed to the crime, none of them were likely to support this during the trial. For example, Rajkunvarba Ravubha, is the mother of Natubha and Jasubha. She stated that on Saturday, when Karsan Kala had been done away with, Jasubha came home and told her about the murder the same night. Another witness was Dhanji Karsanji who was the complainant in the 1968 feud which resulted in the animosity between the deceased and the *darbars* and whose testimony was important to establish motive. Jadav Khoda and Ramdevsinh Wakharsinh gave evidence about the tulsi vivah incident and the role they played in cooling tempers and placating both sides. An important witness was Sukhubhai Kanubhai, to whom an extra-judicial confession had been made by Natubha, implicating seven others involved in the crime.

I contacted the Superintendent of Police, Surat City, requesting him to assist with the arrest of the eight accused, Banubha.

The following day, along with PSI Khunti, I proceeded to Palitana to facilitate the recording of statements of five important witnesses under section 164 CrPC. These included Arjan Dharamshi, Amarshi Jivan and Sukhubhai Kanubhai. A statement made under this section cannot be used as substantive evidence of the facts stated, but it can be used to support or to challenge the evidence given in the court by the person who has made the statement. The inference here is that the police at some point of time thought that the witness may change his or her statement, and therefore it is necessary to safeguard the conclusion of the investigation as reflected in the charge-sheet sent to the court. These individuals lived in the same village and belonged to a stratum of society which was not at par with the *darbars* who were the ruling elite before independence. The pressure that would come to bear on them during trial can easily be guessed and hence such a safeguard was necessary.

On returning to Vallabhipur, I received a message that PSI Local Crime Branch (LCB), Surat City, who was assigned the task of locating the absconding accused by his SP, had succeeded in doing so. He was on his way and arrived in a couple of hours. Banubha was interrogated, he confessed his involvement and cited the threat rendered by the deceased to the *darbars* on the occasion of tulsi vivah as the reason for killing him. The PSI had recorded the statements of five witnesses in Surat regarding the presence of this accused in that city, and I examined the same for its legality and authenticity as Banubha had been formally placed under arrest over there shortly after midnight.

I camped for the night at Vallabhipur, and the following morning arranged for Banubha to be produced before the JMFC and seek police custody. He was remanded to police custody till 13 November, the same time span as the others. Thereafter, post detailed interrogation, he produced the *lathi* under a discovery *panchnama*. The same bore no bloodstains. Around this time the brother of the deceased, Bhura Kala, came to the police station and conveyed that his deceased brother's wristwatch was missing, and he suspected that this may be in the possession of one of the accused. Although this appeared unlikely as the wallet of the victim along with cash was recovered intact, nevertheless I instructed the investigating officer to have their houses searched again. In all likelihood, the wristwatch must have fallen during the scuffle and may have been taken away before the arrival of the police by any of the villagers as several of them had collected near the dead body of the victim.

After spending yet another night at Vallabhipur, the following morning, I interrogated all the eight accused to look for any contradiction in their statements which could throw a new light to the whole episode. Thereafter proceeded to Bhavnagar to question and record the statement of five witnesses, who were relatives of the accused Andubha and Navubha, in order to have a comprehensive picture about their activities while they were absconding.

One of my supervisory duties required me to pay a surprise visit at irregular intervals to police stations under my charge, and check whether they were functioning in a proper way in terms of response to public and attention to their complaints, and checkup whether officers and men were alert. The serious crime I was presently supervising had been detected, and the accused arrested. I could afford to take two hours off. I proceeded to Umrala police station, which was just 12 km away and having arrived at 11:30 PM, discovered that the men had not left for night round which they were supposed to do sharp at 11 PM. I made the necessary entry in the Station Diary and directed that all the defaulters be placed in the Orderly Room. By the time I finished this work it was well past midnight and decided to camp there for the night.

The following day, I reached village Navaniya at 7:30 AM. The Home Minister was visiting the family of the deceased to condole and express solidarity. He came accompanied by the SP and after meeting the family, and other leading citizens of the village, spent some time discussing the work done by the police so far. After their departure, I sat down with Khunti and went through the case papers. The latter was instructed to ensure that articles containing blood stains and control samples are sent to the Director, Forensic Science Laboratory at Junagadh. It is essential that the identity of each article attached by the police in the course of investigation of medico-legal as well as all other cases, should be preserved properly from the commencement of the attachment and the writing of the *panchnama,* up to its production in the court during the trial and through all its intermediate stages, if any, such as while in the custody of the Civil Surgeon or the Chemical Analyser.

The object of a visit by the SDPO to the scene of an offence is personally to ascertain the facts of the case, as far as possible, from the complainant, witnesses, and other sources of information. He must ascertain what investigation the police on the spot have made, assist, and generally direct the investigation, and see that it is being correctly and vigorously pursued by all concerned. It his duty to prevent irregularities on the part of the subordinate police officers, and to encourage and guide them in their enquiries. When a confession has been made, the SDPO is expected to ascertain by enquiry and, if convenient, through conversation with the accused, that no compulsion or inducement has been used by the police in extracting a confession. I spent nine days on this visitation, camped two nights in the village, five nights at Vallabhipur and one night at Umrala, and was satisfied that I had achieved the objective.

# TEMPLE THEFT

On a Tuesday, in the first week of December 1979, I commenced annual inspection of Umrala police station. This important supervisory function can be best discharged when not called away for any other duty. However, the hectic work schedule of a Sub-Divisional Police Officer , barely allows for such a possibility. It was on the third day of the inspection that I received a special report of a house-breaking at a Jain temple in Botad town. Soon thereafter, and certainly within the time limit of two hours prescribed by rules, I left for the scene of crime.

At Botad, I was met by CPI J M Patel and PSI A M Vasava who acquainted me with the facts of the case. The temple was known as Mahavir Swami Temple and was located barely five hundred meters to the east of the police station. From 5 AM in the morning till 12 noon and from 5:30 PM to 8:30 PM in the evening, the premises remained open for devotees to visit. The affairs of the temple were managed by a trust and one Somchand Sonaram Dave functioned as the *pujari* (priest). The previous day he had closed the temple for the night and as per the practice in vogue, had deposited the key with one of the trustees. The following day, when he arrived early in the morning to open the temple, he saw that the main door of the temple had been wrenched open. A metal box where the devotees put coins and small cash had also been broken open. Adjoining the sanctum sanctorum was a room whose door had been broken open. All the cupboards in that room had been ransacked and it was from here that ornaments were stolen. Somchand immediately informed one of the trustees, Rasiklal Vaniya, who then filed a complaint at the police station. Gold and silver ornaments worth ₹ 36,500 had been stolen. In today's time, they would be worth about ₹ 8,75,000.

When I visited the scene of crime, I noticed that to break open the main door, tremendous force would have been required. Further inspection revealed that the line of exit adopted by the culprits was through the door in the back yard which had been forced open. Before my arrival, the premises had been checked for fingerprints, but no sense could be made of them as several people connected with the temple had been going around. The dog-squad apparently also drew a blank. I perused the *panchnama* of the scene of offence prepared by PSI Vasava.

From time immemorial, want and greed have driven even supposed noblemen to resort to embezzling. In a few instances of temple burglary, even the temple administrators or the priests themselves were the culprits—so record temple inscriptions. Therfore, I spent some time questioning the *pujari* in some detail. He hailed from the district Banaskantha in north Gujarat and had been functioning as a priest at the temple for the last ten years. Speaking with him and later with the trustees and given the condition in which the access and exit doors of the temple were found, it was safe to rule out any insider involvement.

Looking around the temple, it was possible to discern that some repair work was underway. It therefore became relevant to question the workmen involved. They turned out to be a father-son team, Shamji Narottam, and Kanji Shamji, who were skilled artisans. A helper assisted them. All three were questioned to ascertain information about any person, who for the purpose of a recce, might have visited the temple and whose conduct and demeanour appeared suspicious to them. They had departed from the temple premises at 6 PM the previous evening having completed their work and were not able to provide any information on that count. Separately, I also asked CPI Patel to run a quick check on their background as well. Shamji's another son Hasmukh was working on a Jain temple not far from the place where the crime was committed, located on Paliyad road. He along with his helper were also called in for questioning. Four individuals, living in Botad, who were previously found to be involved in similar crimes, were located and questioned. These efforts yielded no results. The importance of keeping an eye on men addicted to house-breaking cannot be over stressed. This had been reiterated through a circular issued by IGP Bombay State way back in March 1959. Such persons should receive the most careful attention and therefore Bhanji Harshad, a history-sheeter of Botad police station was summoned for interrogation. The concept of an history sheet needs to be explained.

History sheets are opened for all persons whose names are in the Surveillance Register maintained at the police station, and for no other. The names of all persons required to notify residence under the section 356 CrPC or the Bombay Habitual Offender's Act, 1959; convicts released conditionally or granted furlough under the criminal procedure code; and any other person whose surveillance the SP considers necessary for the prevention or detection of crime, are placed on the Surveillance Register. Persons convicted of house-breaking, robbery or dacoity committed in a professional manner, well-known receivers whether convicted or not, approvers in property cases, coiners, note counterfeiters, professional railway thieves, and persons bound over under section 110 CrPC, are the ones a vigilant SP will order surveillance over with profit. In the case of persons convicted, history sheets must be opened at the time of conviction and not left until the convict is released from jail, when the details of his crime have been forgotten.

The importance of this document can be gauged from the fact that the SP and the Assistant or Deputy Superintendent in charge of a sub-division were under instructions to scrutinise the history sheets whenever they visited a police station, to see that they are properly written up, and that they are not unnecessarily kept open. When a history sheeter dies, orders to destroy his sheet and to remove his name from the Surveillance Register has at once to be sought by the SHO from the SDPO. When a person in respect of whom a history sheet is maintained goes permanently to reside in another State, the officer-in-charge of the police station concerned will send it to his district Superintendent of Police. The latter will then forward the sheet with an English translation thereof, to the district Superintendent of Police of the other State for necessary action. Interestingly, if a person in respect of whom history sheet is maintained was known to have migrated to a province in Pakistan, the document had to be forwarded through proper channel to the government of that province for further action. Similar records of bad characters who were known to have come over to India could be obtained from the concerned provincial governments in Pakistan.

It was clear by now that a determined gang of criminals known to have a certain proficiency in house-breakings had committed the crime. It was learnt that the *"bhats,"* then identified as a criminal community, were based at Ranpur, a small town located 25 km from Botad. They were a nomadic community from Rajasthan. Under the Criminal Tribes Act, 1871, the British had branded them as 'criminals' and later after independence, they were de-notified. CPI Patel was asked to proceed there and tackle them.

That night I decided to camp at Botad. Past midnight I performed night round in the town to check whether firstly, policemen were being deployed for these duties and secondly, to ascertain their alertness. Those were the days prior to the introduction of CCTV camera and performing night-round was an important and critical duties for all ranks up to that of a SDPO. The latter specifically was expected to do it as a surprise. In a circular issued by the IGP back in August 1919, it was mandated that the duty of performing night rounds belonged properly to Assistant and Deputy Superintendents of Police, Inspectors and Sub-Inspector. The Superintendent of Police is expected to occasionally check this work, and that of the patrolling head constables and constables, by doing rounds himself. It was, of course, not necessary for the SP to do this regularly every week as a matter of routine. Assistant and Deputy Superintendents of Police are expected even today to perform night rounds regularly every week, and record in the weekly diary the time of the beginning and ending of the night rounds. Officers, on the day following their night rounds, were, except in exceptional circumstances, excused duty until after midday.

Men were supposed to report at the police station at 11 PM and after recording the details of those deployed that night in the Station Diary, they would be sent to perform night round in different previously earmarked parts of the town. To prevent the occurrence of thefts in the courts of district and subordinate judges, where valuable property has sometimes to be kept, the police on night rounds were to visit, at least once every night, isolated court buildings within their jurisdiction. In places where cash transactions are conducted through banks, and no armed police guards are usually deployed at treasuries or sub-treasuries for guarding the strong rooms, special attention had to be paid by the police on night rounds. I commenced this work that night at 1 AM and continued till 3 AM in the morning. Of the five men deployed that night, two were absent. Normally with a major temple theft having occurred the previous night, and with the presence of senior officers in the town, one would have assumed that all men would be alert. Unfortunately, that was not the case and it pointed towards a casual attitude of the police station staff towards this important duty. I made a note to deal with it separately.

Next morning at 9 AM, I departed for Palitana, located 130 km away and which as recorded earlier, was a major pilgrimage centre for the Jain community. In the past this town had been a focus of temple thieves. Once there, I scrutinised the records of previous such crimes and with the help of Palitana Town police station rounded up as many as we could find, persons who had previously been arrested or found involved in thefts having similar modus operandi. Unfortunately, no headway was made although houses of couple of suspects were also searched. That same evening, I returned to Botad. CPI Patel reported that his visit to Ranpur had not been fruitful. There was absolutely no clue as to who could have or what kind of criminals could have committed this crime. Usually in such a situation receipt of "suggestions" from the District Modus Operandi Bureau becomes the main activity.

DMOB is an important unit of the district police chief's office. Criminology is a science that deals with crime and criminals, whereas investigation is an endeavour to discover the truth by application of that science. The expression "modus operandi" means a plan of work or a mode of operation. It is therefore about various crime patterns and method adopted by different criminals in committing a crime. It is a system that suggests to the investigator the name and description of a probable criminal, largely based on their past criminal activities. The bureau therefore maintains a record of known criminals derived from their individual methods of operation. This is done through the medium of a crime index whose main objective is to assist in the identification of criminals which have come to the knowledge of the police by making use of systematically indexed particulars of known criminals or the crime committed by them. It aims at identifying offenders by any peculiarity in the commission of the crime or a particular story told, or transport used, so on and so forth. This is based on the theory that criminals are accustomed to certain peculiarities which persist despite a long lapse of time. A cheat, for instance, will repeat the same type of offence and is unlikely to become a robber. Although exceptions to this rule exist, it is this trait which gives the criminal away. Even when making a deliberate departure from the patent methods that a culprit normally uses, he is unlikely to go far, and the individual will only make a slight modification to the pattern he is used to. The system is helpful as it narrows down the field of investigation considerably and to that extent helps the investigating officer in tracing the criminals. The bureau therefore kept a record of all criminals previously arrested for cheating, criminal breach of trust, counterfeiting, uttering or possession of counterfeit currency, dacoity, robbery, house-breaking, receiving or disposing of stolen property, and theft. Every police station would have one constable exclusively detailed for this work which would ensure a regular flow of information, in prescribed formats, to the district office. At the state level, the Criminal Investigation Department (CID) with headquarters at the provincial capital, housed the State Modus Operandi Bureau, and maintained similar records for the entire province.

The DMOB, based on the modus operandi used in committing this house-breaking at the temple, had suggested a list of criminals who could be examined for their involvement or otherwise, in the crime. The names contained therein covered a wide geographical area including neighbouring districts, and therefore PSI Khunti, SHO of Vallabhipur police station, PSI Thaker, SHO of Umrala and PSI K K Desai, II PSI Botad police station were summoned to help with the investigation. After conferring with all concerned, the following plan of action was decided upon:

1. CPI Patel and his team were deputed to visit Surendranagar where it was reported that a gang of *baurias,* also known as *'bawarias',* were located residing in small hamlets called a *danga*.

As noted earlier, they engaged only in house burglary and cattle-stealing at night. They are expert at wrenching jewellery off the persons of sleeping women. He was also directed to cover the suggestions received from DMOB concerning Wadhwan in Surendranagar district and Viramgam in Ahmedabad district. The *bhats* were still on the radar, and I asked Patel to tackle them again, having formed an impression that a thorough job was not done during the previous visit to Ranpur.

These instructions were intended to suggest only that they were professional criminals, and it did not ignore the fact that they differed from each other in the specialisation of their criminal activities, their modus operandi, in their codes of conduct, and in modes of signs which they used to carry out their nefarious activities.

2. It was learnt that ten days prior to the occurrence of crime under investigation, some *bawas*, travelling on elephants were roaming in the area. The word "bawa" denotes a person who has chosen active and public practice of religion as a way of life and are often seen on the temple premises or travelling from one part of the province to the other part. They are usually dressed in saffron coloured clothes with their long hair matted and tied on or at the back of their head. It was not unknown for criminals to take this disguise when conducting a survey for their future depredations. PSI Khunti with his men were deputed to locate them. Ground enquiries revealed that they were travelling towards Jasdan, a town in Rajkot district, and Khunti was also directed to tackle the suggestions received from DMOB and residing in that area.

3. Inquiries had revealed that one Ambassador car bearing registration No. GTB 8586 was parked during the night of the

crime at the Vakil Petrol Pump, a prominent fuelling station in the town. However, it departed in the morning without taking any fuel. Since this appeared suspicious, HC K K Vala was deputed to pursue this line.

4. PSI K K Desai and his team were instructed to proceed to Bhavnagar and visit the district jail to speak with some of the inmates who were under trial prisoners and who had been arrested for property crimes. He was also directed to visit the DMOB and the Local Crime Branch and explore possibilities of seeking further information and support.

5. I decided to proceed, along with the investigating officer PSI Vasava, to Amreli district for conducting suitable enquiries, in particular checking the hamlets of *bauriyas,* at Kodinar. The task of locating and questioning suspects whose names were received from the DMOB of this district was also on the agenda.

After another night-halt at Botad and before departing for Amreli, I ensured the preparation of "Hue and Cry" notices to be sent to several police stations notifying the occurrence of the crime. When dacoities, serious robberies, or house-breakings take place in the jurisdiction of a police station, that police station should promptly apprise its neighbouring police stations of such occurrences. In common law, a hue and cry is a process by which bystanders are summoned to assist in the apprehension of a criminal who has been witnessed in the act of committing a crime. The terminology owes its origin to the Statute of Winchester of 1285, which provided that anyone, either a constable or a private citizen, who witnessed a crime shall make hue and cry, and that the hue and cry must be kept up against the fleeing criminal from town to town and from county to county, until the felon is apprehended and delivered to the sheriff. All able-bodied men, upon hearing the shouts, were obliged to assist in the pursuit of the criminal. In the event, the notices were sent to the following police stations, located in the districts of Ahmedabad, Amreli, Bhavnagar, Rajkot and Surendranagar:

'A' Div. Bhavnagar, 'B' Div. Bhavnagar, 'C' Div. Bhavnagar, Amreli City, Barwala, Dhandhuka, Gadhada, Gariyadhar, Gogha, Jasdan, Joravarnagar, Lathi, Limdi, Mahuva, Palitana Rural, Palitana Town, Paliyad, Ranpur, Rajula, Savarkundla, Songadh, Surendranagar, Talaja, Vallabhipur, Vellavadar Bhal, Vinchiya, Wartej.

Thereafter along with Vasava, proceeded to Amreli, a district headquarter town located 112 km away. At the SP's office met PSI Local Crime Branch (LCB). A word about this branch. In order to devote sustained attention and effort to the investigation of important cases and those, in particular, in which the activities of local criminals extend over more than one police station and in order to collect, collate and examine information regarding crime and criminals in the district, a sort of miniature CID known as the Local Crime Branch has been established in districts under the direct control of the district Superintendent of Police. The staff ordinarily consists of a sub-inspector and the necessary number of head constables and constables. During the meeting, details of local criminals of the district who followed identical modus operandi was ascertained. In addition, the PSI furnished a list of 103 Bauriyas and confirmed their location at Kodinar, a town located at a distance of 132 km, near the seacoast. HC Mansingh of the Amreli LCB, a seasoned policeman possessing extensive knowledge of this particular community known for criminal tendencies, was taken on board for further investigation.

R D Tamhane was the district police chief, and I paid a courtesy call on him at his residence. He was 12 years my senior in the IPS and was happy to see the effort that was being put in for detecting a house-breaking by the neighbouring district police. He also appeared to be intrigued to see a directly recruited ASP visiting him in what was then a remote part of Saurashtra. It was winter and as we sat in the outer living room, I remember him sending for his wife and pointing a finger at me, said- "Look, ASP".

Enroute to Kodinar, I stopped at Dhari to take along with me Chitranjan Singh my batchmate who was the SDPO of that subdivision. We reached at about 5 PM and with the help of officers and staff of Kodinar police station, surrounded and raided the *danga* of the *bauriyas*. All the houses were searched, however nothing incriminating was found. We segregated twelve *bauriyas* for detailed questioning and during interrogation it transpired that HC Shivshankar who had accompanied us from Botad, recognised one amongst these twelve persons, namely, Ramprasad Krishna. The HC revealed that a few days prior to the temple theft, during his night-round he had encountered Ramprasad near the Botad Railway Station. After making due enquiries with him, he had escorted him to a *dharamshala*- a building devoted to religious or charitable purposes, especially a rest house for travellers, and asked him to sleep there. Ramprasad however denied this and offered to come to Botad with the police for identification purposes so that the manager of the dharamshala could see him and conclude either way. His father,

Kisan, who was also amongst the twelve people detained, offered to accompany his son.

It was late in the night by the time we finished speaking with each suspect and therefore decided to spend the night at Kodinar. The proximity with hills on the north and sea on the south of the town made the sojourn a pleasant one, a much-needed respite from the rigours of a vigorous investigation.

Nanji Raiya's name figured in the list provided by DMOB. In any case he was a known criminal of the area, and the Kodinar police station staff were familiar with him. The following morning, he was called in for questioning but denied any involvement stating that he had given up criminal activities long back and was now earning his livelihood by working as a casual labourer. Interestingly, his brother, Jiva Raiya along with son Babu also figured on the suspect list. Nanji claimed that he had not been in touch with his brother for a long time. Locating Jiva was important as he was known to have committed temple thefts in the past. Therefore, I proceeded to Una police station and discovered that Jiva had recently been arrested under section 122 of the Bombay Police Act, and having admitted his guilt, he was convicted to four days of simple imprisonment and released about two weeks ago. This section concerns the preventive powers of the police. If any person is found under suspicious circumstances between sunset and sunrise armed with any dangerous instrument with intent to commit an offence, or having his face covered or otherwise disguised with intent to commit an offence, or in any dwelling-house, building, on board any vessel or boat without being able satisfactorily to account for his presence there, he can be arrested without a warrant. Preventive action is an important duty, and in this connection, special attention and efforts must be directed towards resident criminals, wandering gangs, professional criminals, and receivers of stolen property.

Jiva, upon his release, had given village Uchaiyya as his address, and along with Vasava, I proceeded to question him there. However, some 3 km distance from the village, it was not possible for the vehicle to proceed because of waterlogging and therefore we walked that distance. Unfortunately, neither Jiva nor his son were found at their home in the village and inquiries revealed that the son has not been seen for the last six months.

My next destination was Savarkundla, a town located 84 km away and where Lohana Jayantilal Laxmilal, a suspect lived. We arrived at his house only to find him missing. The local police constable who handled DMOB duties revealed that the former was not in a fit mental condition and was often found roaming aimlessly in various parts of the town. I then proceeded to Mahuva, a subdivisional headquarter, 65 km away and located Natwar Magan, a DMOB suspect. Questioning him from various angles ruled out his involvement in the crime. One Praduman Nanjee, another suspect also lived in the same town, but he was not found. His father revealed that he now worked as a farm labourer at village Vavdi under Bagdana police station. Scanning the likely suspects is usually an important function in an undetected property crime. Since an SDPO is the supervisory and not the investigating officer, I wanted to ensure effective compliance before I completed the visitation, which in case of an undetected crime, would last five days. We therefore proceeded towards Talaja, a town located 50 km away, to make enquiries about a few *bhat* women who had been previously arrested there for house-breaking. On the way, I stopped at village Badrada to locate Popat Jatashankar, another suspect, but was informed by his brother that he was away at Surat. At Talaja, we found the bhat women, but their interrogation in the presence of a lady police constable did not yield anything worthwhile.

In pursuing my supervisory functions for tracing this offence, I had hardly been able to pay any attention to other aspects of the same role pertaining to rest of the subdivision. On two occasions during the last four days, a constable had arrived from Palitana carrying mail that had been received in my office and although I had cursorily glanced through them, they needed to be attended to with more diligence. Ideally one was expected to camp at Talaja for the night but as my headquarter town was only 41 km away, I decided to proceed there.

Next day, Monday, I attended to the work in the office that had piled up in the last four days. Case diaries of other serious offences had to be scrutinised, crime registers to be written up, and weekly diaries and crime memos had to be updated and submitted to superior authorities. While I attended to these duties, PSI Vasava proceeded to locate one Pragji Hira Koli, a notorious house-breaker whose name also figured on the suspect list provided by the DMOB. The latter had no information on the temple theft at Botad. His house was searched and nothing incriminating was found. Vasava however found out that one Chaggan Saifa, a known criminal who specialised in house-breakings resided at village Rajpara, under Bodana Nes out-post of Palitana Rural police station. The PSI reached that village but could not find him. He was informed that Chaggan had gone out for fishing about a week ago. A useful bit of information he brought pertained to Jiva Raiya of Uchaiyya village whom we had attempted to trace two days ago. According to Vasava, the latter often came to visit Chaggan at Rajpara village. I suggested that we check the village after nightfall, as often known criminals on the suspect list of the police stay out of their homes during the day, to avoid what they consider unnecessary harassment. That night at 10 PM, Vasava and I left for Rajpara and reached Chaggan's home. He was not found although we were able to speak with his son-in-law, Bhagwan Punja. We returned to Palitana shortly after midnight.

I had developed the practice, that whenever I was up and about late in the night attending to my official duties, I would check men during night-rounds. This is what I did on reaching Palitana and found that all, excepting one police constable, were present. Early that morning I departed for Botad.

At Botad, I took stock of the work done by the other teams that had been despatched with specific tasks.

1. CPI Patel was back after attending to the task assigned to him and he reported that he had visited Muli police station of Surendranagar district and made enquiries. He found one Megha Bhima, a DMOB suspect and questioned him in detail. He next proceeded to Surendranagar and met the SDPO of that division and briefed him about the temple theft at Botad. Patel, on the suggestion of the latter, also checked the railway station in the town, in particular hutments located in the vicinity. The CPI travelled to Joravarnagar police station and then proceeded to Wadhwan police station where he was able to locate one Bipin Sathwara, a suspect on the DMOB

list. A search of the latter's house and his detailed questioning yielded nothing worthwhile. His next port of call was Limbdi police station where too his inquiries did not yield any result. Patel, on the way to Ranpur, stopped at Dhandhuka police station and made suitable enquiries. At Ranpur, he tried to locate a criminal known to commit crime against property, one Deopuri Shankar, but could not trace him. However, while checking on the *bhats*, he was able to locate two individuals, Agru Amra and Bhupat Keshu and questioned them in detail.

2. PSI Khunti, who was tasked to locate the *bawas* travelling on elephants seen in Botad on the day before the night when the offence was committed, reported that they had come from Jagannath temple in Ahmedabad and were legitimate travellers. This information was correct. The temple located in the Jamalpur locality of the city was established about 450 years ago. It is famous for its annual chariot festival, the Rath Yatra, which is the third most important and largest after the Ratha Yatra at Puri. Several elephants are to be seen on the premises of the temple.

3. PSI K K Desai reported that he had gone to Talaja and had interrogated the *bhats* but nothing useful was forthcoming.

4. HC K K Vala was able to partially get some information about the car bearing registration No. GTB 8586, that it did not belong to anybody in Bhavnagar and had come from Vadodara.

In addition to the work enumerated above, between us we had interrogated 37 *wagharies* at Kotada, Kutiyana, Dhandhuka, Vinchiya, Savarkundla, Chuda, and Khas. Unfortunately, these efforts also did not yield any result. Despite being on the job for six days we had not been able to detect the offence. I revisited the scene of crime and spoke again to the witnesses who had already been questioned on the first day to check if we had missed out on anything critical.

By far the most important of the duty of a police officer is to obtain, to the best of his ability, intelligence concerning the commission of cognizable offences or designs to commit such offences, and to take such other steps, consistent with law and with the orders of his superiors as shall be calculated to bring offenders to justice or to prevent the commission of offence. The importance attached to the detection of property crime in those days can be gauged from the extant instructions concerning house-breakings. In 1959, a circular was issued by the IGP directing that a man with three convictions, anyone of which was for house-breaking, should be visited not less than once a week, and that such visits should often be made at night. In addition to the Surveillance Register discussed above, names of all known or those who are likely to revert to crime and whose name did not figure in the former, are entered in the Known Criminals Register. Those who qualified to find mention included thieves, robbers, dacoits and house-breakers, the difference being that whereas a criminal required three convictions for theft to find his name in this register, for all the remaining three categories, one conviction was sufficient. All house-breakings by *rumali* or *kham-nakab*, *bagli* or gimlet and window bar wrenching or bending methods had to be investigated by the SHO himself rather than by a head constable or any other subordinate. Police stations were expected to maintain maps showing the locations of house-breakings. While writing the cognizable crime register, SDPO's were expected to specifically mention the offender's modus operandi. Further, they were required to prepare and submit to the DIG CID, along with copies of their weekly diaries, week by week, a crime statement, giving details of all house-breakings with thefts involving loss of property worth Rs. 1,000 or more.

Details narrated above would give a glimpse of the effort and teamwork brought to bear for tracing property crimes in those days. On the seventh day, after a night halt at Botad, I concluded visitation. Before doing that, I perused the case diaries written by the investigating officer and went through the case papers to ensure that all the statements and the *panchnama*s had been properly documented. Thirty-two years later, in 2012, I could not help but get a sense of déjà vu when I came across a news item that thieves had targeted a Jain *derasar* (temple) in Botad town and decamped with ornaments worth Rs 8,87000. According to police complaint filed in this regard, the thieves took away gold, silver, and diamond jewellery from the temple by breaking the locks and entering the area where jewellery was placed on the idols. The only difference between then and now, is the presence of CCTV cameras and three security guards.

CHAPTER 21

# INFIDELITY

*I*nfidelity, which is being unfaithful in marriage or a relationship, is a violation of a couple's emotional or sexual exclusivity that commonly results in feelings of anger, sexual jealousy, and rivalry. It has existed since times immemorial, and one of the well-known examples often cited, in the ancient Roman tradition, is that of Vulcan discovering his wife, Venus, having an affair with Mars.

Back in Palitana, the weather in March that year in 1980 was salubrious, and having completed a year in independent charge as a sub-divisional police officer, I had acquired a fair degree of grip on the nuances and modalities of a supervisory officer. Understandably, there was an aura of confidence and well-being. That week, I was simultaneously supervising two special report crimes, both registered with Palitana Town police station. One pertained to a twenty-two-year-old married woman who had filed a complaint that she was poisoned by her husband and his mother. The marriage had been solemnized two years earlier, but she had come to live with her husband and his parents about two months ago. Not happy with the situation in that household, she alleged that her husband had stuffed her mouth with a cloth while his mother attempted to feed her poison. The contradiction was apparent, and it was classified as a false complaint. The other visitation pertained to a gentleman from Mumbai who accompanied by his wife and two nephews had come to Palitana for pilgrimage purposes. They had taken two rooms in the Himmat Vihar Jain dharmshala and proceeded up the Shatrunjaya hills to pray at the world-famous Jain temples. About 2 km to the south of Palitana town are twin hilltops with a saddle-like valley and a peak height of about six hundred meters. These are the Palitana hills, historically called the Shatrunjaya hills. The word Shatrunjaya is interpreted as "the hill which conquers enemies". In their absence however, the locked latch had been broken open and cash, gold, and a tape recorder, all estimated at ₹ 5000, had been stolen. This was a case of house-breaking by day.

The district police control room informed me that I was required to visit two more special report crimes which had been registered the previous day at Sihor police station. One was a case of homicide where the aggrieved husband had attempted to kill two individuals who he suspected to have an illicit relation with his wife. One of the two having died, an offence of murder had been registered. The accused Vrajlal Barot was thirty-two years old, and originally belonged to the village Kakidi of Mahuva taluka. For the last two years he had been working as a hired labourer on the farmland belonging to one Ramniklal Vora, generally known as Ramnikbhai Sheth. The latter was a well-to-do person and about three months ago had helped Barot in getting married to one Malini Ruparel (name changed). This lady had been married earlier but was now divorced. From the previous marriage, she had a son and a daughter and, as a part of the divorce settlement, the son was handed over to the previous husband whereas the daughter remained with her. It was second marriage for the Barot as well, who had been convicted earlier to life imprisonment for killing his first wife as he had suspected her fidelity. Having served his term for twelve years and six months, he was released on Gandhi Jayanti as his conduct was rated by the correctional administration as being good.

On arrival at Sihor, I was met by PSI T M Khambholja. He was the complainant in this case, having filed the FIR on behalf of the state. This is normally done when a cognizable crime has been committed and the Police Station Officer either suspects the commission of an offence or has witnessed the commission thereof, but nobody comes forward to file a complaint. In this case there should not have been any difficulty for a relative or a friend coming forth but perhaps given the shock that pervaded after the commission of the crime in full public view, Khambholja must have decided to get the offence registered immediately, lest the late registration of the same should afford the accused person any legal ground of defense.

Barot and his wife Malini along with the latter's daughter from the previous marriage, lived in a hut located in one corner of the farmhouse. While the former worked on the farm, the wife attended to domestic duties within the house. The owner Ramniklal would visit frequently along with a friend of his, Bachubhai Chhantbar. Over a period of time, Barot began to resent their familiarity with his wife and would often rebuke the latter asking her to keep her distance. It transpired that Malini paid little heed to his admonitions and the accused began to suspect an illicit relation between his wife and the owner as well as Bachubhai. The situation deteriorated to such an extent that Barot would beat up his wife. Malini was ignorant about the previous conviction of her husband, a fact that was now conveyed to her by the owner Ramniklal. This revelation upset her considerably and she did not want to live with him anymore. Seven days before the commission of the crime, she along with her daughter left for Porbandar to live with an aunt by the way of a temporary arrangement. Her departure was not known to Barot who began to suspect that she had been moved to some other location by Ramniklal and Bachubhai. Consequently, he began to pester the owner to reveal her location. Ramniklal dismissed him from service and asked him to vacate the premises provided to him when he accepted employment.

Along with the PSI Khambholja, I proceeded to the scene of offence. It was in the *bazaar* which was quite a crowded place. There was a road which ran in the north-south direction while an alley ran in the east-west direction, making an intersection. Nearby on the east side of the road was a cinema and several shops were located on either side of the tar road. A *panchnama* of the scene of offence had already been drawn up and I verified it for accuracy. Next, I met Bhola Bhoga Rabari who owned a tea stall near the scene of offence. Along with this witness, I also examined Narendra Pathak, who owned Prakash *Paan* House. Betel leaves or *paan* form an important part of Indian culture and offering them to guests is a sign of hospitality. All cities and towns in India have outlets where *paan* is available and is quite in demand. It reportedly ends up cleansing the body since the leaves are known to flush out toxins from the internal organs, and boosts metabolism.

On the day of the incident, Barot came to Sihor around 5 PM. He was seething with anger and apparently had lost all sense of proportion in grasping the enormity of what he was about to do. He was carrying a knife. Around 9 PM, he saw Ramniklal accompanied by Bachubhai coming in a car to the bazaar. The former got down near the Prakash *Paan* House even as the latter drove the car into the alley for parking it there. Barot accosted Ramniklal who was in the process of procuring a *paan* and once again asked him about the whereabouts of his wife. On receiving a rude and indifferent reply, the accused whipped out his knife and delivered four blows to this person whom he now perceived to be a tormentor. Standing near the *paan* shop was Nakul Ramsingh, who on witnessing the assault, leapt forward to pull away the accused. As Ramniklal collapsed, Barot ran towards the alley where Bachubhai was parking the car. As the latter turned, after locking the car, to walk towards the main road, Barot stabbed him repeatedly and then fled from the scene of offence.

In the meantime, Nakul displayed extraordinary bravery and started chasing the accused who entered a house in *rabari vaas*, a residential locality predominantly consisting of those who belonged to the Rabari caste and hid himself below a cot. More than two hundred persons collected outside the house, their intention being to lynch the accused. However, Rabari Devshibhai Merabhai who lived there kept them at bay and sent for the police. Barot was apprehended and taken to the police station. Bachubhai, who had sustained serious injuries, died on the spot whereas Ramniklal was dispatched in an ambulance to Sir Takhatsinh General Hospital in Bhavnagar.

The assault on the deceased in the alley was witnessed by Rehmatben Allahrakha and I spoke with her to verify her statement which already had been recorded by the PSI. She was sitting on a cot outside and saw Barot run past her towards the deceased. This witness also knew that the accused was in the employ of Ramniklal. Similarly, the crime was also witnessed by Dolatben Ghulam Hussain who was looking out of the window of the first-floor bedroom of her house located in the alley.

The wife of the accused, Malini, was required to be questioned in order to firmly establish the motive of the crime. While nobody was able to indicate where she was located, it was suggested that she could have found refuge at Gautameshwar Mahadev Temple, a well-known place of pilgrimage in Sihor. However, inquiries established that she was not available there. The next important witness to be questioned was Ramniklal and I proceeded to Bhavnagar to speak with him. The medical officer on duty reported that the latter was in a serious condition. In that event, it was important to record his dying declaration as soon as he was in position to speak, and I arranged for an executive magistrate to be available. Later that evening, Ramniklal's statement was recorded, and he corroborated what the investigation had revealed so far. Nakul, the witness who had tried to apprehend the accused at significant risk to his personal safety, was also admitted to the same hospital, having suffered injuries during the scuffle. I examined him and he confirmed the details narrated above. On completion of this work, I returned to Sihor and interrogated the accused. He confessed to the crime and blamed both the deceased as well as Ramniklal for his marital problems. A formal communication was sent to JMFC Palitana to record a confession of the accused under section 164 CrPC.

That evening I reflected on the dramatis personae involved. The accused belonged to the Barot community which neither has martial traditions nor is known for violence. They traditionally worked as historians, genealogists, and mythographers, and are also known as "vahivancha barots". The word *vahivancha* literally means "one who reads a vahi". *Vahi* means a ledger or a book in general. The vahivanchas traditionally maintained genealogies, told stories and recited bardic poetry. The term "Barot" was originally used as an honorific title for vahivanchas and was gradually adopted as a caste appellation. His wife Malini was a *lohana*[1] which is essentially a trading and a mercantile community. They are found in large numbers in Gujarat, mostly in Saurashtra, Kachcch, Ahmedabad and Vadodara. Many are also settled in Maharashtra in Mumbai, Mulund, Pune, and Nagpur. Lohanas claim to be descendants of Lav, son of Bhagwan Ram, and thus their lineage is the Raghuvanshi dynasty. Ramniklal was a *vaniya (bania)*, an upper caste community known for their prowess in business, banking, and commercial matters. As per the societal rules in practice there was absolutely no scope for social interaction amongst them. And yet lust is a powerful emotion which influences human behaviour. Often the consequences are violently disastrous.

The following day, inquiries were made about Malini but strangely, nobody could say anything about her whereabouts. Inquiries were made at the Tapibai Mahila Vikas Gruh at Bhavnagar but to no avail. This was a non-profit organization that operated independently of the government, to address social or economic issues of destitute women. The institution was known to take in women who had nowhere to go. By evening, however information was received that Malini and her daughter were in Porbander. I also visited the farmhouse of Ramnik Sheth and discovered an unlicensed .32 caliber revolver. In the result, an offence under section 25 (1) of the Arms Act was registered in this regard.

Studies have since found that men are more likely to engage in extramarital sex if they are unsatisfied sexually, while women are more likely to engage in extramarital sex if they are unsatisfied emotionally. However, no such sophisticated understanding existed in those days, and it was assumed that the wife was impressed by the affluence of the owner and his deceased friend. What constitutes infidelity depends on expectations within the relationship. In marital relationships, exclusivity is commonly assumed. Infidelity can cause psychological damage, including feelings of rage and betrayal, low sexual and personal confidence, and even post-traumatic stress disorder. Barot must have felt exploited, and even cheated, as he was known to work diligently on the farm. Jealousy is an emotion that can elicit strong responses. Cases have been commonly documented where sexual jealousy was a direct cause of murders. People of all genders can experience social consequences if their act of infidelity becomes public, but the form and extent of these consequences often depends on the gender of the unfaithful person. The abrupt and callous responses to his queries regarding the whereabouts of his wife unleashed in him uncontrollable rage. It is not often that a low paid employee decides to murder his master as the accused did in this case. PSI Khambholja must have realised the impact of such a happening on the local area and therefore instead of waiting for any relative of the deceased or Ramnikbhai Sheth to come forward to file a complaint, he decided to do so himself on behalf of the state.

Here was a unique case where a husband killed his first wife suspecting infidelity on her part and then, after he marries again, kills the paramour of his second wife.

The arrest of the accused from *rabari vaas* after the commission of the offence had to be properly documented and therefore the statements of Rabari Devshibhai, from whose house he was picked up and that of Rabari Bababhai Virabhai, who was present there at that time, were recorded. So far, the vital ingredients required to secure a conviction had either been gathered or the process was set in motion for acquiring the same. This in effect achieved the objective of a visitation by a supervisory rank and I therefore decided to conclude the visitation. The investigating officer was given a set of directions for scrupulous and immediate compliance, amongst them being recording the statement of Malini and to obtain record of the previous conviction of the accused for inclusion in the charge-sheet to be filed in a court of competent jurisdiction.

Two months later I was to visit another such case in which a 20-year-old young married woman had committed suicide by throwing herself in front of a passing train, along with her three-year-old son. Infidelity can also provoke unreasonable behavioural patterns either because of a sense of remorse or because the person concerned has nowhere to go, given the societal stigma attached to it. The lady in question Savitaben (name changed) resided at her parental home at Savarkundla, a taluka town in Bhavnagar district. All of sixteen years old, there she met Bhikhalal Mohanlal, a *koli* by caste and fell in love with him. The parents and members of the family were averse to such a union and therefore she eloped with the latter to Dhola, an out-post of Umrala police station and a railway junction. Bhikahlal found employment in a diamond polishing factory, acquired a rented accommodation near the railway station, the couple got married and a year later their son was born who they named Dipak. About six months prior to the incident, the factory closed and the husband had no option but to accept employment as a casual labourer at Dhasa, a flourishing village located 30 km away. Savita stayed back at Dhola with their son. The husband sometimes would return after four or five days because the nature of his employment on the agricultural land required continuous work and constant vigil.

In many parts of Gujarat in those days, there was a shortage of drinking water and although wells were available in the village, the people living near a public utility visited it to fetch water. This is what Savita used to do. She would go to the railway platform with an earthen pot to fetch water. There was another reason also. Trains were pulled by steam engines then, and often, the engine driver would throw out some lumps or pieces of coal, by the way of being helpful, which was then taken home by women living in the surrounding area of a railway station or a railway crossing for the purpose of using it as a fuel to cook food. During such visits, she met Kanaiyalal Vanmalidas, a railway employee who operated the signals. He had a glad eye, and soon developed a special interest in Savita. It appears that the long absences of her husband facilitated similar interest in the latter, which then took the form of an extramarital relationship. Kanaiyalal would ensure that she was not wanting in the supply of drinking water or coal, illegally provided of course. Savita also began to take the initiative of informing her paramour about the departure of her husband when she came to the railway station. In rural India, visits by a male member of the community, in the absence of the husband to a married woman is socially not allowed. Therefore, even though both resorted to certain subterfuges to conceal the reason for Kanaiyalal's visit to the residence of the lady, this soon became public knowledge. Bhikhalal also heard about it and confronted his wife. After the usual denials and realising that her relationship with another man was more widely known than she had imagined, she confessed to the same and pleaded to be forgiven. The husband on the other hand, as I discovered when I questioned him, had held back the confrontation fearing in the deep recesses of his mind that it might be true. However, once the unfortunate fact came out, he decided to leave home. On the day of the incident, Bhikhalal told Savita that he was going to Dhasa to look for rented accommodation for himself and that she was free to go wherever she desired. The latter pleaded with him not to do so. She had nowhere to go, having cut-off all relations with her parents after she married Bhikhalal against their wishes. He conveyed that he did not want to have anything to do with her. After the departure of the husband, Savita picked up her three-year-old old boy, proceeded to the railway track and as the 24 Down Somnath Mail coming from Ahmedabad arrived, she flung herself along with her child in front of the train.

A special report about the above suicide-cum-murder was received by me at Palitana where I was already visiting a case of dacoity with murder registered with Palitana Rural police station. One of the longest visitations undertaken, I had been on the job for the last fourteen days, two accused had been arrested and we were on the lookout for the remaining culprits. I therefore concluded the visitation in order to proceed to Umrala. Even as I was about to leave, I was advised by district police control room at Bhavnagar that I also had to supervise a murder case previously registered with Paliyad police station. As the distance between Umrala and Paliyad is 73 km, there seemed to be a mistake in the instructions conveyed. Nevertheless, giving priority to a homicide over a suicide, I headed for Paliyad. However, after travelling 110 km to that town, I was informed that the visitation of that case had been handed over to CPI C K Jha. Shortly before midnight, I arrived at Umrala and camped there for the night.

The following day I began my work by visiting the scene of the crime. Blood stains, broken bangles and torn pieces of sari could be seen lying around. The investigating officer, as usual, had already drawn the *panchnama* of the scene of offence, recording the places where the severed heads of both the mother and son were found. Savita had chosen a place which was between a stone marked 1/10, located next to the railway track about 1 km from Dhola railway station and Jaliya Railway Station. The complaint had been filed by Ratilal Vaja, the Station Master, and I spoke to him to ascertain more details. He revealed that the engine driver had seen the deceased throwing herself on the railway track along with the son, and therefore the train had halted briefly. It thereafter proceeded to Jaliya Railway Station and although there was no scheduled halt, it stopped there to enable the Guard of the train to give a memo to the station master over there. The latter in turn, informed PSI Dhola Railway Station, who first having registered an offence under section 302, 309 IPC, later transferred the case to Umrala police station as the scene of crime fell within the jurisdiction of the latter.

I discussed the application of the law with SHO Umrala. There was no confusion in my mind about the application of section 302 which was regarding murder. The deceased had caused the death of her son so this provision of law was applicable although it is open to debate whether a more appropriate provision could have been section 304 which is culpable homicide not amounting to murder. In fact, the definition of both culpable homicide and murder contained in the IPC is both complex and subtle. One of the best distinctions came in a 1932 judgement of Bombay High Court delivered by Justice Melvill in the Govinda case. Since the decision rested on the knowledge that the act is likely to cause death against the knowledge that the act is so imminently dangerous and that it must, in all probability, cause death, and since Savita knew that her son will die, a charge of murder against her was appropriately made out.

But I was not sure how section 309 which dealt with attempt to commit suicide was applicable. In this case the attempt had succeeded, and the person had died. To my mind this section was not relevant. I used to carry with me a copy of Indian Penal Code authored by Ratanlal and Dhirajlal. I consulted the same and was even more convinced about the correctness of my understanding. Nevertheless, the practice was to apply that section as well, on the specious ground that the attempt had preceded death. It appears that nobody, including the office of the Superintendent of Police, found anything wrong with the procedure, and I was too new to the system and lacking in experience to attempt any changes. In any case, at the end of the investigation, police would be submitting a closure report known as the Final Report, as the accused had died.

Speaking with the husband Bhikhalal was not a pleasant experience. He understandably looked distressed, partly I presume for the loss of his wife and son in this manner and partly from a sense of remorse regarding the manner in which he had handled the situation. He was a slim, tall person, law abiding by nature and must have found it difficult to come to terms with his wife's infidelity. During questioning, he admitted that he had become violent and beaten her and had also abused her. He, however, never expected her to take this extreme step. I also questioned the paramour Kanaiyalal who admitted to having entered into a relationship with the deceased. That apart, his demeanour indicated that he was least bothered.

Not a single person in the village or in the neighbourhood claimed any knowledge about the alleged extramarital affair, although they were the ones who had alerted the husband. On the contrary most said that there was no discord between the husband and wife. I had dispatched the investigating officer to Savarkundla to meet with the parental family members of the deceased. He questioned her two brothers who simply stated that because their sister had developed "illicit relations" with Bhikhalal and had eloped, they had never made any attempt to connect with her. Similarly, the husband's parents were also contacted who said that they were not in contact with their son for the last three years.

It was thus a case of murder and suicide. There was nothing much to be done accepting recording the statement of the Station Master at Jaliya Railway Station and scrutinising the post-mortem report. The document brutally declared that Savitaben died "because of the cutting apart of the torso from the head." Similar finding was recorded for the young child.

On conclusion of the visitation, as I began my return journey to Palitana, the plot of Leo Tolstoy's Anna Karenina, a book which I had read earlier, came to my mind. The novel begins with Anna as the faithful wife of the stiff, unromantic, but otherwise decent government minister Aleksei Karenin with whom she has a son, Seryozha. But Anna, who imagines herself as the heroine of a romantic novel, allows herself to fall in love with an officer, Aleksei Vronsky. Schooling herself to see only the worst in her husband, she eventually leaves him and her son to live with Vronsky. There is an inevitability about the tragic fate that hangs over the adulterous love of Anna and Vronsky. Anna pays not so much because she transgresses the moral code but because she refuses to observe the proprieties customarily exacted in such liaisons by the hypocritical high society to which she belongs. As the novel progresses, Anna, who suffers pangs of conscience for abandoning her husband and child, develops a habit of lying to herself until she reaches a state of near madness and total separation from reality. She commits suicide by throwing herself under a train. The realization that her understanding of life was far from reality, comes to her only when she is lying on the track, and it is too late to save herself.

CHAPTER 22

# THE OFFENCE OF HOUSE-BREAKING

*O*ne crime that concerns the common citizen most often is the offence of house-breaking. The frequency, effort, and difficulty of controlling this crime places a great demand on the police. In the earlier times, one of the yardsticks of police performance based on yearly statistical data was the occurrence and detection of this particular crime. In the 1970s, it was generally believed that 20% to 30% detection was good enough as that was the annual average everywhere. It was never expected though that no house-breakings would occur in any given police district. What was reasonable however was to expect sincere efforts in tracing the criminal gangs that went about this business in a professional manner.

Property crime in the Indian Penal Code have been dealt with in a scientific manner in chapter XVII. The categories listed there include theft, extortion, robbery, dacoity, misappropriation of property, criminal breach of trust, cheating, receiving stolen property, mischief, and criminal trespass. Having earlier read Erle

Stanley Gardner, the American lawyer and author, best known for the Perry Mason series of detective stories, I had come across terms like burglary, larceny, and felony. According to the English law, burglary is feloniously breaking into or out of a dwelling house during the night, while house-breaking is feloniously breaking into any house or outhouse during the day as well as the night. The word burglary has not been used in the IPC. As a young officer trying to grasp the ingredients of the eighty-five sections contained in that chapter, I was confused why the category of mischief, which included killing or maiming animals or diverting water used for irrigation purposes, was included as a property crime. Similarly, the difference between criminal trespass and lurking house-trespass had to be ingested. However, as I began to grasp the scheme followed in the Code and implemented its substance practically on the ground, the logic became clear. The authors of the Code had observed:

> *"We have given the name of trespass to every usurpation, however slight, of dominion over property. We do not propose to make trespass, as such, an offence, except when it is committed in order to the commission of some offence injurious to some person interested in the property on which the trespass is committed, or for the purpose of causing annoyance to such a person. Even then we propose to visit it with a light punishment unless it be attended with aggravating circumstances."*

House-breaking has been defined in section 445 of the code in a detailed manner in six distinct categories. For example, if a person enters or quits a house or a dwelling by any passage which he knows to have been fastened against such entrance or departure, and the same is unfastened by that person, the offence is deemed to have been committed. So, it was not only about breaking a lock or wrenching open a door or window. This would show how much care was taken in drafting the law, which received the assent of the Governor General on 6th October 1860.

As mentioned earlier, Palitana is a major center of pilgrimage for the Jain community. Consequently, the area around the Shatrunjeya hills saw several dharamshalas coming up which provided decent accommodation at a reasonable cost to the pilgrims who came from all over India, and especially from states where the Jain community existed in large numbers. Anandji Kalyanji Trust[1], the largest and the oldest Jain trust, founded somewhere around 1787 AD, managed the temples. In addition, they owned guesthouses and hostel accommodation for the devout. The normal practice would be for the inmates to leave early in the morning, climb up the hill, a journey of about one hour, and return in the evening after having visited the temples and performed rituals that they chose to follow. Most of the house-breakings by day occurred during this time and the modus operandi was breaking open the lock of the front door. Sometimes, the inmates would be away for the whole night having decided to visit Talaja, a town located 54 km away. Here the Jain temple was established by Chalukya king Kumarpal during the 12th century and is considered a holy place of the Shatrunjay *panchteerth*, part of the Shatrunjay hills. These pilgrims became the victims of house-breakings by night. In those cases sometimes a window on the back side is wrenched open or a hole is made in the wall to gain entry.

In April 1980, there was a series of house-breakings which kept me immensely busy as all such crimes, with theft involving property of Rs. 5,000 or more, were a special report crime, visitable by the SDPO. Shantilal Rupchand Jain, a resident of Bombay as the metropolis was then called, had come to Palitana with his extended family on the occasion of *Akhatrij*. Also known as *Akha Teej*, it is an annual Hindu and Jain spring festival. It is considered auspicious in many regions of India and Nepal for new ventures, marriages, expensive investments such as in gold or property, and any new beginnings. Shantilal had booked with the Anand Bhuvan dharamshala and had occupied a big hall, a kitchen, and a storeroom. He had also brought along with him a cook. The hall was used for resting and sleeping purposes. One early morning at about 4 AM, one of the ladies of the family, Rasilaben, opened the store-room where luggage, condiments and food items were stored, for the purpose of preparing breakfast. On entering, she found that the room had been ransacked, clothes thrown here and there, and all the trunks and boxes opened. She raised an alarm and as others arrived, it was noticed that a window in the back wall had been wrenched open and beyond that a hole had been bored in the compound wall. This must have become necessary for the culprits to gain entry as the wall was quite high and contained a barbed steel wire fence on the top.

I visited the scene of crime and discovered that the culprits had stolen ₹ 7565/- worth of cash, clothes, and ornaments, and had also partaken of the sweetmeats kept in the storeroom. This indicated a cool-headed gang which was aware that the family was sleeping in the adjoining hall and yet had the audacity to not only steal but also find the time to consume food. They also must have quickly surveyed the property that they were about to decamp with and decided to discard all the clothes that they had initially taken. These were found outside the compound wall. The investigating officer, while drawing up the seizure *panchnama*, had placed their value at ₹ 5440/-. Questioning the members of the family including Shantilal on whose complaint an offence had been registered, revealed that the weather being warm, all had slept on cots outside in the open yard in the front, and not in the hall. Every dharamshala has a manager locally called *munim*. However, he and the watchman on duty could offer no clues nor did they report sighting any strangers near the dharamshala. The cook mentioned that he too had gotten up at 4 AM to prepare breakfast for everybody and entered the storeroom only after Rasilaben raised an alarm.

The modus operandi revealed the involvement of local *wagharies*. One of the prime suspects was Waghari Jora Jivraj and without loss of time, I decided to go with the police party headed by PSI Dave of Palitana Town police station, sent to locate the former at his house at Khodiar Gala, not far away from the town. He was not found, and therefore we went ahead to the *waghari vaas*, where some listed suspects resided. Although four whose names figured in the Known Criminals Register were found there, their examination did not lead to any worthwhile clue.

The following day I was back at the scene of offence looking for any clue that could give a direction to the investigation. It was important to establish whether the crime had been committed with skill and planning, or without such an attribute simply because the location offered that possibility. The latter is not difficult to recognise and whoever has visited several scenes of the offence of house-breaking, can soon tell whether the offence has been committed in a methodical manner or whether it was a hurried act. We had not yet been able to conclude about the kind of the implement used for the break-in, and this was important to address as that would point in the direction of a gang having similar modus operandi. While we were busy with this work and also interrogating the munim and his son who helped him with his duties, the dog squad arrived from Ahmedabad. The canine moved here and there, after having smelt certain objects in the storeroom, but to no avail.

In the afternoon, while still at the scene of the crime, I was informed about another house-breaking, this time by day, which had occurred that very day between 9 AM and 12 noon. This was certainly startling as the presence of the police, it seemed, had absolutely no effect on the criminals operating in that area. Since the place of offence was nearby, I proceeded there immediately.

A Nasik resident, Rameshbhai Vaniya, along with his family had come to Palitana for the purpose of pilgrimage around the middle of that month and had taken accommodation in Jain Harivihar dharamshala. They had occupied two rooms which were interconnected. When they were away, culprits obtained access by strongly pushing one of the doors which was latched from inside and which opened as the latches were not secured properly. Property worth ₹ 21,925/- was stolen including gold ornaments and cash. Munim of the dharamshala was informed after which they reported the matter to the police. This was a crime that had occurred only about two or three hours ago, and the dog squad was still with us, helping with the house-breaking at the Anand Bhuvan dharamshala. The scent of the criminals would be fresh, and it was hoped that the canine would be able to help us. Indeed, after sniffing around the scene of offence, it first led us to the office of the Anandji Kalyanji Trust and from there walked right up to the Chela Chakala gate. The canine did not go any further and it was left for us to guess where the culprit could have moved away. Since the canine had entered the premises of the Anandji Kalyanji Trust, a line-up of all its employees as also of the Jain Harivihar dharamshala was organised for being sniffed at, and hopefully identified by the dog squad, in case the culprit was amongst them. Unfortunately, this also did not yield any result.

Detailed questioning was done of every resident currently staying or working on the premises. Enquiries revealed the presence of a man who was about thirty years old, had a paunch, was slightly fat with dark hair and wearing a *kurta* and pyjama. He was noticed by a lady witness, Mohanbai Pukhraj, occupying an adjoining room. She had seen the person walking around the previous day as well as early that morning. The munim confirmed that no such person was a lodger at the dharamshala. The possibility of the suspect being still in Palitana was not ruled out and therefore not only a thorough checking was done at the State Transport bus depot but also checkpoints were put up on the road to Gariadhar, Bhavnagar, Gheti and Talaja. Buses were stopped and vigourous checking was done, much to the inconvenience of the innocent passengers travelling in them. A team was constituted headed by a head constable who was directed to visit every lodge and dharamshala in Palitana to locate the person matching the description. More men were requisitioned from neighbouring police stations, and they were given the task of checking the trains departing that evening from the railway station. Plainclothes men were detailed on the street to look out for the suspect.

Over the next three days, every person who was a history sheeter or whose name figured in the Known Criminal Register or about whom suggestions were received from the DMOB were located and interrogated. The geographical area that was covered for the purpose of this enquiries, keeping Palitana as the center point, covered a radius of 50 km and included the towns of Talaja, Songadh and Sihor. Specifically listed criminals from the *waghari* community were targeted and one Dharamshi Jeraj was now shortlisted as a likely offender. Although we were investigating two separate house-breakings each with a different modus operandi, it was decided to trace both categories of criminals simultaneously in the hope of at least succeeding in tracing one offence. It must be appreciated that the detection of such cases does not enthuse the police force and it is important for the supervisory officer to himself actively get involved in the effort that he is directing. Therefore, four teams were set up, one each headed by a PSI, one by the CPI and the fourth one by me. In those days there were no cell phones and even landline telephone services were limited to those towns where a telephone exchange was available. Therefore, the only alternative was to begin in the morning, travel, and work extensively during the day, questioning suspects, visiting villages, and then converging in the evening at Palitana for a review. As many as twenty-five suspects were found and thoroughly questioned but to no avail. Two men from the district LCB also joined the probe and they, along with plain-clothes men provided from the subdivision itself, were also asked to do intensive local enquiries.

Although members of those communities traditionally known to commit such crimes are the object of police investigation, individuals belonging to the so-called upper caste are not above suspicion as well. The Jains are known for affluence and prosperity and a pilgrimage center like Palitana was bound to attract a fair share of cheaters and fraudsters. In fact, the names of Jitendra Nanavaty, Vinod Shah and Dilip Shah were gleaned from the earlier records, and it was discovered that their last known location was in Ahmedabad and Surat. A communication was sent out to the Police Commissioner, Ahmedabad city and the Superintendent of Police, Surat, with a request to trace them and question them about their involvement, if at all. Look-out notices were also sent to several police stations within Bhavnagar district and Amreli district. Since a visitable offence is to be investigated by the SHO of the concerned police station, PSI Dave was investigating officer for both the house-breakings. I directed him to hand over the investigation of the Anand Bhuvan dharamshala to his second PSI, as in this case most of the stolen property had been recovered and instead focus on the Jain Harivihar dharamshala case. He was specifically tasked to find the suspect Dharamshi Jeraj and sent to Talaja for this purpose.

The DMOB has albums containing photographs of persons with previous criminal history in property crime. There is nothing mysterious or esoteric in the working of the bureau. It is simply a formation of properly indexed record of criminals previously arrested for crime against property, and arranged such that it is easily available to police officers "to catch thieves on paper". The principle on which such a record is framed is that it should serve a definite purpose and should not absorb more than a limited amount of the time of the police staff. Any tendency to magnify the importance or utility of the scheme is to be avoided if it is to be useful. I spoke with the Home Police Inspector, the supervisory officer of the bureau, requesting him to dispatch the albums by special messenger. It was hoped that such a scrutiny might perhaps confirm the involvement of a specific individual. However, the photographs were not to arrive until the following day, and in the meantime the lady witness had left for Ahmedabad to catch the night train to Mumbai. Another witness, Susheela, who appeared sharp enough to assist with such a scrutiny, was scheduled to leave in the evening, enroute to Madras. These were faraway places and missing such an opportunity would delay or even deny the possibility of detection. I therefore dispatched PSI Dave to proceed to Bhavnagar, collect the albums and then proceed directly to Ahmedabad to enable both the witnesses to peruse them before their departure.

On the fourth day, suspect Dharamshi Jeraj was traced to the state transport bus depot at Trapaj, an important village, 50 km from Palitana. A Jain temple, Mulnayak Shree Chintamani Parshwanath, is also located there. He was interrogated intensively, during which time he confessed to a house-breaking by night committed within the limits of Vallabhipur police station. However, regarding the house-breakings under investigation, he maintained deniability. In the meantime, those who frequented the dharamshala on a regular basis or lived around it, were also questioned. Of special interest was the washerman (*dhobi*), Vrajlal Nathubhai, who had unfettered access to the premises, going from room to room collecting and depositing clothes. He and similar tradespersons were questioned for any clue without any success.

The following day plainclothes men picked up one Koli Raisingh Amarsingh from near the Shetrunji Dam on suspicion. To my utter surprise, he revealed that the house-breaking at the Jain Harivihar dharamshala was committed by one Koli Chhagan Mohan, himself, and one another. When taken to the scene of the offence for him to show which room they had broken into, he was unable to do so, explaining that his role was to stand outside the premises and keep an eye while the other two accomplices went in. The suspect further revealed that they all belonged to Khambhat, a taluka headquarter town, 184 km away in Kheda district of central Gujarat. Of the descriptions that he provided of his two partners in crime, one matched with that provided by the lady witness Mohanbai Pukhraj. He further revealed that on arrival at Palitana, all three of them had stayed at the Sarvajanik dharamshala. It became necessary therefore to check the cash-book and register of that lodge but no entries were found matching their names. However, there was an entry in the name of one Shantilal Ishwarlal and two others with a Botad address. A telephone call was at once placed to PSI Botad police station to verify the antecedents of these persons. By evening, it was learned that both the names and the address were fake. The munims who are responsible for the day-to-day affairs of the dharamshala would have known from the demeanour of the suspects that the details such as name and address may not be genuine and yet there was little that they could do as in those days the concept of an identity card did not exist. It is also possible that the former were not interested in such details as their primary interest would be in letting out the rooms.

PSI Dave had returned from Ahmedabad after showing the photo albums. That effort did not yield any result. The following day he went ahead to Khambhat, along with Raisingh, to trace Koli Chhagan Mohan who was now the main suspect. He returned the following day to report that the suspect was found and questioned but did not seem to be involved. Dave further conveyed that during this journey Raisingh went back on his words saying that he had made up the story fearing physical intimidation from the police. Nevertheless, the formality of searching the houses of both the suspects was undertaken and nothing incriminating was found.

I had been visiting and supervising the investigation of this serious crime for six days now and we had not succeeded yet. As I was applying my mind to the next course of action, a special report arrived informing me of yet another house-breaking by day, a third one in fact in that week. The scene of offence this time was the Moti Sukhiya dharamshala, and the crime had occurred four days ago but reported only that morning. Kamlaben Mulchand, a resident of Indore had come to Palitana about a month ago. She was joined by her daughter and son-in-law from Surat. On the Monday of 21st April 1980, at 7 AM in the morning, the son-in-law Balindra Shah had left the dharamshala to climb up the sacred hills while Kamlaben accompanied by her daughter and two others had proceeded to Talaja to visit the temples there. When they returned at 6 PM in the evening, on entering their room, it was discovered that the suitcase was open and property consisting of cash, gold, and a watch worth Rs. 16,250/- had been stolen.

I visited the scene of offence. The family had in fact taken two rooms with a common bathroom in between. Adjoining the bathroom on one side was the kitchen with a low wall separating both. It appeared that the kitchen door which opens on the outside was left ajar by mistake and the culprits, having gained entry there, jumped over the wall into the bathroom and from there entered the bedroom. The suitcases from where property was stolen, were not locked. The complainant informed the munim who told them that it was not necessary to approach the police and that local enquiries would be made to recover their property. When even after four days nothing happened, Kamlaben lost patience and filed a complaint with Palitana Town police station. It transpired that the munim knew HC Bharatsinh Jashwantsinh Gohil, who was on the strength of the town police station and therefore sent word to him. The intention was to enlist his help and to solve the issue unofficially. The head constable questioned all the servants working on the premises, but nothing came of it. Normally, he should have reported this matter to the SHO so that an offence could be registered. He did not do so. Concealing a cognizable crime of this magnitude was a serious matter and hence an enquiry was ordered in this regard.

The investigating officer was PSI Parmar and along with him, I questioned as many as thirty persons. These included servants, employees, watchmen and support staff. None of them reported any suspicious activity or doubted the presence of any individual on the premises. It was noticed that the culprits had left footprints on the wall of the bathroom and although four days had elapsed and they appeared smudged, photographs of the same were taken. An attempt was made to compare these foot markings with those of persons working on the premises during the time of offence, but that too did not yield any result. From the facts surrounding the incident, it appeared plausible that the culprit could be one of the pilgrims staying on the premises and who by now would have gone as far away as possible from the scene of offence. A list of pilgrims was obtained, and scrutiny discovered that they came from Madhya Pradesh, Maharashtra, and Gujarat. There was, however, no reason to suspect anybody on the list nor could we devise a criterion to shortlist names who could perhaps be contacted for information. Over the next three days, officers, men of the police station, and I along with them, continued to pursue our attempts to trace the house-breaking. Several suspects and history sheeters were contacted and questioned. Persons who were arrested for having committed an offence with similar modus operandi were also examined. It was discovered that *math bawas* were camping opposite the bus station in town. Several of them were questioned. They had been coming to Palitana regularly over the last few years and engaged in begging, or making plaster statues which they sold as a form of living. None of them, however, appeared to be involved in the crime under investigation.

The above is as vivid a description as is possible, to provide a glimpse of how earnestly visitable property crime was investigated in those days. The offences were not detected in many of the cases. However, the effort made was sincere. With the advantage of hindsight and experience, I can now see that there was perhaps a meeting of minds amongst various categories of criminals operating in Palitana and even amongst the munims of various dharamshalas. A comprehensive approach by classifying the localities and the modus operandi, specific to this pilgrimage town, would have yielded better results. For example, the inspection of the scene of offence is often done in a cursory manner by a low-grade officer who is content with a summary description of the spot where the thief has broken into. While details of articles stolen are reflected in the papers of investigation, the place from where he made good his escape is rarely documented. An FIR lodged or an entry in the case diary would often mention that no trace of the culprit has been found. Scientifically speaking this would be incorrect for nearly every case, as the thief always leaves an important trace of his passage, namely, the manner in which he has committed the crime. Every house-breaker has a characteristic style which he rarely departs from and which he is incapable of completely getting rid of. At times, this distinctive feature is so visible and striking that even a novice can spot it without any difficulty. However, a novice, and I was certainly that, does not know how to group, differentiate, or utilise what he has observed. Often the character of the procedure is not always easy to recognise. Only a practiced, intelligent, and a fervent observer can distinguish the delicate but always identical things which characterize a theft.

That is why the Bombay Police Manual provides that particular attention should be paid to the delay in visiting the scene of offence, and for ascertaining whether the SHO went himself or sent a head constable and whether he was justified in so doing. A perusal of the case papers should show how house-breakings are committed, how the different methods can be classified and consequently, who was responsible for them. House-breaking is a common and objectionable form of crime which specially requires collective treatment. Another element that is usually missed is the "style" of the culprit. It is either the actual or the pretended occupation of the criminal at the time of, or immediately prior to the commission of the offence, and does not refer to the method of committing the crime. It must not be confused with the trade or calling adopted by the criminal before he engaged in the crime. Sometimes, the style and actual occupation may be identical, such as a hired cart driver absconding with property entrusted to him. Sometimes a criminal, when accosted by a third person or when disposing of stolen property to a dealer, pawn-broker or a casual acquaintance will mention his alleged trade or profession to inspire confidence and allay suspicion. In such cases, what the criminal is guised as, for instance, a glassware-hawker or a building contractor, is to be regarded as his style. Similarly, statement made by the criminal, often prepared beforehand to cover up his tracks or to avoid suspicion or to impress people with his bona fides, is important. It generally supports his "style" and becomes part of his make-up for the purpose of committing the offence. It is critical that the tale should be obtained from the people victimized or from the neighbourhood, and no part of the tale should be considered too insignificant to be recorded.

# MUSINGS

*A* direct recruit of the IPS while under training, whether institutional or in the field, aspires to and looks forward to being appointed a Superintendent of Police in-charge of a district. Presumably, this is where power, status and glory are to be found. In the process he or she often overlooks the importance of proper investigation of crime which normally is a function of the officers and men of the concerned police station. When posted to an independent subdivision, a direct recruit believes that this assignment is merely transitory meant only to prepare him or her for the next higher role of a SP. It is true that he or she is quite inexperienced and lacking in procedural knowledge of the investigation of crime. Some even describe it as an extended training schedule. That is why a directly recruited ASP, is required to, unless specially exempted by the Director General of Police, investigate every year personally, assisted by a sub-inspector or inspector, at least six important cases, whether occurring at the headquarters police station or outside of it. This duty is to be done diligently, preparing, and signing all diaries and documents about those cases, and generally attending to them to completion in all their stages, including the proceedings in court. In practice however, most direct recruits get away from this important learning process by not taking it seriously, and largely leaving it to their subordinates so far as recording of statements and preparation of case papers are concerned.

On the other hand, an SDPO who has risen from the ranks has a proper grip of management of crime occurring in his area. This is not an easy task. There is a common misconception that every crime is intrinsically soluble, that there is always sufficient evidence available to reveal the identity of the criminal, and that the perpetrator always leaves traces at the crime scene which will lead inevitably to his door. It is for this reason that a citizen becomes indignant at the inability of the police force to locate unerringly the perpetrator of a mysterious robbery or a house-breaking, from amongst thousands of inhabitants of that area. Many crimes are not susceptible to solution by reason of the fact that the evidence is insufficient. The absence of eyewitnesses, discernible motives and physical clues will obviously provide an obstacle unless the malefactor confesses. Often the *corpus delicti* or the fact that a crime was committed cannot be established, and even a confession is of little value.

Apart from Palitana, there were two other subdivisions in Bhavnagar district. K L Trivedi was the SDPO of Mahuva sub-division whereas J M Mehta, headed the Bhavnagar sub-division. Both had joined the police force as sub-inspectors in the bilingual Bombay State and had about twenty-five years of experience behind them. On the other hand, on the day I joined duties as SDPO Palitana, I had no experience of practical police work. And yet when Z S Saiyed, SP Bhavnagar proceeded on earned leave from 13 April 1979, I held additional charge as officiating Superintendent of Police of the district. I had been on the job for a little over two months. This was because a directly recruited IPS officer in the junior time scale of pay and designated as Assistant Superintendent of Police are above the Deputy Superintendent of Police in the official hierarchy. While at that time I liked it, in retrospect my conclusion is that such a system is counter-productive and frankly not conducive to the development of a good order. The charge in officiating capacity of the district police chief should have been held by Mehta who was higher in inter se seniority than Trivedi. An ASP is promoted to the senior time scale on completion of four years of service which is inclusive of the training period and posted as SP in charge of the district. When that happens, he or she can rightfully assume that position. Before that whoever, whether ASP or DySP, has served in that rank for a longer period, must take precedence. Three weeks later, on 3rd May, when Saiyed returned from leave, I handed over charge back to him. Mehta, being the SDPO of the headquarters subdivision was also present. I heard him comment that it is strange that the district charge is handed over to a greenhorn ASP instead of more experienced personnel. He was right.

*****

**Zulfiqar** Ali Saiyed, the district police chief had joined the Gujarat police in 1963 as a directly recruited Deputy Superintendent of Police. Selections to this rank are done through the state public service commission and they are borne on the cadre of the Gujarat Police Service. He had worked for several years as a DySP before being elevated to the rank of an SP and was therefore an experienced hand. More than others of his ilk, he took interest in crime work and was keen to build a reputation of being a thorough professional. I was eager to impress him as well but for reasons of certain human failings on both sides, by the time I completed a year as SDPO, we had fallen out. On his part, while scrutinising the weekly diary submitted by me along with the crime memos pertaining to the serious crimes visited, he made observations which began to convey an impression that despite my putting in a lot of hard work, he was not satisfied with its outcome. In doing so he did not fathom the impact such correspondence would have on the inexperienced mind of a freshly posted police officer. On my part, I did not display the patience required to absorb such an attitude and chose to reply point by point to his queries, a behaviour not expected from a newly minted police officer. He would have been happy if I had simply not replied, or pretended humility. In the result, the matter was escalated to the IGP. The gentleman was N H Sethna, who had joined the Indian Army during World War II as an emergency commissioned officer and, after the war, joined the police through a special recruitment procedure. He had a no-nonsense kind of reputation. On a sweltering summer day of May 1980, I met him in Ahmedabad where the office of the state police chief was then located. He heard me out briefly, quickly grasping the reasons for the discord. He then directed me to return to my headquarters. I later learned that prior to this meeting, he was briefed by the Deputy Inspector-General of Police, Rajkot Range, H K Vasavada. The latter was Saiyed's superior officer. Three months later when I promoted to the senior time scale and posted as Superintendent of Police, Amreli, it was clear that nothing that the SP wrote about or against me, came in the way of my elevation.

*****

**Rajkot** Range was a huge territorial jurisdiction consisting of Rajkot, Surendranagar, Bhavnagar, Jamnagar, Junagadh, Porbandar and Amreli districts. This is Saurashtra, also known as Kathiawar, a peninsular region of Gujarat located on the Arabian Sea coast. Its *prakrit* name Sorath, literally means "good country", and covers about a third of Gujarat state. After India's independence, 217 princely states of Kathiawar, including the former Junagadh state, were merged to form the state of Saurashtra on 15 February 1948. This was merged into Gujarat when the state was carved out of the bilingual Bombay State in 1960. Kachchh district was also included in Rajkot Range. H K Vasavada was the DIG in-charge of this range and responsible for law-enforcement in these eight districts. He belonged to the old school having been directly recruited as a Deputy Superintendent of Police in Saurashtra state. After assuming charge as SDPO Palitana, I had the occasion to call on him at Rajkot during my visit to that city. He had less than two years of service left before superannuation and came across as a kindly soul. I do not now recall if he gave me any specific advice. When I moved to Amreli on promotion as SP, he became my immediate superior. During a major law and order situation in the district, he camped there for two days providing me with necessary guidance required in handling disturbances which we apprehended might occur due to a call given by a political party. At the end of the same year, he retired from service and settled down in Vadodara.

*****

**Babubhai** Jashbhai Patel was the Chief Minister of Gujarat. He held the office twice, the first time from June 1975 to March 1976 as the leader of the Janata Morcha, and the second time from April 1977 to February 1980 as leader of the Janata Party. In the third week of April 1979, he visited Palitana and after completing that day's activity he retired to the guesthouse located on the Shetrunji Dam for the night. Security arrangements at the site consisted of one head constable and three police constables each armed with a .303 rifle. Since the premises were located within the limits of Palitana Rural police station, the SHO was asked to remain present. There were no arrangements beyond this in those days. Next day the Chief Minister was to leave early as 7 AM, and I along with the Sub-Divisional Magistrate went ahead to the guesthouse to see him off. This duty came upon us as we were the senior most civil servants in the subdivision. I had till then never met a politician whether in power or out of it, and frankly did not think much of them. However, I knew for certain that Babubhai Patel was the apex authority in the state government and deserved to be treated with respect and deference. He came out of his room sharply at the appointed hour in the morning dressed in *dhoti* and *kurta* and was first greeted by the Sub-Divisional Magistrate. Next, I clicked my heels together and saluted him. He was a small statured man with a quiet demeanour and came across as a dignified person. He looked at me, nodded his head gravely, sat in the car and drove off. SHO Palitana

Rural police station was to pilot the Chief Minister through his jurisdiction after which further responsibility would be that of the neighbouring SHO. There was no special vehicle piloting the Chief Minister nor there was any escort car carrying personal security officers. Those were simple days when politicians did not throw their weight around nor did the bureaucrats chase them hankering after choicest postings. I later learnt that Babubhai had joined Indian independence movement in 1930 when he was in college and had been sent to jail seven times by the British.

*****

**As** is evident, most of the districts are divided into two or more sub-divisions, each in charge of an SDPO of the rank of Assistant or Deputy Superintendent of Police. Every important sub-division has, in addition, one or more Circle Police Inspectors attached to it mainly for the purpose of supervising the investigation of crime. Duties of Circle Police Inspector included quarterly inspection of a police station. The CPI is usually an officer who has risen to the position he holds owing to his ability to deal with crime and criminals. He should, therefore, be employed entirely on crime work and the supervision of bad characters and gangs in the circle. He would thus supply a much-needed check in supervising and co-ordinating the crime work of the different police stations in his circle.

Palitana sub-division consisted of Palitana circle which had under its ambit five police stations, and Botad circle which included six police stations. G S Ahuja oversaw the former whereas J M Patel, the latter. Both these individuals had joined as directly recruited sub-inspectors of police and by the time they picked up their next rank of an inspector they had more than twelve to fifteen years of service under their belt. Whether for the IPS or for recruitment to the Gujarat Police, I had the impression that men selected during the 1950s and 1960s were tall well-built male specimen with a confident demeanour. Ahuja and Patel were no exceptions and carried themselves in an impressive manner. Amongst this cadre there was a certain reverence for IPS officers of the rank of SP and above and benign tolerance for those like me who were doing their first independent assignment and therefore were learning the ropes.

The rank of CPI remains underestimated in comparison to the duties that they perform. This included visiting the different police stations and out-posts as often as possible to see that the men are working properly, ensuring that the surveillance registers are properly kept, ascertaining that the police are acquainted with bad characters, including knowledge of their places of abode and manner of living, and verifying that crime is being properly reported, registered, and investigated. A CPI is expected to tour regularly and remain present during the investigation of serious crimes, such as murders, dacoities, highway robberies, and crime suspected of being the work of gangs or professional criminals. Motor accidents involving loss of life occurring in rural areas require him to visit the scene of the offence and direct and advise the sub-inspector and his staff. The system of visiting the scene of every serious offence was not to be adhered to rigidly. It is open to the SP to employ them for more useful purposes such as in co-ordinating the activities of two or more police stations in relation to a crime. They are also required to stay connected with the village police and see that patrolling by the district police is being properly performed, and that information likely to lead to the prevention and detection of crime is being systematically picked up.

Another expectation from the CPI was to educate his subordinates to realise that old time-worn methods in preventive and detecting crime will not, in the days of fast transport and improved communications, suffice in dealing with crime and that no amount of surveillance over local bad characters, however effective, will make up for failure to cope with criminals from outside the police station limits, ranging from bad characters residing within the limits of a neighbouring police station, to criminals from other states moving about in disguise or under false pretences. I am not sure how much of this education Ahuja and Patel imparted to their subordinates but as far as I was concerned, they were keen to share their professional knowledge mainly to impress me with their prowess, and partly to educate me recognising my lack of experience so far as duties of an SDPO were concerned. This was a strange situation. *De jure,* I was their superior officer expected to direct and guide them in their work. *De facto,* both the CPIs were far more knowledgeable in every aspect of policing and in the investigation of crime. However, what I did not lack was commitment and energy, and pride in wearing a uniform. It is possible that the long hours that I put in, and the extensive tours that I undertook, may have been looked upon by both the worthies with amusement and attributed to the zeal and enthusiasm of a new entrant.

*****

**Indira** Gandhi came to Sihor on 18th May 1980 for addressing an election rally. I was at Junagadh supervising the investigation of a dacoity which had occurred within the limits of Palitana Rural police station when I received a message, on 15th May, from the SP's office about the Prime Minister's election meeting within the limits of my subdivision. Originally, she was to address a public meeting at Bhavnagar, but the venue was shifted to Sihor at short notice. Gandhi and her Indian National Congress had won the general elections in January that year to the seventh Lok Sabha. Following this the Gujarat legislative assembly was dissolved, and fresh elections ordered. This was the first time that I would participate in such an event and departed immediately for the location where I camped continuously from 16th May onwards. The state government had detailed Majbootsinh Jadeja, then head of CID, Gujarat State for overall supervision. He was an officer of unimpeachable integrity and remarkable competence. This was also the first time when I oversaw the preparation of a makeshift helipad near the open ground where the election meeting was to be held.

The Prime Minister arrived, accompanied by Madhavsinh Solanki, former Chief Minister of Gujarat. The Collector and the Superintendent of Police were present on the occasion. After delivering her speech and before proceeding to board the waiting helicopter, she was asked by the Joint Director, Intelligence Bureau, who was in-charge of her security, and had accompanied her from New Delhi, as to whether she would like to go around in an open jeep and meet the crowd. I was standing next to her and initially saw her hesitate, not being sure, but soon she agreed and went around waving at the crowd, before departing. She appeared frail to me although the thought soon perished when I recalled how India under her leadership had scored one of the greatest military victories since World War II, resulting in the creation of Bangladesh in 1971. In the event, the Congress won the assembly elections with a huge tally of 141 seats out of 182, a record that remained unbroken for the next four decades. However, the voters of Sihor chose Dalsukhbhai Godani, a Patidar leader who contested from the Janata Party.

*****

**There** was an official accommodation available for the incumbent SDPO at Palitana. This was a simple colonial type of bungalow, albeit small, located next to the office. However, my predecessor continued to occupy it for nine months after handing over charge. I therefore had no option but to stay in the government guest house whenever I was in the headquarters town. Uniquely this was known as Readymoney guest house, named after Sir Cowasji Jehangir Readymoney, who was a Parsi community leader, philanthropist, and industrialist during the nineteenth century based out of Mumbai. He must have contributed towards the cost of constructing it. In any case I was travelling extensively, visiting serious crime across the subdivision hence I was barely at Palitana for more than a week or ten days in a month. When I finally moved to the house, I had to furnish it with some basic stuff such as a bed, a table, and chairs. While under training at Rajkot, a year earlier, I had been provided government accommodation, the furnishing of which was done from what I got from my parental home in Ahmedabad. This consisted of a sofa set, a steel cot, a dining table and four chairs.

SDPO's are provided with two orderlies to assist them with their official and personal affairs so that they are fully available for government work. Bachumiya Subalmiya was one such personnel allotted to me and I distinctly remember him because he used to travel with me during all my visitations with a "kitchen box." This was different than the kit box which was supplied to the constabulary for storing their accoutrements. The kitchen box was made of wood and consisted of vertical compartments of assorted sizes to carry therein such items as stove, cooking oil, rice, flour, salt, pepper, chilies, and such other dry items normally required for cooking a meal. Vegetables and milk were purchased fresh at the place of camp and Bachumiya would on reaching the destination, which was usually a government guest house and could sometimes even be a school classroom, unload the box from the vehicle and set about making preparation for the next meal. I followed this practice rigidly as I did not want to avail of the hospitality of the local SHO. Sometimes, especially during inspection of the police station, I was camping there for five days, and it was by no means appropriate to impose the burden of oneself and one's staff, which consisted of the police driver and Bachumiya, on the local officers. Unlike the kit box, maintaining the kitchen box was not a government directive, and it appears to have been conceived several decades ago by an enterprising officer to facilitate extensive touring by district officers.

I retained this box even after my promotion to the rank of an SP and utilised it during my district tours for inspection purposes.

*****

**Prabhat** Kumar Datta was the Superintendent of Police, Rajkot City under whose guidance and direction I had completed my practical training before being sent to an independent charge as SDPO, Palitana. He was one of the most charismatic, remarkable, and an extraordinary police officer that I have ever met, and it was my good fortune to be trained by him. Belonging to the 1963 batch of the IPS, he was a true leader in every sense of the word and honest to the core. My regard for him emanated from the heart, a sentiment that I developed for a few more officers who I met during my career. These were outstanding officers with whom I had the pleasure to work with and for whom I had, and continue to have, great respect. It was the last day of inspection of Palitana Rural police station and during the note-reading, I received a message from Botad police station indicating that Datta along with other members of a committee set-up to buy horses for the equitation wing of Gujarat police had arrived. I was immediately excited and thrilled at the prospect of my mentor visiting my subdivision although he was 110 km away from Palitana. There was no expectation that I undertake a journey involving a two and a half hours drive, only to meet him. Those were the days of phone calls made through a telephone exchange, and I spoke to him including mentioning that I was concluding that day the inspection of the police station. However, the fact is, that I was not able to concentrate. My "guru" was within my jurisdiction, and I could not have possibly conceived of any circumstance under which I would not go across to meet him. As the note reading progressed, the SHO of the police station PSI Karamta sensed that while physically I was there, mentally I was in Botad. Karamta was an old timer having joined the police as a constable. He was a solid, reliable and a kindly soul, and yet firm when required while attending to his official duties. He suggested that the rest of the note reading could be done later, and I may like to consider going across and pay my respects to Datta Saheb. The Reader PSI Dabhi seconded this. I needed no other persuasion.

I recall proceeding to Botad immediately and was happy to meet Datta who was camping there for the night. Admittedly I did not obtain permission of my SP for this travel, nor did I consider it necessary as I was travelling within my own jurisdiction. Nevertheless, this was a journey undertaken out of a sense of gratitude for a teacher who taught me the best that was to learn about the police as a service.

*****

**An** assessment of the magnitude of work that a SDPO is expected to do, would help in putting in perspective the seminal contribution of this rank. Not counting a month spent on leave, in a period of eleven months during the assessment year 1979-80, I had visited seventy serious crimes reported across the subdivision and the district. This would work out to an average of six visitations in a month, most of which required travelling outside the headquarters and camping, within a radius of 8 km, at the scene of the offence. Although this was my first independent charge after joining the IPS and therefore I lacked the requisite experience, the perseverance that I displayed while visiting these serious crimes, had resulted in the solving of three undetected murder cases, one each registered with Vallabhipur, Talaja and Datha police stations. Of these, the last two police stations were part of the neighbouring Mahuva sub-division, revealing thereby that it did not matter whether a serious crime, which was the subject matter of a visitation, was part of the SDPO's jurisdiction or not. The essence and spirit of the enabling provisions of the police manual would apply regardless, and one would put in sustained hard work to trace the offenders.

There was emphasis in those days on enforcing the dry law and ensuring that gambling activities did not take place. I had personally carried out twenty-two raids on liquor dens, and thirteen raids on gambling joints. This had a salutary effect so far as the public perception of the police was concerned. Both, the DIG Rajkot Range and SP Bhavnagar, had conveyed their appreciation while commenting on the entries recorded by me in the weekly diary concerning the same. However, when I proceeded on earned leave or was away attending the Basic Terminal Training Course at the National Police Academy, Hyderabad, these prohibited activities would commence again, clearly because of the connivance of the local staff. In fact, on my return from Hyderabad, the SP sent me a petition submitted by a group of citizens to him listing the places where these activities had begun in my absence and urging him to have me posted back.

Apart from supervising serious crime and conducting raids, I inspected eight police stations, enquired into thirty-six applications received from the SP, held twenty-two Orderly Rooms, and performed patrolling during the night on twenty-seven occasions in different police stations. The mandatory requirement of personal investigation by a directly recruited IPS officer during his tenure as SDPO was met when I took over for investigation six cases, two of which were murder cases, two of attempt to murder, and one each of house-breaking and simple theft.

*****

I received my first letter of appreciation for the detection of a house-breaking and theft which occurred on the premises of the Ambaji temple at Mota Khuntavada, Mahuva sub-division. Gold and silver ornaments worth ₹ 25,000 had been stolen. As mentioned earlier in this book, house-breakings are the most difficult to detect. However, with about a year's experience under the belt, I had acquired sufficient knowledge and grip in tracing property crime. In this case, not only did we succeed in apprehending a gang of *baurias*, but we also recovered the entire stolen property. It was discovered that the gang was operating out of Kodinar town, then in Amreli district, since the last fifteen years. The SP had sent a wireless message to IGP Gujarat state and DIG CID, informing them of the detection. The latter responded by sending the following message:

> *Reference your signal No. 7/RB/92 dated 22-1-80 regarding Ambaji temple theft at Mota Khuntavda. Please accept my heartiest congratulations for detection of the offence and recovery of entire stolen property. Please convey my thanks and appreciation to ASP Palitana and others who with their sustained efforts on the correct lines contributed to the detection of this offence.*

Majbootsinh Jivaji Jadeja, was the CID chief then. Known throughout the state for his prowess in detection of crime, appreciation coming from him meant a lot to all of us. This incident would convey how much attention, for a mere housebreaking, was paid even at the state level in those days. An enduring memory of the effort put in for detecting this crime was the acquaintance I made with Vanrajsinh Krushnasinh Zala. During the Second World War, he had joined as a commissioned officer in the Indian Army, and after independence, he was specially inducted as a DySP in the police force of Saurashtra state for apprehending and neutralising Bhupat, a notorious dacoit of those times. He had retired, in April 1977, as DIG Rajkot Range and settled down at Rajkot. Earlier, during his tenure as SP Banaskantha, a district in north Gujarat, he had acquired a remarkable ability in controlling crimes committed by the *baurias*. Over a period, they had developed such regard that they would conceal nothing if questioned by him. While I had succeeded in tracing the crime to this gang, their leader would not, despite intensive interrogation, tell us where the stolen property was stashed away. On a hunch, I proceeded to Rajkot along with the latter and the investigating officer and called on Zala. He received me with the courtesy typical of those days. After hearing my request, he took the criminal aside to another room and came back five minutes later to convey that the latter had confessed and would produce the gold and silver ornaments stolen from the temple. And this is exactly what happened.

*****

**My** tenure as SDPO drove home the point that that there are natural limitations to human testimony and that no human faculty is infallible. I had the opportunity of speaking with, questioning or interrogating scores of witnesses, suspects, and victims. Gradually, it dawned upon me that human testimony has three stages of development- preception, fixation in the mind of what is seen, and expression. As these powers vary from person to person, some discrepancies are bound to crop up amongst the versions of different witnesses even regarding the same incident. The investigating officer should check if the discrepancies are vital and go to the root of the matter. Minor discrepancies, however, do not take away a case; rather they go to prove the genuineness of the occurrence. Dove-tail precision is only possible in concocted cases. It is not possible for every witness to remember all the details. Some differences and discrepancies in details are generally found even in the case of honest witnesses and unless the contradictions are material they need not necessarily be disbelieved. On the contrary, slight differences in the story of the same event shows that the witnesses are giving their own account and not reciting a tutored agreed upon story.

Identifying and apprehending criminals has never been an easy task. Even then, and certainly now, many criminals were and are more sophisticated and, in many cases, "post-graduates of the penal system". An SDPO must have an eye for detail, and the ability to recognise and evaluate evidence. Equally important is the ability to interview and interrogate different types of personalities, he or she may encounter. The job requires a certain tenacity and perseverance to achieve results. For a directly recruited Assistant or Deputy Superintendent of Police, these traits if imbibed early would go a long way in converting them into competent police officers. Tact is indispensable, true courage is required in many situations, and he or she must always be ready in an emergency to risk health, if the cause so requires. I have no doubt in my mind, that the kind of work that I did, the challenges that I faced both within and outside the police department, and the long hours that I devoted to my work in the subdivision, stood me in good stead as I progressed in my career as a police officer.

*****

# NOTES

## Foreword

*designated as 'visitable crimes', or 'grave crimes' or 'special crimes', in different states.

## Chapter 2

[1] A taluka is a revenue unit below the Subdivision. In North India, it is called a Tehsil.

## Chapter 4

[1] Kunbi is a generic term applied to castes of traditional farmers in western India which includes patels (patidars) of Gujarat.

[2] Bhil is a scheduled tribe in western and central India and are found in the states of Gujarat, Madhya Pradesh, Chhattisgarh, Maharashtra, and Rajasthan.

## Chapter 6

[1] This nomenclature has been taken from Panchayat Raj which is one of the oldest systems of local government originating on the Indian subcontinent. The word 'raj' means rule and 'panchayat' means assembly (ayat) of five (panch). Traditionally, panchayats consisted of wise and respected elders chosen and accepted by the local community. These assemblies settled disputes between both individuals and villages.

[2] The Criminal Tribes of India, K. M. Kapadia, 1952

Notes

## Chapter 10

[1] In K.R. Lakshmanan v. State of Tamil Nadu, the Supreme Court defined a 'game of skill' to mean "one in which success primarily depends on the superior knowledge, training, attention, experience, and adroitness of the player". Games like golf, horse race betting and chess are "games of skill". It is interesting to note that while horse race betting is assumed to require skill, betting in cricket is prohibited.

[2] Imperial Gazetteer of India, v. 15, p. 165.

[3] A bucket shop is a business that allows gambling based on the prices of stocks or commodities.

[4] The Difficulty of Being Good by Gurcharan Das

## Chapter 11

[1] The word 'burking' is unique to the police lexicon of bi-lingual Bombay State. It means to suppress or extinguish quietly or stifle.

[2] Assistant and Deputy Superintendents of Police were required to maintain and write up day by day, as the facts come to be known in their own handwriting, for each week commencing on Sunday and ending on Saturday, a diary in a bound book stamped, paged, and endorsed by the Superintendent of Police, of their movements and proceedings.

[3] Section 36- "Police officers superior in rank to an officer in charge of a police station may exercise the same powers, throughout the local area to which they are appointed, as may be exercised by such officer within the limits of his station."

## Chapter 12

[1] The Narcotic Drugs and Psychotropic Substances Act, 1985 had not been enacted then.

[2] This includes offering intermittent prayers for protection of the dead body from negative energy, putting cow dung on the floor before putting the dead body down, putting Gangajal in the mouth of the deceased and close the openings of the nose and ears by inserting tulsi leaves in them.

## Chapter 13

[1] I. G.'s No. 10720, dated 30th November 1896

## Chapter 14

[1] Karadiya caste (Serial No. 102) was included in SEBC list as per Government Resolution No. SSP/ 1194/ 1411/ A Dated 25/7/1994.

## Chapter 15

[1] Prescribed number of days for inspection is four days if the sanctioned strength of the police station is up to 50, five days if it was between 50 to 100 and six days if the sanctioned strength exceeded 100.

[2] This pertains to taking security for good behaviour from suspected persons and habitual offenders, and for keeping peace.

## Chapter 16

[1] David Ludden (2013)- India and South Asia: A Short History.

## Chapter 21

[1] According to historian Richard Burton, Lohanas originated in Lohanpur in Multan district of Punjab (now in Pakistan)

## Chapter 22

[1] Initially founded to manage the Shatrunjaya Palitana temples, it now manages numerous Jain tirthas and temples belonging to the Shvetambara tradition.

www.ingramcontent.com/pod-product-compliance
Lightning Source LLC
LaVergne TN
LVHW091621070526
838199LV00044B/882